John Swett

Methods of Teaching

A Handbook of Principles, Directions, and Working Models for....

John Swett

Methods of Teaching
A Handbook of Principles, Directions, and Working Models for....

ISBN/EAN: 9783337167547

Printed in Europe, USA, Canada, Australia, Japan

Cover: Foto ©Paul-Georg Meister /pixelio.de

More available books at **www.hansebooks.com**

METHODS OF TEACHING

A HAND-BOOK OF
PRINCIPLES, DIRECTIONS, AND WORKING MODELS
FOR COMMON-SCHOOL TEACHERS

BY

JOHN SWETT

PRINCIPAL OF THE SAN FRANCISCO GIRLS' HIGH SCHOOL AND NORMAL CLASS

"Special preparation is a prerequisite for teaching."—HORACE MANN

NEW YORK ∴ CINCINNATI ∴ CHICAGO
AMERICAN BOOK COMPANY

PREFACE.

This book is intended—

(1.) For use in normal schools and normal classes as a basis for instruction in methods of teaching.

(2.) For the use of those who intend to become teachers without taking a course of professional training.

(3.) For experienced teachers who believe there is something to be learned from the suggestions of others.

The characteristic features claimed for this manual are:

(1.) Its strict limitation to the essentials of common-school instruction.

(2.) Its condensed and specific directions.

(3.) Its working models for beginners.

The attempt to reduce teaching-methods to condensed statements and bird's-eye views is beset with many difficulties readily appreciated by practical educators. But what the young teacher most needs is *a definite direction or method;* he will learn to make for himself all necessary qualifications and exceptions in schoolroom practice. My chief purpose has been, therefore, to make, not an exhaustive treatise on education in general, but a volume of principles, directions, and working models for the practical guidance of the rank and file in the great army of common-school teachers.

In the statement of general principles in education, I have quoted from the thinkers and writers of the present rather than the past, in order fairly to present advanced ideas, and to give the young teacher occasional glimpses of a modern educational literature outside of mere hand-books and text-books. The practical directions, drawn largely from the common stock of school methods, are substantiated by opinions quoted from eminent living American teachers and superintendents. The working models are made up of exercises that were prepared for use, and were actually used for several years, in a large public school. The whole book, indeed, owes its existence to the practical needs of a normal class-room.

Personal experience in teaching is a good school, but a slow and costly one. Looking back over a varied experience of thirty years, I deeply realize how great would have been my vantage-ground had I begun with a more thorough professional training and a wider acquaintance with educational literature. If I have failed to seize upon essentials, the failure is not from lack of opportunity to observe the need of them. In a new state, I have taken a part in the organization of a school system almost from the beginning. My personal experience includes actual teaching in country, city, ungraded, half-graded,

graded, evening, primary, grammar, high, and normal schools, and several years' service in state and city superintendence. Though not so good as I would like to make it, this book is submitted with the hope that it may save some beginners from wasting time and efforts in unprofitable empirical experiments, and that some veteran teachers may find in it a confirmation of principles and methods arrived at in the course of their own life-work.

For criticisms and suggestions I am under special obligations to Professor George W. Minns, of Concord, Mass., and to John Muir, of California.

J. S.

CONTENTS.

PART I.
GENERAL PRINCIPLES OF EDUCATION.

CHAPTER I.
SCHOOLS AND SCHOOL-TEACHING.

	PAGE
I. GENERAL REMARKS	1
II. THE SCIENCE OF TEACHING	2
III. THE ART OF TEACHING	5
IV. THE PROFESSION OF TEACHING	10
V. THE NEXT STEP	13
VI. THE SCHOLARSHIP OF TEACHERS	16
VII. TEACHERS' ASSOCIATIONS	19
VIII. EDUCATIONAL POWER	20
IX. THE COMMON-SCHOOL SYSTEM	21

CHAPTER II.
PHYSICAL TRAINING.

I. ITS IMPORTANCE	23
II. WAYS AND MEANS	27
III. PRACTICAL DIRECTIONS	28
IV. INDUSTRIAL TRAINING	31
V. TECHNICAL EDUCATION	32
VI. SCHOOL HYGIENE	34
VII. RULES OF HEALTH FOR PUPILS	37

Chapter III.
MORAL TRAINING.

		PAGE
I.	General Remarks	39
II.	The Sphere of School	40
III.	Possibilities and Conditions	42
IV.	General Directions from Herbert Spencer.	44
V.	Practical Hints.	45

Chapter IV.
INTELLECTUAL TRAINING.

I.	Classification of the Intellectual Faculties	54
II.	The Perceptive Faculties	55
III.	The Expressive Faculties	58
IV.	The Reflective Faculties	59

Chapter V.
SCHOOL GOVERNMENT.

I.	Corporal Punishment	64
II.	Self-control	66
III.	Public Opinion of the School	67
IV.	Emulation	67
V.	School Discipline	68
VI.	Obstinacy	69
VII.	School Despotism	69
VIII.	General Principles from Herbert Spencer.	70
IX.	Condensed Directions.	71
X.	Punishment	75

Chapter VI.
SPECIAL DIRECTIONS FOR SCHOOL-ROOM MANAGEMENT.

| I. | Special Directions and Suggestions for Principals. | 78 |
| II. | Special Directions for Assistants | 85 |

CONTENTS.

		PAGE
III.	MANAGEMENT IN GENERAL	88
IV.	CONDENSED DIRECTIONS FOR THE CLASS TEACHER	91
V.	METHODS IN RECITATIONS.	95
VI.	THE MINIMUM OF RULES.	98
VII.	SPECIFIC DIRECTIONS FOR PUPILS	98
VIII.	DIRECTIONS ABOUT WRITTEN EXAMINATIONS	99

CHAPTER VII.
THE MANAGEMENT OF UNGRADED COUNTRY SCHOOLS.

I.	GENERAL REMARKS.	101
II.	THINGS ESSENTIAL.	103
III.	MISCELLANEOUS THINGS	110
IV.	MINOR MATTERS	113
V.	ADVANTAGES OF COUNTRY SCHOOLS	115
VI.	CONDENSED DIRECTIONS.	117

PART II.
CONDENSED DIRECTIONS FOR TEACHING COMMON-SCHOOL ESSENTIALS.

CHAPTER I.
GENERAL PRINCIPLES FROM

I.	JOHN STUART MILL.	121
II.	THOMAS H. HUXLEY.	121
III.	SUPERINTENDENT ELIOT.	122
IV.	ALEXANDER BAIN.	122

CHAPTER II.
CONDENSED DIRECTIONS FOR TEACHING READING.

I.	DIRECTIONS	123
II.	QUOTATIONS FROM EDUCATORS.	129

Chapter III.

CONDENSED DIRECTIONS FOR TEACHING SPELLING, WORD-ANALYSIS, AND DEFINING.

I. SPELLING................................. 132
    (1.) SPELLING......................... 132
    (2.) SPELLING-GAMES.................. 134
    (3.) WRITTEN EXERCISES FOR PRIMARY CLASSES . 135
    (4.) WRITTEN EXERCISES FOR GRAMMAR GRADES. . 136
    (5.) ORAL EXERCISES FOR GRAMMAR GRADES. . . 136

II. WORD-ANALYSIS.......................... 136
    (1.) DIRECTIONS....................... 137
    (2.) WORD-MATCHES.................... 138

III. DEFINING................................ 139

Chapter IV.

CONDENSED DIRECTIONS FOR TEACHING ARITHMETIC. 141

Chapter V.

CONDENSED DIRECTIONS FOR TEACHING LANGUAGE-LESSONS, GRAMMAR, AND COMPOSITION.

I. LANGUAGE-LESSONS AND GRAMMAR......... 150

II. ENGLISH COMPOSITION................... 155
    (1.) DIRECTIONS FOR TEACHERS.......... 155
    (2.) DIRECTIONS TO BE GIVEN TO PUPILS.... 156

Chapter VI.

CONDENSED DIRECTIONS FOR TEACHING GEOGRAPHY.

I. DIRECTIONS............................. 157
II. GEOGRAPHY MATCHES.................... 161
III. GEOGRAPHICAL EXERCISES............... 162

Chapter VII.
HISTORY OF THE UNITED STATES.

I. Directions	164
II. Class Exercises	167

Chapter VIII.
OBJECT-LESSONS AND THE ELEMENTS OF NATURAL SCIENCE.

I. Hints on Object-lessons	168
II. Elements of Natural Science	171
III. Quotations from Educators	176

Chapter IX.
WRITING AND DRAWING.

I. Hints on Writing	178
II. Hints on Drawing	180
III. Quotations from Educators	182

Chapter X.
MISCELLANEOUS MATTERS.

I. Music	184
II. Manners	184

PART III.
WORKING-MODELS IN ESSENTIALS.

Introductory Note 187

Chapter I.
WORKING-MODELS FOR READING-LESSONS.

I. Lessons in Word-making	189
II. Lessons for Primary Grades	190

CONTENTS.

		PAGE
III.	Miscellaneous Exercises	191
IV.	Lessons for Lower Grammar Grades	191
V.	Lessons for Higher Grammar Grades	194

Chapter II.
WORKING MODELS IN ARITHMETIC.

I.	Lessons for Beginners	196
II.	Lessons for Second Term or Year	207
III.	Lessons for Third Term or Year	212
IV.	Drill Exercises in the Four Rules	213
V.	Working Models in Common Fractions	215
VI.	Fractions for Grammar-school Grades	219
VII.	Working Models in Mental Arithmetic	224
VIII.	Working Models in the Tables	227
IX.	The Metric System	230

Chapter III.
WORKING MODELS IN GEOGRAPHY.

I.	Globe Lessons for Beginners	233
II.	Second Series of Globe Lessons	236
III.	Lessons in Local Geography	239
IV.	Climate and the Zones	242
V.	Questions on Local Weather Conditions	243
VI.	Local State Geography	244
VII.	Compositions on Geography	246
VIII.	Facts about Our Own Country	249
IX.	Facts about the Continents	251
X.	Physical Features of the Globe	253
XI.	General Review Questions	255

Chapter IV.
LANGUAGE-LESSONS AND COMPOSITION FOR BEGINNERS.

(a.) Copying Short Stories	258
(b.) Sentence-making	262

CONTENTS.   xiii

		PAGE
(c.) Letter-writing	. . . .	264
(d.) Short Compositions	. . . .	265

Chapter V.
PRACTICAL COMPOSITION IN GRAMMAR GRADES.

I. Narration and Description	. . . .	269
II. Letter-writing	. . . .	270
III. Imaginative Letters	. . . .	270
IV. Abstracts from Memory	. . . .	271
V. Stories of the Imagination	. . . .	271
VI. Short Descriptions of Trees	. . . . . .	272
VII. Metals and Minerals	. . . .	272
VIII. Manufactured Articles	. . . .	273
IX. Geographical Compositions	. . . .	273
X. General Exercises	. . . .	274
XI. Biographical Sketches	. . . .	274
XII. Historical Sketches	. . . .	276
XIII. Natural History Sketches	. . . .	277

Chapter VI.
WORKING MODELS IN SENTENCE-MAKING.

I. The Simple Sentence	. . . .	279
II. The Complex Sentence	. . . .	287
III. The Compound Sentence	. . . .	293
IV. Examination Questions in Language-lessons and Grammar	. . . .	295

Chapter VII.
PUNCTUATION OF SENTENCES.

I. The Simple Sentence	. . . .	300
II. The Complex Sentence	. . . .	303
III. The Compound Sentence	. . . .	304
IV. Quotation Marks	. . . .	306

Chapter VIII.
RULES FOR WRITING GOOD ENGLISH.

I. Words	307
II. Order of Words	310
III. Brevity	313
IV. Figurative Language	314

Chapter IX.
REVIEW QUESTIONS ON THE HISTORY OF THE UNITED STATES 319

Chapter X.
PRACTICAL HINTS IN SCHOOL ETHICS.

I. Lessons for Younger Pupils	322
II. Lessons for Older Pupils	323
III. A Teacher's Minimum Library	325

METHODS OF TEACHING.

PART I.

GENERAL PRINCIPLES IN EDUCATION.

Chapter I.
SCHOOLS AND SCHOOL-TEACHING.
I. GENERAL REMARKS.

THERE is a profession of law, of medicine, and of theology: is there a profession of teaching? The skilful practice of any pursuit is termed an art: is there an art of teaching? There seems to be a popular opinion handed down from the past that anybody who has been "educated" can teach school; and that there *is* no art of teaching, no science underlying the practice of teaching, and therefore no profession of teaching. In most parts of our country, the impression prevails that anybody who can pass an examination and get a certificate is a duly qualified teacher, and, consequently, that no specific preparation for teaching is necessary other than personal experience derived from actual work in the schoolroom. And there is some ground for this opinion. Out of 300,000 teachers in the United States, not more than one in ten is a graduate of the normal school; of the remaining nine tenths, some have fitted themselves by thorough self-culture to do the best kind of professional work, but more are merely unskilled school-keepers. Of this latter class, most have gained little by experience except a narrow conceit in their own empirical methods. Knowing nothing whatever of modern investigations in physiology, biology, and sociology, they sneer at all attempts at formulating the principles of teaching into a *science*.

In our educational centres, however, it is evident that the opinion is steadily gaining ground that education is based upon scientific principles, and that there ought to be a profession of teaching. The number of normal schools grows larger year by year. In several cities only normal graduates are employed as teachers; and in many places the preference is given to professionally trained teachers. Moreover, teachers' institutes and associations are diffusing a professional spirit more and more widely; the number of men and women who read educational journals and imbibe their progressive spirit is far in excess of former times; and, at length, some school-officers, and a few thinkers among citizens at large, begin to give evidence of a nebulous perception of the truth that teachers, as well as lawyers, doctors, clergymen, and artisans, need special training for their business.

II. THE SCIENCE OF TEACHING.

"In every department of human affairs," says John Stuart Mill, "practice long precedes science; systematic inquiry into the modes of action of the powers of nature is the tardy product of a long course of efforts to use those powers for practical ends."

The science of teaching is a classification of principles derived by observation, investigation, and experience from a knowledge of things to be *taught*, and from a study of the child to be *trained*. The object of school education is to *aid* the mental, moral, and physical development of the child by means of appropriate training and instruction in the kinds of knowledge required by existing social conditions as an outfit for the duties of life. From age to age school instruction has been modified to meet the new wants of each succeeding generation occasioned by each successive advance in civilization.

The child, too, is a variable factor. It is an old saying that human nature is the same in all ages the world over; but this proverb, despite the wisdom of our ancestors, is a fallacy. The child is not plastic clay in the hands of the potter, nor a sheet of blank paper to be written upon; on the contrary, it is a bundle of inherited tendencies and capacities. Education merely *aids* development, and directs latent tendencies; it cannot *create* powers, and often fails to *control* them. Teaching, therefore, must depend in a great measure upon the transmitted nature of the child to be taught. The child of prehistoric man, born in some cave at the close of the last glacial period, had little except form in common with children now living in New York, London, or Berlin. It is evident that the child of an Apache Indian or an Australian savage cannot be trained successfully by the educational processes which are adapted to the hereditary capacities of children that represent the highest type of human development.

Hence no one particular age can prescribe the methods of education for succeeding ages; no one nation for all other nations; no one race for all other races. Schools are an organic growth of society. They represent, more or less perfectly, the wants and spirit of a nation. Modern methods of teaching should therefore represent the existing state of knowledge and civilization, not the obsolete learning or methods of past ages; but traditional culture, like customs, manners, habits, and laws, too often holds sway long after the causes that organized it have ceased to act. "Like political constitutions," says Herbert Spencer, "educational systems are not *made*, but grow, and within brief periods growth is insensible."

While it cannot be claimed as yet that teaching is a fully developed science, great progress has been made in formulating the principles that underlie the best of our present methods of instruction. Educational history is full of errors, most of which were the result of empirical methods. Experience in this field, as in every other, in order to be of any value, must be the result of experiments directed by the light of science, and must have for its objective point the welfare of every child in the nation. "No matter how limited the strictly scientific domain of education is considered to be," says Mr. Soldan, of St. Louis, "it cannot be denied that there *is* such a science; and it should be mastered before the practical duties of teaching are assumed. In other pursuits the tyro may be allowed to spoil and waste the first piece of work, but in teaching the material is too precious to admit of useless experiment."

"Our teachers," says Mr. E. L. Youmans, Editor of the Popular Science Monthly, etc., "mostly belong to the old dispensation. Their preparation is chiefly literary. Their art is a mechanical routine; and hence, very naturally, while admitting the importance of advancing views, they really cannot see what is to be done about it. When we say that education is an affair of the laws of our being, involving a wide range of considerations—involving, in short, a complete acquaintance with corporeal conditions, which science alone can give — when we hint of these things, we seem to be speaking in an unknown tongue; or, if intelligible, then very irrelevant and unpractical."

"The teaching method," says Professor Bain, "is arrived at in various ways. One principal mode is experience of the work: this is the inductive, or practical, source. Another mode is education from the laws of the human mind: this is the deductive, or theoretical, source. The third and best mode is to combine the two; to rectify empirical teaching by principles, and to qualify deductions from principles by practical experience."

III. THE ART OF TEACHING.

"Art," says Professor Joseph Le Conte, "is the result, at first, of the empirical method; science always of the rational method. Art leads upward to the comprehension of science; but science, when sufficiently perfect, turns again and perfects art."

The art of school-teaching consists in the skilful application of the great body of rules and methods deduced from science, observation, experiment, and practice. In other words, the art lies in teaching according to laws based upon a scientific knowledge of the nature of the child to be instructed.

"Successful teaching," says Mr. Dickinson, Secretary of the Massachusetts Board of Education, "is the product of knowledge, skill, and experience. The teacher must have a good knowledge of the mind, of the facts he is to teach, of the sciences which rest upon them, and of the end to be secured by school-work. He must have skill in applying his method, or he will fail to awaken right ideas, or he will do for the pupil what the pupil should do for himself, or he will talk too much, or spend time in teaching what is not worth knowing. He must have experience, or he will be liable to violate all the principles of good teaching in attempting to apply them."

It is an axiom in the art of teaching that *it is what the child does for himself and by himself, under wise guidance, that educates him.*

Now, the untrained and unskilled teacher, ignorant of the laws of mind, believes that children are educated mainly by what they are *told*, or by what they commit to memory from books. He fills all children to the brim with facts. Like Gradgrind and M'Choakumchild in Dickens, he seems "a kind of cannon, loaded to the muzzle with facts, and prepared to blow the boys and girls clean out of the regions of childhood at one discharge." His fetich is the school text-book. It is ugly, but he worships it, and makes his pupils bow down before it. To him the child has but one intellectual faculty, and that is *memory*. He enlists *pain* in his service, and drives his pupils by main force.

Mill says that if there is a first principle in education, it is this: "That the discipline which does good to the mind is that in which the mind is active, not passive; the secret of developing the faculties is to give them much to do, and much inducement to do it." Tyndall says, "The exercise of the mind, like that of the body, depends for its value upon the spirit in which it is accomplished." Spencer says, "The child should be told as little as possible, and induced to discover as much as possible." But the unskilled teacher blunders along as if Mill, Spencer, Tyndall, Froebel, and Pestalozzi had never lived, thought, observed, discovered, and written. He recognizes no educational authority but himself. He teaches in the "good old way" handed down by imitation from the past—a "way" still perpetuated, not only in common-schools both in the city and country, but also in not a few high-schools and colleges.

Agassiz said the worst service a teacher could render a pupil was to give him a ready-made answer; but the school-keeper tells everything in advance. Spencer, Bain, Comenius, and other educators agree that in every branch of study the mind should be conducted to principles through the medium of examples, and so should be led from the particular to the general, the simple to the complex, the concrete to the abstract, the indefinite to the definite, the empirical to the rational or scientific. But the unscientific teacher violates all these rules. In arithmetic, he begins with definitions, continues in abstractions and mechanical rules, and ends in puzzling problems. In grammar, he omits the actual use of language in expressing thought, and devotes his attention to the technicalities of parsing and analysis. In geography, he is content to have his pupils memorize names regardless of ideas. In history, he strings dates like wooden beads upon the thread of memory. In reading, he trains pupils to call words without much reference to meaning. In botany, he takes books before flowers, and in physics omits experiments. Object-lessons he regards with disdain. In fact, he does not educate at all; that is, he does not draw out, train, and discipline; he does not awaken curiosity, nor excite inquiry, nor develop discrimination.

In view of the charlatanism and empiricism so widespread in methods of instruction, we may well be tolerant towards those who assert that there is, as yet, in our common-schools, neither an art nor a science of teaching. "Our schools," said Agassiz, "are the treadmills of knowledge, while they might be made the living sources of knowledge."

Mr. Dickinson, of Massachusetts, says, in his recent report, "The old methods of teaching are still generally practised. Lessons to be committed to memory are still assigned from books; and then the teacher, by question and answer, conducts the recitation."

A state superintendent, who had made, during a four years' term of office, hundreds of visits to country schools, recently stated that he never once saw a teacher conducting a recitation without a text-book in hand; that he seldom saw either teacher or scholar at the blackboard; that he never saw a school globe actually in use; that pupils seemed to know nothing of local geography, and when asked to point north, uniformly pointed overhead to the zenith; that he saw but one school cabinet; that he never saw a teacher give an object-lesson; and that he never found a school where pupils had been taught how to write a letter either of business or friendship.

An examiner in one of the ten largest cities of our country says that he found many classes of children in the primary department who, after attending school three years, had never made a figure or letter upon the blackboard; that oral lessons were copied into blank-books and memorized by pupils; that the school globe was used only to show that the earth is round; that most of the teaching consisted in hearing verbatim recitations; that in more than half the recitations written answers were required; that pupils were worried by frequent written examinations; and that the anxiety of teachers seemed to be not to develop the faculties of pupils, but to get them through the annual official written examination into the next higher grade. This crude teaching was the result, partly of bad supervision, and partly of untrained teachers. Such work is the natural outgrowth of the popular notion "that anybody can keep school." And it is hopeless to expect that teachers who are ignorant of their own ignorance, who have grown wrongheaded from haphazard experience, and conceited from their narrow-mindedness, will ever become anything more than machine teachers, marking their pupils with a stencil-plate. It is this class of pedagogues that Carlyle has so graphically made immortal in the following paragraph:

"My teachers were hide-bound pedants without knowledge of man's nature, or of boys, or of aught save lexicons. Innumerable dead vocables they crammed into us, and called it fostering the growth of the mind. How can an inanimate mechanical verb-grinder foster the growth of *anything*, much more of mind, which grows, not like a vegetable by having its roots littered by etymological compost, but, like a spirit, by mysterious contact with spirit-thought kindling itself at the fire of living thought! How shall he give kindling in whose own inward man there is no live coal but is burned out to a dead grammatical cinder? My professors knew syntax enough, and of the human soul this much—that it had a faculty called memory, and could be acted on through the muscular integument by the appliance of birch-rods."

The greatest waste of time and money in our school-system comes from the employment of untrained teachers who, finally, learn how to teach after a fashion; but who spoil a great many classes before they learn how to teach at all. The true economy of school management is the employment of professionally educated teachers, and the exclusion of itinerants and bunglers. "The chief function of the normal school," says Thomas Hunter, President of the New York Normal College, "is to prevent machine teaching." Our common-schools need not more laws, rules, and regulations, but better-trained teachers in the school-houses. "A good school," says President Eliot, of Harvard University, "is a man or a woman."

IV. THE PROFESSION OF TEACHING.

Except in a few colleges and universities, it cannot be said that there is in our country a *profession of teaching*. There are, it is true, many men and women who have made teaching their life-work; but they have little or no legal recognition as professional teachers. The peripatetic pedagogue is found only in the remotest rural districts on the borders of civilization, yet all teachers are still regarded by law and by custom as itinerants. In many states "the law" requires teachers to be examined annually for a certificate "to teach a common-school one year." In every state of the Union, law—or custom stronger than law—requires that teachers shall be appointed *annually* "for the term of one year." But in no state does "the law" require any professional training whatever as a prerequisite "for teaching a common-school one year." The legal status of the teacher is strictly in accordance with the popular fallacy that anybody who can, in any way, get a certificate is fit to keep school. In a few states and cities there is a protozoic indication of an order of development higher than that of the single-cell certificate; but, before teachers can gain a professional footing, there must be some general system of permanent diplomas authorized by state law, as are medical diplomas, or licenses to practise law.

Have we not reached such a stage of progress that a normal-school diploma may safely be taken as *prima facie* evidence of fitness to teach, or that the life diploma of one state may be legally recognized in every other? Must local exclusiveness stand forever a Chinese wall in the way of the school-teacher? Must all teachers, when they change their residence, forever be compelled by legal enactments to halt at every state line, or city limits, or district boundary, and submit to an "examination," in order to prove that they are not educational "tramps?" As long as "the law" requires teachers to submit to frequent and humiliating examinations, so long will school officials regard them, if not with contempt, with "a certain condescension."

The annual election or appointment of teachers is another legal barrier against teaching as a profession. It is not possible to dignify as a profession an occupation in which men and women are subject to an annual loss of place at the caprice of ever-changing school-boards. Even under our civil-service system, by which places are parcelled out as spoils by the victors, the tenure of position is at least four years. There is need of school-service reform as well as of civil-service reform. There is only one large city in our country in which the tenure of a teacher's place is during good behavior; everywhere else appointments are made annually "for the term of one year."

Among the minor influences tending to prevent the

recognition of teaching as a profession are the short terms of school officials, the multiplicity of state laws and city ordinances, the low rates of teachers' salaries, and the almost total lack of any discrimination in wages between trained teachers and raw recruits. Before there can be a supply of professional teachers, there must be some demand for them by the people whose children go to school. There is still another stumbling-block in the way of the professional teacher in the large cities where boards of education are elected by direct vote at general elections, and that is the influence of ward politicians in securing places for friends and relatives as a reward for political or partisan services. In the days of his power, Tweed was a dictator of school appointments in New York, and in smaller cities innumerable smaller *Tweeds* are still dictating appointments. As long as there is a public disposition to regard school departments as charitable institutions where needy and politically useful persons can be respectably pensioned, just so long will it be impossible to secure professional teachers.

People are apt to put too much faith in systems, and too little in devoted, educated, and skilled men and women. "It will be a sorry day for the development of American life," says Superintendent Hancock, "when school authorities shall come to consider organization and method in our school system, however perfect, a substitute for brains and character in the educator, or to look on mechanic as the equal of dynamic teaching." "If there be one profession," says Tyndall, "of paramount importance, I believe it to be that of the schoolmaster."

John D. Philbrick, Ex-Superintendent of the Boston Schools, says, "We cannot too often repeat the great fundamental maxim, 'As is the teacher, so is the school.' In the administration of a system of public instruction, therefore, it should be the first and foremost aim to select superior teachers, to retain them in service, and to insist upon constant progress in excellence. I trust the time is not far distant when no teacher will be permitted to assume the responsibility of conducting a primary school who has not been first thoroughly trained to the art in a model school."

V. THE NEXT STEP.

It must be evident that the weakest point in our school system is the very general employment of untrained teachers. The sheet-anchor of our hope for improvement is in the establishment by legal enactments that only those persons shall be eligible to secure teachers' certificates who, as a prerequisite, shall have graduated from a normal school, or shall have pursued in some other school a satisfactory course in the science and art of education, all holders of existing certificates to be ranked as professionals. In the outset, this plan can be carried into full effect only in the larger cities and towns. It will be impracticable to establish such a standard of attainments, for a long time to come, in the ungraded country schools, kept open only a part of the year; but to bring public opinion up to this point should be the objective aim of every educator. There are persons born with the natural capacities to make superior instructors, but there are no "born" teachers; *they* are the product of technical training superadded to education. Emerson's general statement applies with special fitness to the education of the teacher:

"Our arts and tools give to him who can handle them much the same advantage over the novice as if you extended his life ten, fifty, or a hundred years. And I think it is the part of good-sense to provide every fine soul with such culture that it shall not, at thirty or forty years, have to say, 'This which I might do is made hopeless through my want of weapons.'"

It is true that not all graduates of medical schools become good physicians; not all graduates of theological schools become eloquent preachers; not all graduates of art schools become great artists; and not all graduates of normal schools become efficient teachers; but in all these cases there is a far greater probability of success than there would be with persons both *untrained* and *untried*. Professional schools do send out teachers with some knowledge derived from the experience of educators, and some conception of right methods of instruction.

There are in the United States about 100 public normal schools which graduate about 2000 teachers every year. Into the standing army of 300,000 teachers there are enlisted annually at least 20,000 raw recruits who have to learn how to teach at the public expense. These facts do not indicate that the people have yet been educated up to the belief of Horace Mann, "that normal schools are a new instrumentality in the advancement of the race."

We need not on this account, however, despair of the future. From the very nature of the school systems, our progress must be slow. We have a multiplicity of state laws, hundreds of city charters and city boards of education, thousands of town committees, and tens of thousands of district trustees. Uniform advancement is impossible. The school district is the unit of political organization, and every district is, in school affairs, an independent republic, or rather a local democracy. The schools are improved only by the pressure of public opinion, and cannot rise higher than the average intelligence of the community of which they are the outgrowth. But being under the direct control of the people, they are vitalized by the American spirit, and their progress is as certain as the advancement of civilization.

In addition to the present system of normal schools, the colleges and universities—especially those maintained by the state—should establish professorships of the science and art of education, and provide postgraduate courses for those who intend to become school-teachers or superintendents. It is true that a college course, of itself, may fit a graduate for some kinds of special teaching; but it certainly fails to prepare one to become a good general teacher or principal of a public school. "Professors of the theory, history, and practice of education" have been appointed in the universities of Edinburgh and St. Andrew's, Scotland; and there is a movement to establish similar chairs in some of the English universities. In our own country, this measure has been urged by many prominent educators who consider it essential to the future well-being of the common-school system. "Mr. William Harold Payne has been recently appointed Professor of the Science and Art of Teaching in the University of Michigan. The University of Wisconsin maintains a course of lectures in Didactics. The University of Iowa has maintained her normal department, with modifications and improvements on the original plan, uninterruptedly since 1855. The University of Missouri established a normal professorship in 1856, and a normal college in 1867." The colleges and universities, combined with state and city normal schools, and normal classes in connection with high-schools, could in twenty years supply the nation with a corps of trained and enthusiastic teachers. With a body of professional teachers under the wise supervision of trained superintendents and inspectors, the common-schools would be well equipped to educate the people.

Meanwhile, in many parts of our country still under rude social conditions, we must expect the statement to hold true that was made by Roger Ascham, "scholemaster" to Queen Elizabeth:

"And it is pity that commonly more care is had, yea, and that among very wise men, to find out rather a cunning man for their Horse than a cunning man for their Children. For to the one they will gladly give a Stipend of two hundred crowns by the year, and are loth to offer to the other two hundred Shillings. God that sitteth in Heaven laugheth their choice to scorn, and rewardeth their Liberality as it should. For he suffereth them to have tame and well-ordered Horses, but wild and unfortunate Children; and, therefore, in the end they find more Pleasure in their Horse than Comfort in their Children."

VI. THE SCHOLARSHIP OF TEACHERS.

Before teaching can take rank as a profession, teachers must command respect for their scholarship. If they confine themselves to the schoolroom; if they write nothing, say nothing, and do nothing—society will estimate them for value received. Teachers who would stand high in public opinion must read, study, think, observe, and take an active part in the affairs of society outside of school lessons.

"The hardest thing to do in the world," says Emerson, "is to think." But the true teacher must do more—he must take the step from thought to *action*. His work is done, not in the retirement of the closet, but in living contact with other minds. The best teacher is not the one who has devoured the most books, but he who can best kindle young hearts into enthusiasm by a spark of electric fire from his own soul. "The first principle of human culture," says Carlyle, "the foundation of all but false, imaginary culture, is that men must, before every other thing, be able to *do* somewhat."

Mere learning is often mistaken for scholarship, and a walking library for an electric battery of thought. "No person can be called educated," says Whipple, "until he has organized his knowledge into faculty, and can wield it as a weapon."

The scholarship of the teacher ought to be liberal, embracing some knowledge of many things; and any teacher can make his culture liberal if he uses rightly the leisure time which his pursuit affords. It is a good thing to be many-sided; but the teacher must be a specialist in whatever relates directly to the science of education. He is judged by his success as a *teacher*, not as a scientist, writer, lecturer, or poet. In his own profession, when he rises above his routine drudgery, he gets into the region of hard thinking. Climbing mountains is hard work, and the strain is hardest near the summit. The teacher who gets out of the sphere of imitation into that of invention and discovery will find ample scope for his powers. One reason why self-educated men so often succeed is, they concentrate their energies upon what they need to use. Like Napoleon, they fight without tents or baggage. They acquire a concentrated force of character, that stamps its impress upon everything with which it comes in contact.

Above all things, the true teacher should avoid recasting everything in the mould of his own egotism. Dealing mostly with young and immature minds, he is in continual danger of overestimating his own powers. Seldom questioned in his assertions, he is peculiarly liable to become dogmatic and opinionated. Everybody knows of pedantic pedagogues whose conceit is insufferable and ineffable. They *look* wiser than it is possible for any mortal to become. They gain credit, like Wouter Van Twiller, for knowing a vast deal by saying nothing at all. The egotistical teacher reverses the old maxim "*All* men know more than *one* man" so that it reads "*One* man knows more than *all* men," he himself being that one man. But the true teacher will not dream his life away, like a Hindoo god, in contemplating his own perfections.

It is often said that teaching school belittles a man and sours a woman. It *may* be so; it sometimes is so; but not from any law of nature. It can never be true of any teacher made *alive* by keeping his intellectual and spiritual faculties and emotions in healthful play. "The original and proper sources of knowledge," says Blackie, "are not books, but life, experience, personal thinking, feeling, and acting." These sources are open to the teacher all his life. By imparting knowledge he enriches himself, and the freshness of childhood becomes to him a fountain of youth. "All really superior teachers," says Mr. Philbrick, "are every day growing better." "The teacher," says Mr. William Russell, "is himself a primary observer, authority, and reporter in the science of mind. His work is that of a living philosopher in *act*."

Aside from the course of general reading which every teacher ought to pursue, there must be some regular study of the science and art of teaching. For general principles in education, let him read the works of Herbert Spencer; for rugged practical suggestions, Bain and Huxley; for enthusiasm, the life and works of Horace Mann. He should peruse all such good books on teaching as those of Russell, Page, Phelps, Hart, G. B. Emerson, Wickersham, and Orcutt; and also all the school reports he can get; and all the educational journals he can afford to pay for. Let him critically examine all new text-books in the various branches of study; he will glean some new method from each one. He ought to attend teachers' conventions, institutes, and associations, and to take part in the proceedings. The original thinkers, the discoverers, and inventors may be few; but the efficient workers are many, whose mission is to aid the progress of the race by earnest, skilful, intelligent teaching. "Be ashamed to die," said Horace Mann, "until you have won some victory for humanity."

VII. TEACHERS' ASSOCIATIONS.

It is no wonder that the solitary teacher in some rural district, surrounded by the protoplasm of humanity, his labors unappreciated, his motives misunderstood, his services half paid—it is no wonder that he sometimes becomes moody, loses his enthusiasm, and imagines that the sky is only a vast concave blackboard upon which he is doomed to work out the problem of a bare subsistence. He needs the pleasant intercourse of professional gatherings to make the heavens brighten with the stars of hope and glow with the aurora of enthusiasm. As well expect a hermit on a desolate island to advance in civilization as to suppose that an isolated teacher can rise far above his surroundings. Association is the motive power of progress in civilization, science, and art. The world's industrial expositions are dignifying mechanics and artisans. Farmers hold their state or district or county fairs for the purpose of improving their live-stock: they organize as "Grangers" to improve themselves socially and politically. Printers, carpenters, machinists, and laborers, all have their societies and trades-unions for defence and offence. The lawyers, the doctors, the dentists, the clergy, the Masons, the Odd-fellows, all have their societies for charitable or protective purposes.

If teachers would exert any marked influence, they must wield it through the consolidated power of organized societies, associations, conventions, and institutes.

VIII. EDUCATIONAL POWER.

The true teacher must have the faith of martyrs. In the limited horizon of the schoolroom, he can dimly see only the beginning of the effects of his teaching upon his pupils. The solid results, the building-up of character, the creative power of motives, become evident only in the work of a lifetime in the wider circle of the world. Hence the power of the teacher, like that of the silent and invisible forces of nature, is only feebly realized.

I once visited a quartz mine of fabulous richness. Deep in the bowels of the earth, rough miners were blasting out the gold-bearing rock; above, the powerful mill was crushing the white quartz with its iron teeth. In the office, piles of yellow bars, ready to be sent to the mint to be poured into the channels of trade, showed the immediate returns of wisely invested capital and well-directed labor. An hour later, I stepped into a public school, not half a mile distant, where a hundred children were at work on their lessons. What does the school yield, I asked, on the investment of money by the State? The returns of the mine are made monthly, in solid bullion; the school returns will be made in the far future, and they cannot be expressed in dollars.

I go out from my school daily into the crowded streets of a great commercial city. I hear everywhere the hum of industry, and see the stir of business. The results of business are solid and tangible; but when I go back to my classes, after witnessing the mighty play of industrial forces, it seems as if the teacher were only a looker-on in the bustling life around. But when I pause to consider that intelligence is the motive power of trade; that the steamship is navigated by means of science, and is built as a triumph of art; that science surveyed the converging lines of railroads, and that skill runs the trains freighted with the products of industry and art, then I begin to perceive the connection between schools and the material results of civilization. I realize that the life of a nation is made up of the mothers that guard the homes, and the men who drive the plough, build the ships, run the mills, work the mines, construct the machinery, print the papers, shoulder the musket, cast the ballots; and it is for all these that the public schools have done, and are now doing, their beneficent work.

IX. THE COMMON-SCHOOL SYSTEM.

"Whatever you would have appear in the life of a nation you must first put into the schools," holds true pre-eminently in a republic. Our free-school system has its shortcomings and its defects; but, taken as a whole, it is the broadest and the best ever organized. It is the duty of every true teacher to strive to remedy its defects, and never to submit to them as incurable. When taxes are high and times are hard, the school system will be subject to a running fire of criticism all along the line; but only timid and despairing souls are frightened into the belief that the foundations of society are breaking up on account of over-education in the common-schools. Neither representatives of the caste of Capital nor the caste of Culture can convince the American people that vice, crime, idleness, poverty, social discontent, are the legitimate results of an elementary education among the workers of society, or that the schoolmaster is a public enemy. The sentiment of most Americans is that of Daniel Webster, who once said, "If I had as many sons as old Priam, I would send them all to the public schools." If our schools fail to meet the needs of changing social conditions, the *kind* and *quality*, not the *extent*, of education must be changed. Neither the free high-school nor the free state university must be lopped off. "No system of education," says Huxley, "is worthy of the name unless it creates a great educational ladder with one end in the gutter and the other in the university."

It is only by means of skilled labor, wisely and intelligently directed, that a people can become or can remain permanently prosperous and happy; it is only by means of intelligent and honest voters that law and liberty can be preserved and maintained; and it is only by means of a still more complete education of all classes that humanity can rise into a higher type of social evolution. There is no slavery so oppressive as that of ignorance.

Chapter II.

PHYSICAL TRAINING.

I. ITS IMPORTANCE.

One of the most hopeful features of modern education is the growing recognition of the importance of physical training in school. By thinkers and educators the necessity of a trained body as the instrument of a trained mind is fully recognized, though by the mass of teachers it is, as yet, feebly acted upon.

"To the wise educator," says W. T. Harris, Superintendent of the schools of the city of St. Louis, "nothing is more certain than that the child is an animal with the possibility of reason." "To be a nation of good animals," says Spencer, "is the first condition of national prosperity." "No perfect brain ever crowns an imperfectly developed body," says Dr. E. H. Clarke, of Boston. That tough old sceptic Montaigne says, "We have not to train up a soul, nor yet a body, but a man, and we cannot divide him." "Physical training and drill," says Huxley, "should be a part of the regular business of school. There is no real difficulty about teaching drill and the simpler kinds of gymnastics. If something of the kind is not done, the English physique, which has been, and still is, on the whole, a grand one, will become in the great towns as extinct as the dodo."

"When we have mastered the laws of physical education," says Professor Youmans, "we have the essential data for dealing with questions of mental education, and those steps are the indispensable preparation for an enlightened moral education." It is true that the leading purpose of the public school is intellectual training, and true that physical condition depends largely upon home surroundings and inherited constitution. It may be true also that, considering education strictly as a science, physical health does not fall within its domain, but is to be assumed as an essential prerequisite of education. Nevertheless, though the teacher has no direct control over pupils in respect to diet, clothing, exercise, rest, sleep, work, or play, yet the school must not, on that account, shirk its appropriate share of responsibility in relation to bodily development. As an abstract proposition, no teacher will deny that sound health is the true basis of mental and moral culture; the difficulty is how to secure it.

There are certain negative duties which are evident and easy. Teachers should at least protect their pupils against impure air, too long confinement, over-work, and the deadening effects of mental worry, caused by severe competitive written examinations. A great deal more than this ought to be done; but in many schools not even this is attempted.

It is the duty of every teacher, whether in the primary, grammar, or high school, whether in city or country, to impress upon pupils, by emphatic iteration, the laws of health in relation to food, air, sleep, rest, exercise, play, work, and personal habits in general. Teachers should give attention to the encouragement of games, plays, and amusements, in addition to calisthenic drill.

"Play," says Froebel, "is the development of the human

mind, its first effort to make acquaintance with the outward world. The child, indeed, recognizes no purpose in it, sees not the end that is to be reached; but it expresses its own nature, and that is human nature in its playful activity."

In the German schools, children are systematically trained to gymnastics, and the result is a national taste for athletic sports. English schools are noted for football and cricket, and Englishmen are famous for pluck. But in our own country, we must confess there is some truth in the remark made by a foreigner, "that the only popular recreation of the American is business."

Moreover, it is a first principle in the science of education that the best results in intellectual training can be secured only by a correlative physical development. Childhood is the season of animal growth. Playfulness is as much an instinct of children as of kittens or puppies. Even in the icy winters of the Arctic regions, Dr. Kane found the hardy little Esquimaux boys playing ball on the frosty snow-fields. It is a mistaken notion of some pedagogues that the chief end of children is to go to school and study lessons from books. It is painful to witness, in many schools, how the plastic, growing bodies are cramped, how natural impulses are repressed, how the laws of nature are systematically violated. Not many children, perhaps, are killed outright by mental high-pressure; but, now and then, some delicately organized boy, brilliant and ambitious, whose vitality all tends to brain instead of body, drops out of school into the grave, and his death is attributed to Providence instead of to schoolmasters. High-school diplomas, not a few, are gained at the expense of sound health, and girls, not a few, are annually made life-long invalids by over-stimulated ambition, long lessons, short hours of sleep, and a lack of healthful amusements.

Physicians know this, though teachers and parents shut their eyes to the painful facts. Not all the girls in public schools or private seminaries have round shoulders, crooked spines, and dyspepsia; but how much greater might be their physical stamina if physical training received a small share of the attention given to music and mathematics? If these girls need mental culture in order to make their future homes pleasant and attractive, do they not also need bodily culture to enable them to bear the burdens of domestic life? In the struggle for existence, it is generally the strong, active, vigorous boys that come out ahead, and it is the healthy and beautiful girls that win the prizes of life.

After admitting all this, it is often urged that systematic drill soon becomes irksome to children; that boys dislike the gymnasium, and that girls find calisthenics wearisome; that it is not natural for children to use wands and dumb-bells; and that boys and girls should be left to follow their own inclinations and impulses about exercise and amusement.

But school drill is designed not to supersede, but to supplement, the natural games and plays of children. If we leave physical culture wholly to natural impulse, why not leave mental culture to take care of itself? In mental training, we recognize the principle that intellectual development is attained only by repeated, long-continued, and systematic exercises. Mental school gymnastics are rigidly enforced for many years. The same law holds true in physical development; yet children are too often crowded into small rooms, and cramped in hard seats—

their muscles weak and relaxed, and their vital energies all concentrated on an overworked brain.

Would not the physique of a class of boys under judicious gymnastic training for ten years be superior to that of a class left to run wild? And would not their accumulated stock of trained muscular power be quite as serviceable to them through life as a great deal of what is called mental discipline? Business men, mechanics, artisans, and farmers know that success depends, not upon intellectual attainments so much as upon sound health and power of endurance. Sinewy frames as well as trained minds are essential to the sons of workingmen who must make their own way in the world. For them muscular power means food, clothing, and a living. Their only capital in the struggle for existence is an elementary education and a sound body. "Health is the first wealth," says Emerson. The plain truth is that no education is worth having at the expense of health and physical vigor. "I am a poor man," said a friend to me, "because in a business crisis I was sick, and did the wrong thing; and I was sick because of neglected physical training at school."

II. WAYS AND MEANS.

Admitting the importance of physical training in school, how shall we set about it? Doubtless, in some schools nothing whatever can be done. In city schools the need is more pressing than in country schools. After many years of experience in directing physical exercises, I am inclined to think that the possibility of doing something depends in a great measure on the interest, enthusiasm, and tact of the teacher. The pleasantest recollections of my earlier years of teaching are connected with gymnastic classes of active boys who could, with me, kick foot-ball, play base-ball, lift dumb-bells, swing clubs, climb ladders, vault bars, walk twenty miles on Saturday, and roast a beefsteak on a pointed stick over an improvised camp-fire. As I meet those boys, now grown up into rugged manhood, I know by the way they grip my hand and speak of the "splendid times we used to have," that they think of me, not as a mere schoolmaster, but as the friend who shared their sports and entered into the spirit of their boyhood.

My later experience in a girls' high-school, numbering eight hundred pupils, has convinced me of the very great value for girls of systematic calisthenic drill. In his Boston report so long ago as 1860, Superintendent Philbrick said, "The principal remedy which I would suggest is the introduction into all grades of our schools of a thorough system of physical training as a part of school culture." "Gymnastic exercises," says Secretary Dickinson, "give grace and beauty to the body, and good training to the mind."

III. PRACTICAL DIRECTIONS.

In every school, whether in city or country, there should be given a daily drill of five or ten minutes in free gymnastics. Without apparatus and without music, a skilful teacher can secure very good results from what may be termed "free-arm movements," executed by counting in time. To these there may be added "breathing exercises," and concert exercises in vocal culture or in singing.

Both wands and dumb-bells can be used in any school-room. Wands will cost about ten cents apiece, and light wooden dumb-bells about twenty-five cents a pair. If there is a piano in the schoolroom, the light gymnastic drill can be made quite varied and thorough with no other appliances. If there is a hall, wooden rings should be added for girls.

For the larger boys, there should be some inexpensive gymnastic appliances in the yard. A movable horizontal bar, a circular swing, hanging rings, parallel bars, iron dumb-bells, and Indian clubs can all be obtained for a small expenditure.

Any young lady, even if not previously trained in calisthenics, ought to be able to lead a class after a few weeks' study of any one of several good manuals on the subject. Any man, unless superannuated, ought to be able to lead, or at least *direct*, gymnastic exercises in the yard, at recess, intermission, or after school.

The man who understands boys will either join with them or will encourage and direct them in their games of ball and foot-ball; in skating, coasting, and snow-balling; and will take an interest in their games of marbles, in kite-flying, and top-spinning. On pleasant Saturdays, or after school in the long summer days, he will head excursion parties to the fields, woods, or hills after collections for the cabinet, or to see nature, or merely to have a good time.

The woman who understands little children will invite them to pleasant walks with her for the same purpose. The games of the primary children must not be forgotten. By a little attention to the playground, their sports may be regulated and made delightful. Marbles, tops, kites, balls, and hoops are all a part of educational apparatus.

A visit to a kindergarten and a careful study of some kindergarten manual will be very suggestive in the direction of play and amusements. Teachers must study variety, for monotonous repetition soon becomes distasteful. Notice how marbles succeed tops, and kites follow ball, and one play another, as often as the moon changes.

The cold, formal, precise, unsympathetic teacher should never set foot on the playground. An owl frightens singing birds. The only teachers who succeed well in directing children in calisthenics, gymnastics, or games are those who can enter into the spirit of girlhood and boyhood. "He was always a boy, and he will die one," was the remark I once heard made about one of the best teachers I ever knew.

The indirect lessons of the playground are often more valuable and more lasting than the formal teachings of the class-room. For in the hours of play, when off duty, the teacher can best win the confidence and love of children. What man or woman would not be remembered by pupils as a sharer of their amusements, a director of their games, a sympathizer with their impulses, rather than as nothing but an expounder of text-books and a taskmaster of lessons? It is on the playground, too, that boys get their first lessons in social life outside of the family circle.

"You send a boy to the schoolmaster," says Emerson, "but it is the schoolboys who educate him. He hates the grammar and *Gradus*, and loves guns, fishing-rods, horses, and boats. Well, the boy is right, and you are not fit to direct his bringing up if your theory leaves out his gymnastic training. Provided always the boy is teachable, foot-ball, cricket, climbing, fencing, riding, archery, swimming, skating, are lessons in the art of power which it is his main business to learn." "Moreover," says Charles

Kingsley, "they know well that games conduce, not merely to physical, but to moral health; that in the playing-field boys acquire virtues that no books can give them; not merely daring and endurance, but, better still, temper, self-restraint, fairness, honor, unenvious approbation of another's success, and all that 'give and take' of life which stands a man in such good stead when he goes forth into the world; and without which, indeed, his success is always maimed and partial."

IV. INDUSTRIAL TRAINING.

And, in connection with physical training, there is the question of industrial or technical education in the great cities. In the country, boys work on the farm half the year, and girls work in the house all the year through. The country pupils combine mental and physical work, and are the better for it.

Children are not content with reading and thinking; they burn to be *doing* something. The kindergarten supplies this want with the little children; but from the age of six to fifteen there is at present, in the city public school, little for boys but books. There is no doubt whatever that many boys get a distaste for school, and leave it as soon as they can find any work to do, and before they have obtained any education beyond the ability to read, write, and cipher a little. How the combination of head-work with hand-work can be effected, if at all, is one of the educational problems of the future. It is not safe to assert that it cannot be done. On this subject, John Hancock, of Ohio, speaks as follows:

"But to impart in the schools of our cities and large towns all this general knowledge and training without the slightest abatement, and to add, not the knowledge of a trade, but such a knowledge of the uses of tools and materials as shall enable the scholar readily to adjust himself to several trades, seems to be something worth striving for. That this can be done, and without greatly lengthening the period of school life or enormously increasing school expenses, has been pretty well established by the experiments made within the last two or three years at the Boston School of Technology. Indications are strong that the education of the brain and of the hand are, at no distant day, to run on side by side, mutually strengthening each other in the race. To unite a thinking brain with a skilful hand is the way to make labor respectable, and any other way than this there is not under the sun."

"Froebel did not value manual work for the sake merely of making a better workman," says Emily Shirreff, " but for the sake of making a more complete human being. His teaching rested upon the principle that the starting-point of all we see, know, are conscious of, is *action*, and, therefore, that education must begin in *action*. Book-study, in his system, is postponed to the discipline of the mental and physical powers through observation and work."

V. TECHNICAL EDUCATION.

As yet, technical education can hardly be said to form a part of our common-school system, except in one state, and in some cities where a beginning has been made in the evening schools. I dismiss this part of the subject by giving a few quotations to show the drift of opinion among prominent educators:

"Technical education, in the sense in which the term is ordinarily used, means that sort of education which is specially adapted to the needs of men whose business in life it is to pursue some kind of handicraft. . . . Moreover, those who have to live by labor must be shaped to labor early. The colt that is left at grass too long makes but a sorry draught-horse. Perhaps the most valuable result of all education is the ability to make yourself do the thing you have to do when it ought to be done, whether you like it or not: it is the first lesson that ought to be learned; and, however early a man's training begins, it is probably the last lesson that he learns thoroughly."—*Huxley.*

"A knowledge of some form of industrial labor is as necessary as a knowledge of books, and the state which acknowledges its obligation to teach children to read cannot logically deny its obligation to teach them to work. . . . Do I think it possible to attach workshops to all our public schools? Certainly not. But I do think it possible to have public workshops where boys can learn trades, as well as public schools where they can learn letters. And just as we transfer the *few* from the state school to the state college, where they learn to be *thinkers*, I would transfer the *many* from the city school to the city workshop, where they would learn to be workers."—*Superintendent Newell*, of Maryland.

"I hold it to be a correct principle that, while the common-school does not aim to make farmers or mechanics, but leaves this to the special schools, it is the business of the common-schools to teach the elements of technical knowledge, both scientific and artistic."—*Superintendent Carr*, of California.

"I have given what I believe a good reason for the assumption that the keeping at school of boys who are to be handicraftsmen beyond the age of thirteen or fourteen is neither practicable nor desirable; and it is quite certain that, with justice to other and no less important branches of education, nothing more than the rudiments of science and art-teaching can be introduced into elementary schools; and we must seek elsewhere for a supplementary training in these subjects, which may go on after the workman's life has begun. . . . The great advantage of evening technical classes is that they bring the means of instruction to the doors of the factories and workshops."—*Huxley.*

VI. SCHOOL HYGIENE.

1. "The laws of health," says Dr. Willard Parker, "are the laws of God, and are as binding as the Decalogue." "The fact is," says Spencer, "that all breaches of the laws of health are physical sins." "Nature's discipline," says Huxley, "is not even a word and a blow, and the blow first; but the blow without the word. It is left for you to find out why your ears are boxed."

2. No education is worth the cost if gained at the expense of health and cheerfulness, or under the penalty of nervous weaknesses, dyspepsia, or near-sightedness.

3. A sound body is the groundwork of sound intellectual faculties. A morbid condition of body leads to dulness of mental perceptions and weakness of the intellectual faculties. Excessive or premature mental development checks the growth of the body; over-development is antagonistic to growth.

4. "The physiological motto is," says Dr. E. H. Clarke, "Educate a man for manhood, a woman for womanhood, both for humanity. In this lies the hope of the race." "Get health," says Emerson, "for sickness is a cannibal which eats up all the life and youth it can lay hold of, and absorbs its own sons and daughters."

5. "Mental labor, rightly directed," says Dr. Lincoln, of Boston, "is a most healthful occupation; and there is no real reason why this should not be true at all periods of school life. But the difference between *forced* and *spontaneous* action is of great consequence to the health and mental energy of the child."

6. "At college," says Horace Mann, "I was taught the motions of the heavenly bodies as if their keeping in their

orbits depended upon my knowing them; while I was in profound ignorance of the laws of health of my own body. The rest of my life was, in consequence, one long battle with exhausted energies."

SUGGESTIONS TO TEACHERS.

1. Children under ten years of age ought to have no lessons whatever assigned for home study. Whatever time they can spare from play ought to be spent in reading suitable library books. Boys and girls from ten to twelve years of age ought not to have more than one lesson for home study. And girls from fourteen to sixteen years of age, in high-schools, ought not to study more than one hour a day out of school. From ten to sixteen is the golden period for the reading of good books; and any course of school-work that deprives pupils of time to read by keeping them all the time at the drudgery of text-book lessons is a mental wrong and a physical sin.

2. Do not exhaust the vitality of weak, nervous, brilliant, ambitious children by too rapid promotion. Put on the brakes, even if you have to oppose ambitious and ignorant parents. Of what use is it to let them gain a year in school and lose a lifetime?

3. If possible, keep your schoolroom well ventilated; but do not run to the foolish extreme of subjecting your pupils to strong draughts of cold or damp air from open windows. In winter, regulate the temperature by a thermometer.

4. Do not allow children to sit in school with wet feet or damp clothing. Let them get warm and dry around the stove before you begin work.

5. When children suffer from headaches, send them

home. They cannot *think* well, and the attempt to study leads to bad mental habits.

6. In pleasant weather, compel girls as well as boys to go out of doors to play at recesses and intermissions; and do not allow them to take their books with them for the purpose of studying when they ought to play.

7. By means of window-shades, carefully attended to during the day, protect the eyes of your pupils from excessive light, and from the direct rays of the sun. Caution your pupils against habits of holding books in ways that lead to near-sightedness.

8. Require your pupils to sit erect and to stand erect, and explain to them the reason *why* you do so.

9. Explain *why* loose clothing is healthful, and tight clothing is harmful.

10. Tell pupils what articles of diet are, in general, wholesome; what, in general, are unwholesome.

11. Teach them that it is better to *prevent* sickness by attention to the laws of health than to be continually dosing themselves with medicines.

12. Teach them the importance of preserving their teeth and of chewing their food.

13. Charge them not to sit up late at night to study. The more active the mind, the greater the need of sleep. From the age of twelve to eighteen, boys and girls need from eight to ten hours of unbroken sleep every night.

14. Impress upon them the fact that they must take care of their bodies, or suffer the penalty of neglect in the form of sickness; that suffering is sure to follow transgression; and that nature remits no punishments.

15. If you are teaching in a girls' school, read Clarke's *Sex in Education,* Clarke's *Building of a Brain,* Miss

Studley's *What Girls Ought to Know*, and Miss Brackett's *Education of American Girls*.

VII. RULES OF HEALTH FOR PUPILS.

NOTE.—The following rules are given as a model for additional ones. The teacher can make each direction the topic for a short lesson by giving the reasons for it.

1. Retire early, and sleep from eight to ten hours every night. *The harder you study, the more sleep you need.*
2. Exercise in the open air and sunshine is second in importance only to sleep.
3. Ventilate your sleeping-room at night either by an open door, or a window slightly open both at top and bottom.
4. Avoid hot cakes, hot bread, strong tea, and strong coffee. In hot weather, avoid fat meats. Avoid eating between meals, and especially beware of lunches just before going to bed. If you want a clear head for good mental work, take light breakfasts. Do not study immediately after a hearty meal. If possible, avoid studying before breakfast.
5. Take care of your teeth; you need them both for ornament and use.
6. Wear loose clothing, and loose-fitting boots and shoes.
7. Keep the feet warm and dry, and you will avoid a great many colds and headaches. In cold or wet weather wear thick boots and shoes.
8. Keep the whole body clean by bathing according to season and climate.
9. Do not study out of school more than from one to two hours. No education is worth getting at the expense of health.

10. Take care of your eyes. When they ache, stop reading or writing at once. Any abuse of the eyes is sure to be followed by a severe penalty in later life.

11. Avoid cross lights. If possible, sit so that the light shall fall over your left shoulder.

12. Never sit in school with a ray of sunshine streaming into your face or upon your desk. Ask your teacher to lower the shade, or to allow you to change your seat.

13. When you read, sit erect, and hold your book *up*, not flat upon the desk.

14. Avoid books in fine print. Do not read at twilight, nor before breakfast by lamplight or gaslight.

15. Unless you wish to ruin your eyes, never read in bed.

16. Never study later than nine o'clock at night. Milton, when young, used to sit up till midnight; result, blindness in old age.

17. For weak eyes, an extra hour's sleep every night is the best remedy.

18. Pain in the eyes is often caused by a disordered stomach. Be careful about your diet.

19. If you wish to avoid being near-sighted, hold your book at a reasonable distance from your eyes when reading.

20. Do not wear colored glasses, except by the advice of a physician.

Chapter III.
MORAL TRAINING.
I. GENERAL REMARKS.

INTELLECTUAL development is the most prominent object of common-school instruction; but moral training is not less important, though its results are not so immediate and tangible. "The vital part of human culture," says Russell, "is not that which makes man what he is intellectually; but that which makes him what he is in heart, life, and character."

"That education," says President Chadbourne, of Williams College, "which does not make prominent justice as well as benevolence, law as well as liberty, honesty as well as thrift, and purity of life as well as enjoyment should be stamped, by every true educator, as a waste and a curse; for so it will prove in the end."

"The common-school," says Rev. A. D. Mayo, "is the place, of all others, to inculcate the great industrial, social, and civic virtues of honesty, chastity, truthfulness, justice, responsibility for social order; all the moral safeguards of national life."

What we term moral culture, which concerns the feelings, the emotions, the will, the conscience, must always be, to some extent, the result of the teacher's indirect tuition of manner, character, and example. Lessons in arithmetic, grammar, and geography may be given by formal methods, or may be learned from text-books; but good moral training is of a higher and more complex character. "Creeds pasted upon the memory," says Spencer, "good principles learned by rote, lessons in right and wrong, will not eradicate vicious propensities, though people, in spite of their experience as parents and as citizens, persist in hoping they will." "The difficulties of moral teaching," says Bain, "exceed in every way the difficulties of intellectual teaching." In the child's moral nature, *sympathy* is the ruling impulse, and *influence* the controlling power. The teacher must be a trusted and affectionate guide, not a bundle of philosophical ethics.

It is true the child's moral tendencies are largely the result of home influences or of hereditary transmission; nevertheless, the school cannot shirk its appropriate share of responsibility.

II. THE SPHERE OF SCHOOL.

Unfavorable home influences must be counteracted as far as possible at school, and the moral faculties must be called into daily exercise until habits of right-thinking result in habits of right-doing. The strict discipline of school is in itself a powerful means of moral culture. Pupils are trained to habits of order, regularity, punctuality, industry, truthfulness, obedience, regard for the rights of others, and a general sense of justice. The influence of school, continued for a series of years, in these respects, is very powerful in the formation of habit and character.

But beyond these incidental and indirect results, what is it possible to accomplish in the way of moral development? In the past, moral training was very generally confounded with religious instruction; and some still hold that there can be no moral culture not based on specific religious instruction or sectarian faith. In our public schools, purely secular instruction is the rule, both by law and custom; religious exercises the exception. For the purpose of practical consideration, then, we may remand religious teaching to the home, the Sunday-school, and the Church.

The reading of the Bible, still required in some schools as a formal morning exercise, may or may not be an aid in moral training, according to the manner and spirit in which the exercise is conducted. The same holds true of morning or evening school prayers. Unless marked by earnestness on the part of the teacher, and attentive reverence by pupils, it is better to omit them. With regard to such devotional exercises, considered by many to be on the border-line of religious instruction, teachers must be guided by local custom and regulations; but they should bear in mind that there is a growing tendency to make the public schools purely secular; that the present is an age of the broadest personal liberty in respect to religious belief; and that they must manifest in school a tolerant regard for the conscientious scruples as well as the legal rights of both Jew and Gentile, Catholic and Protestant, Liberal and Churchman.

"It is not merely by hearing the Bible read," says Professor George W. Minns, "or by learning Bible lessons or theological dogmas, or by any forms or ceremonies, that the religious spirit cometh. All these, at their best, are only means to an end; they are not the end itself, and they often defeat it. Motives are the springs of all actions. We judge of a man's conduct by his motives; the spirit with which a man works, the motives which prompt his conduct—these show and constitute the man, and these are moral qualities springing from and dwelling in the heart."

Professor Bain, in his late work, *Education as a Science*, thus clearly draws the following dividing line:

"Morality is not religion, and religion is not morality; and yet the two have points of coincidence. Morality cannot be the same thing without religion as with it; religion, working in its own sphere, does not make full provision for all the moral exigencies of human life. The precepts of morality must be chiefly grounded on our human relations in this world as known by practical experience; the motives, too, grow very largely out of those relations. Religion has precepts of its own, and these are all the more effectively worked when worked in separation."

"I wish to be distinctly understood," says W. T. Harris, "as claiming only that public-school education is moral, and completely so, on its own basis; that it lays the basis for religion, *but is no substitute for religion.* It is not a substitute for the State because it teaches justice; it only prepares an indispensable culture for the citizen of the State. The State must exist; religion must exist, and complement the structure of human culture begun in moral education."

III. POSSIBILITIES AND CONDITIONS.

Leaving out of consideration all religious forms and observances in school, what is it possible to accomplish in the way of *moral training?* There are some who think nothing can be done if distinctive religious instruction is omitted, and that moral training must necessarily be disregarded; but this, in the words of Huxley, "is burning the ship to get rid of the cockroaches."

If moral training consisted merely in *telling* children what is right and what is wrong, and in dealing out ethical maxims and proverbs; if it were enough to tell children it is wicked to lie, steal, or swear; if it would make boys truthful and honest to learn commandments by rote —then the teacher's task would be an easy one. "Did you ever give a lesson on honesty?" asked Horace Mann of a teacher in England. "Oh no," was the ready reply, "that isn't necessary; they have the commandment in the catechism, you know."

But the fact that true moral development depends on complex conditions is no reason why the whole matter should be practically ignored, as seems to be the case in some schools.

Moral development depends partly on the clearness of the intellectual faculties, and partly upon physical conditions; partly on hereditary traits, and partly on educational bias. It is influenced by the pupil's associates, home discipline, by school government, and by religious instruction in the family, the Church, and the Sunday-school.

There can be no sound moral character not based upon a sound understanding capable of forming correct judgments upon thoughts and acts. Emotions, appetites, passions, and will must be under the control of intelligent mental perceptions. Sound health is an important factor. "Every man is a rascal as soon as he is sick," says Dr. Johnson. As the child should be made to feel, in physical training, that every violation of the laws of health is visited by swift and inevitable punishment, so in moral training the central idea should be to make the child realize the natural penalty upon himself of every violation of the law of right.

"The tendency of each new generation," says Spencer, "to develop itself wrongly indicates the degree of modification that has yet to take place. Those respects in which a child requires restraint are just the respects in which he is taking after the aboriginal man. The selfish squabbles of the nursery, the persecutions of the playground, the lyings and petty thefts, the rough treatment of inferior creatures, the propensity to destroy—all these imply that tendency to pursue self-gratification at the expense of other beings which qualified man for the wilderness, and which disqualifies him for civilized life."

IV. GENERAL DIRECTIONS FROM HERBERT SPENCER.

1. "There are in all children tendencies to good feelings and actions, and also tendencies and impulses to wrong-doing. These tendencies, whether good or bad, are the result of hereditary transmission and of surrounding circumstances."

2. "Do not expect from children any great amount of moral goodness."

3. "Do not attempt to force young children into precocious moral goodness. Be content with moderate measures and moderate results."

4. "Bear in mind the fact that a higher morality, like a higher intelligence, must be reached by a slow growth."

5. "Leave children, whenever you can, to the discipline of experience."

6. "Be sparing of commands; but whenever you *do* command, command with decision and firmness."

7. "Let your penalties be like the penalties inflicted by inanimate nature—*inevitable.*"

8. "The aim of your discipline should be to produce a

self-governing being, not to produce a being to be governed by others."

9. "Do not regret the exhibition of considerable self-will on the part of children. The independent boy is the father of the independent man."

10. "Always remember that to educate rightly is not a simple and easy thing; but a complex and extremely difficult thing, the hardest task that devolves upon adult life."

V. PRACTICAL HINTS.

Methods of conducting moral lessons in school must be gathered up by experience and observation. They cannot be stated like rules of syntax or mathematical demonstrations. A warm heart, a genial nature, an even temper, a beaming eye, a cheerful countenance, a sincere voice, an earnest manner—these are the potential agencies by which you can win, direct, and control your pupils.

1. *The Emotions.*—Keep fresh in mind your own feelings, passions, emotions, impulses, sympathies, and experiences when a child, and you will avoid the grievous mistake of applying to school children the moral philosophy suited only to adult metaphysicians. "Put yourself in the place of your pupils" is a good motto. ".We might as well expect children," says Rousseau, "to be ten feet high as to have judgment in their tenth year." "Young children," says Pestalozzi, "cannot be governed by appeals to conscience, because it is not yet developed. *Sympathy* must be gradually superseded by the rule of right, and children must be led from good feelings to right principles."

The opinions of children are influenced, not so much by reason as by emotion—their likes and dislikes. "The education of the child," says Bishop Jebb, "is principally derived from its own observation of the actions, the words, the voice, the looks, of those with whom it lives."

"What children see constantly done by those whom they respect and love," says the famous German educator Niemeyer, "they very soon come to think is what ought to be done. Thus it is that the manners and morals of nations, as well as of smaller societies and of families, are perpetuated."

"Whatever moral benefit *can* be effected by education," says Herbert Spencer, "must be effected by an education that is *emotional* rather than perceptive. If, in place of making a child *understand* that this thing is *right* and the other *wrong*, you make it *feel* that they are so; if you make virtue *loved* and vice *loathed;* if you arouse a noble *desire* and make torpid an inferior one; if you bring into life a previously dormant *sentiment;* if you cause a sympathetic *impulse* to get the better of one that is selfish; if, in short, you produce a state of mind to which proper behavior is natural, spontaneous, instinctive —you do some good. But no drilling in catechisms, no teaching of moral codes, can effect this. Mere ideas received by the intellect, meeting no response from within, are quite inoperative upon conduct, and are quickly forgotten upon entering into life."

2. *Doing.*—Children must not only be taught what is right, they must also be made to *do* what is right. The school is a miniature world. In one way or another it affords opportunities for the practice of most of the moral virtues. Strict discipline trains pupils to habits of obedience and order, corrects bad habits, and compels the lawless to respect the rights of others. It is possible for the

teacher to breathe into a school a spirit of honor, truthfulness, and honesty that shall control every new scholar that comes under its influence. This spirit will put down profanity, vulgarity, slang, slander, tattling, lying, and meanness generally.

"Character is formed," says Dunning, "by *training* rather than by teaching. A teacher cannot lecture a child into good manners, nor change habits of any kind by the longest speech. Habits are changed only by a repetition of doings, and it is in these *doings* that training consists."

3. *Specific Topics.*—It is a good plan to have a regular time, as Monday morning or Friday afternoon, for a lesson on some topic, such as honor, honesty, truthfulness, etc., given out to pupils a week in advance, for them to think about. The subject taken up may be discussed and illustrated by anecdotes, incidents, stories, fables, poetry, or historical facts. Gow's *Morals and Manners* and Cowdery's *Moral Lessons* will aid the teacher in giving such lessons. But such lessons must be conducted with great skill, in order to be productive of good results. Bain, in his *Education as a Science*, says,

"For boys and girls above twelve, we may, as a rule, pronounce that moral lecturing, except in actual discipline, is misplaced; and only a very roundabout approach to the subject can be borne. In the higher schools and universities, direct moral teaching is, by common consent, disused as part of the ordinary class-work."

4. *Stories.*—One of the most effective ways of giving moral lessons is through the medium of well-selected stories. "A moral lesson," says Bain, "may be wrapped

up in a tale and brought home with an impetus. Stories of great and noble deeds have fired more youthful hearts with enthusiasm than sermons have." "To hear about good men," says Richter, "is equivalent to living among them. For children, there is absolutely no other morality than example, either seen or narrated." When you read a story or fable, let your pupils draw their own inferences and do their own moralizing. It is not best for you to spoil the effect by drawing conclusions.

Every teacher should keep a scrap-book for storing up material gleaned from the newspapers for these lessons. Miss Alcott's *Stories* are good hand-books for the teacher's desk. If there is a school library, make good use of it by calling the special attention of pupils to the biographies and story-books that you think fitted to become your assistants in morals and manners. Tyndall says he was made a scientist by reading Emerson and Carlyle. The golden grains of thought gleaned from good books will spring up in the youthful mind and yield a rich harvest of noble sympathies and right emotions. "Let a child read and understand," says Horace Mann, "such stories as the friendship of Damon and Pythias, the integrity of Aristides, the fidelity of Regulus, the purity of Washington, the invincible perseverance of Franklin, and he will think differently and act differently all the days of his remaining life." "A large part of the tactics of the teacher," says Bain, "is determined by the natural repugnance of human nature to the whole subject. Pupils would much rather be instructed in knowledge than be lectured on virtue; while, as regards knowledge, want of liking is not so fatal to the end. The use of the fable, the parable, the example, is evidently meant to avoid direct lecturing, and to reach the mind by insinuation and circumvention."

In urging this point upon the attention, Professor Minns remarks, "The lives of men deserving the name of great and good; every instance of self-sacrifice in the cause of justice, truth, country, or humanity; every noble utterance of poet or preacher or orator; everything in nature and art that appeals to our best and highest feelings and 'touches the heart to finer issues;' every act of kindness, of charity, of sympathy—will feed the soul with pure and generous and lofty thoughts, will lift it into a serener and diviner air, will place Deity upon his lawful throne, will broaden and deepen the sentiment of love to God and man until it shall come to be a well-spring of everlasting joy in the heart, and will bring nearer the day when all mankind shall become brothers—the children of one Heavenly Father."

5. *Time and Place.*—Advise, correct, and discipline at the right time and in the right way. The events of a school-week will often furnish practical illustrations for a short but effective talk to the pupils on manners or morals. Omit no fitting occasion to impress a principle upon the moral feelings. Whether an offender is to be reproved publicly or in private, you must determine. "A few words of earnest advice or remonstrance," says Quick, "which a boy hears at the right time from a man whom he respects may affect that boy's character for life. Here everything depends, not on the words used, but on the feeling with which they are spoken, and on the way in which the speaker is regarded by the hearer."

"Do but gain a boy's trust," says Spencer; "convince him by your behavior that you have his happiness at heart; let him discover that you are the wiser of the two; let him experience the benefits of following your advice, and the evils that arise from disregarding it; and fear not; you will readily enough guide him. Not by *authority* is your sway to be obtained; neither by *reasoning;* but by *inducement.*"

Joshua Bates, Master of the Brimmer School, Boston, for thirty-three years, remarked, at the close of his school teaching,

"There is no part of my professional career that I look back upon with more pleasure and satisfaction than the practice I always pursued in giving, each Saturday morning, familiar talks on such subjects as would conduce to make my pupils happier and better men. I have been more fully assured of the benefit resulting to many of my pupils from letters received, and conversations I have had with past members of the school, who uniformly write or say, 'Much of what I studied in school is forgotten; but the words then spoken are treasured and remembered, and they have influenced, and ever will influence, me while life lasts.'"

The true teacher will keep steadily in mind the fact that character outweighs mere intellect; that high percentages in examinations are but as dust in the balance compared with the moral qualities that constitute manhood and womanhood. Prince Albert, when drawing up the conditions of the annual prize to be given by the Queen at Wellington College, determined that it should be awarded, not to the cleverest boy, nor to the most bookish boy, nor to the most precise, diligent, and prudent boy; but to the noblest boy—to the boy who should show the most promise of becoming a large-hearted, high-minded man.

Character ought to rank in school, as in society, above all attainments of the intellect or accomplishments of art. A just, upright, truthful, pure, and magnanimous character, guided by principle and inspired by good-will to all, is worth all the learning in the world.

6. *Books and Reading.*—If there is no school library, advise your pupils what books to draw from the public libraries, if they have access to any; and, if not, what books to buy for themselves when they have any money to buy with. See to it that they do not poison themselves with sensational and trashy stories and novels, the blood-and-thunder tales of which too many boys are fond, and the sentimental love-stories devoured by too many girls.

7. *The Main Thing.*—There are no keener critics upon sham character and moral pretence than children. "The divine method of moral instruction in a common-school," says Mayo, "is that a cultivated and consecrated man or woman should rise upon it at nine o'clock in the morning, and lead it through light and shadow, breeze and calm, tempest and tranquillity, to the end. All special methods flow out of him, as the hours of the day mark the course of the sun through the vault of heaven."

The moral power of the teacher will be measured largely by his own reserved forces of character and life, and this central idea has been so fully and eloquently set forth by Rev. F. D. Huntington, in his classic paper on *Unconscious Tuition*, that I conclude this chapter in his words:

"My main propositions are these three: 1st. That there is an educating power issuing from the teacher, not by voice nor by immediate design, but silent and involuntary, as indispensable to his true function as any element in it.

2d. That this unconscious tuition is yet no product of caprice, nor of accident, but takes its quality from the undermost substance of the teacher's character. And 3d. That as it is an emanation flowing from the very spirit of his own life, so it is also an influence acting insensibly to form the life of the scholar. . . .

"We are taught, and we teach, by something about us that never goes into language at all. I believe that often this is the very highest kind of teaching, most charged with moral power, most apt to go down among the secret springs of conduct, most effectual for vital issues, for the very reason that it is spiritual in its character, noiseless in its pretensions, and constant in its operation. . . .

"It is time, then, to pronounce more distinctly a fixed connection between a teacher's unconscious tuition and the foregoing discipline of his life. What he is to impart, at least by this delicate and sacred medium, he must be. 'No admittance for shams' is stamped on that sanctuary's door. Nothing can come out that has not gone in. The measure of real influence is the measure of genuine personal substance. How much patient toil in obscurity, so much triumph in an emergency. The moral balance never lets us overdraw. If we expect our drafts to be honored in a crisis, there must have been the deposits of a punctual life. To-day's simplest dealing with a raw or refractory pupil takes its insensible coloring from the moral climate you have all along been breathing. Celestial opportunities avail us nothing unless we have ourselves been educated up to their level. If an angel come to converse with us on the mountain-top, he must find our tent already pitched in that upper air. Each day recites a lesson for which all preceding days were a preparation. Our real rank is determined, not by lucky answers or some brilliant impromptu, but by the uniform diligence. For the exhibition-days of Providence there is no preconcerted colloquy — no hasty retrieving of a wasted term by a stealthy study on the eve of the examination."

Chapter IV.
INTELLECTUAL TRAINING.

PHYSICAL culture is important, moral training is essential; but, by common consent and practice, intellectual development is made the leading object of the common-school. As succeeding chapters of this book relate mainly to methods of intellectual training, this branch of the subject is here dismissed with a few brief allusions to the classification of the mental faculties, which seem to be necessary, in order that the directions, hints, and suggestions hereafter given may be made more clearly comprehensible. It is not necessary that every teacher should be a metaphysician; but it is desirable to know the elements of mental philosophy. The teacher ought to know, not what *may* be successful, after experiment, but what *must* be successful because based on the laws of nature.

I. CLASSIFICATION OF THE INTELLECTUAL FACULTIES.

The classification of the intellectual faculties which follows is, in the main, that of Professor William Russell.* I have adopted this, partly on account of its clearness, and partly from the partiality which a pupil feels for the work of his former teacher.

The three main divisions of the intellectual faculties

---

* Russell's *Normal Training.*

are (1) the *perceptive*, (2) the *expressive*, (3) the *reflective*. In education all these groups of powers are exerted, to some extent, simultaneously; but with very different degrees of relative activity and strength in the successive stages of school life. In the beginning, the perceptive faculties are most active; then the expressive faculties come into freer play; and, finally, the reflective or reasoning powers are developed by slow degrees.

II. THE PERCEPTIVE FACULTIES.

The modes of action of these faculties are sensation, perception, attention, and observation; their impelling force is *curiosity*, and the result of their action is *knowledge*. These faculties are exceedingly active in childhood; hence, in the order of nature, the first years of the child in school should be mainly devoted to such things as will best secure perceptive development. These processes consist of object-lessons; of exercises in color, form, measure; of writing and drawing; of reading and speech; of the elements of natural science; and, in general, of exercises in observation which include examination, analysis, inspection, comparison, discrimination, and classification, begun and carried on to a limited extent. "Mind," says Bain, "starts from *discrimination*. Our intelligence is absolutely limited by our power of discrimination."

"*Analysis*," says Russell, "is the grand instrument in all the operations of the perceptive faculties; and of all the implements of science, it is the keenest in its edge, the truest in its action, and the surest in the results which it attains. It is the key to knowledge in all departments of intelligence."

Principles in Training.—"*Sensations*," says Payne,

"constitute the elements of knowledge, and *sensations* grow into *ideas*."

"*Knowledge*, with children," says Russell, "is what they have experienced in their own intellect, by means of their own observation; in other words, it is the accurate interpretation of the facts of sense in matters usually of color, form, number, weight, or sound, and the relations these bear to one another."

Pestalozzi says, "If I look back and ask myself what I have really done towards the improvement of elementary instruction, I find that, in recognizing *observation* as the absolute basis of all knowledge, I have established the first and most important principle of instruction." The distinguished German educator Niemeyer says, "What is perceived by the senses is fixed in the mind more firmly than what is merely said over even a hundred times. It is not the shadows of things, but *things* themselves, which should be presented to youth."

In order to train pupils to habits of observation, the teacher must make every effort to secure the fixed attention of every pupil in the class to whatever is *inspected*, to whatever is *done*, and to whatever is *said*. The main instrument in securing an attentive examination of things is by means of skilful questioning. "The faculty of perception," says Niemeyer, "united with the endeavor to attain clear consciousness of the ideas received by means of exerted attention, is the life of thought; without it, all teaching, all machinery for communicating ideas to the young, are useless. They may have ears and all the other organs of sense, but they will neither hear, nor see, nor perceive; *for they will pay no attention*."

It is easier to secure the attention of young children to

actual things than to spoken descriptions of things; hence the value of object-lessons as a means of instruction. Things are learned more quickly and accurately through the eye than through the ear. Without the object, the teacher may spend a long time in endeavoring to convey to a class, through the ear by description, an idea of what may be understood at a glance of the eye; and, after all his pains, he may give his pupils the wrong idea.

Kindergarten training is admirably adapted to call the perceptive faculties into appropriate exercise, while, at the same time, it calls into play the expressive faculties. The careful study of a Kindergarten manual, together with a few visits to a Kindergarten school, will supply every young teacher with ideas upon which to build a rational system of primary teaching. "Froebel," says Emily Shirreff, "makes discipline of the moral and intellectual faculties his direct aim. He cares more for the *habit* of observing than for the *matter* of the observation; more for the correctness of the reasoning than for the subject on which it is exercised; more for strict accuracy of thought and expression than for the amount of knowledge."

In order to secure the best possible results in training young children to habits of attention and observation, there must be a frequent transition from one subject to another, and the hours of school confinement must not be too long. For children under eight years of age, the school-day ought not to exceed four hours, and those hours should be broken by two twenty-minute recesses. As to the limit of time in fixing the attention, the following is an approximate statement: A child from five to seven years of age may be able to give unflagging attention to one lesson or subject for from ten to fifteen minutes; from seven to ten years of age, from fifteen to twenty minutes; from ten to twelve years of age, from twenty to thirty minutes; from twelve to sixteen years of age, from thirty to forty minutes.

It is well to bear in mind the irrevocable law of nature, *that work in excess of the power of the system adds nothing to the result achieved.*

III. THE EXPRESSIVE FACULTIES.

The modes of action of these faculties are emotion, imagination, fancy, imitation, personation, representation, language, and taste; their impelling force is *feeling;* and the result of their action is *communication.* The educational processes consist of exercises in language—words, reading, grammar; of practice in oral speech and written expression; of studies in natural science and art.

Principles in Training.—The first impulse of the child, on making some discovery by means of the senses, is to express its surprise or satisfaction to others. Speech, in its early stages, is almost unconsciously acquired by imitation. The process is a long and slow one; but by long-continued repetition it is effective. Here again the Kindergarten system is suggestive of natural methods of training, as opposed to the old repressive system summed up in the formula "Study your book; don't ask questions." Well-conducted oral recitations afford the most effective means of securing correctness and readiness of oral expression. "It is an obvious defect in teaching," says Bain, "to keep continually lecturing pupils without asking them, in turn, to reproduce and apply what is said."

Readiness in written expression is a more difficult attainment than correctness of speech. Training in composition should begin as soon as the child can write at all, and should be continued during the whole period of school life. "The ability to define our thoughts," says Currie, "and to express them in a clear and orderly manner, may be taken as a practical test of an intellectual education." "A child," says Horace Mann, "must not only be exercised into correctness of observation, but into accuracy in the narration or description of what he has seen, heard, thought, or felt; so that whatever thoughts, emotions, memories, are within him, he can present them all to others in exact and luminous words."

Imagination.—The first step is to train the pupil to observe facts; the next, to reproduce clearly the *conception* of facts, which power may be classed under the term *imagination*, as that word is used to include the whole work of remembering, reproducing, and modifying the pictures of direct perception. The imagination may be specially cultivated by the recitation of suitable poetry, by the speaking of dialogues, by declamations, by compositions upon subjects which exercise the inventive faculty, and by the perusal of the best works of creative genius.

IV. THE REFLECTIVE FACULTIES.

The modes of action of these faculties are included under the heads of memory, conception, consciousness, reason, understanding, and judgment; their impelling force is *inquiry;* and the result of their action is *truth.* The educational processes are language and grammar, composition and rhetoric, geography and history, mathematics and natural science, or whatever is made a subject of thought.

Principles in Training.—Memory, as the basis of the eflective faculties, consists, not so much in remembering words to be repeated as in the power of retaining in the mind what has been experienced, observed, or conceived. In childhood, the memorizing of words is easy; but the memory of ideas and principles and experiences is weak. As the pupil advances in years, memory rises to a higher order of power, until it finally begins to act through the exercise of the *judgment*.

"The retentive faculty," says Bain, "is the faculty that most of all concerns us in education. All improvement in the art of teaching depends on the attention that we give to the various circumstances that facilitate acquirement, or lessen the number of repetitions for a given effect."

The foundation of memory is *attention*. "*As is the earnestness of attention, so is the duration of remembrance, or the distinctness and readiness of recollection.*"

Throughout the entire course of school training, the chief reliance of memory must be the freshness and force of attention both to *things* and *words*. "The more force we can throw into the act of noting a difference," says Bain, "the better is that difference felt, and *the better it is impressed*."

In cultivating the memory, the teacher should bear in mind: (1) That children must be trained to habits of attention in every school exercise; (2) that this attention must not be too long-continued; (3) that pupils must be accustomed to memorize poetry, dialogues, descriptions, and definitions, provided they first comprehend what they learn; (4) that they must be trained to remember words as well as ideas; (5) that what is told them by the teacher, or is read aloud in the class, is better remembered than what they read silently from the printed page; (6) that there must be frequent reviews of ideas already acquired, in order to fix them permanently in the mind; (7) that what they do for themselves is better remembered than what is told them by the teacher; (8) and that constantly doing children's thinking for them is the worst possible way of making them reflective.

"Experience teaches us," says Dr. Schwab, of Germany, "more and more, from day to day, that a child will retain in its memory only what is incorporated into its life. It will forget what it has seen or heard, but rarely or never what it has accomplished through its own efforts."

The teacher must also take into consideration the fact that the inherent power of memory in different children is a variable quantity; and this fact constitutes one of the difficulties in the management of large classes. No method and no teacher can impart to every pupil a retentive memory. But no teacher should, on the other hand, push to extremes those who are gifted by nature with great power of retaining.

"The absolute power of retentiveness in any individual mind," says Bain, "is a limited quantity. There is no way of extending this limit except by encroaching on some of the other powers of the mind, or else by quickening the mental faculties altogether, at the expense of the bodily functions. An unnatural memory may be produced at the cost of reason, judgment, and imagination, or at the cost of the emotional aptitudes. This is not a desirable result."

The reflective faculties are not fully developed during the period of school life, and a consideration of *reason* and *judgment* hardly comes within the scope of this chapter.

"*Reason, reasoning,* and *giving reasons* are intellectual

operations," says Bain, "not far removed from some of the meanings of judgment." "Mankind," says Faraday, "are willing, generally, to leave the faculties which relate to *judgment* almost entirely uneducated, and their decisions at the mercy of ignorance, prepossessions, the passions, or even accident. Society, speaking generally, is not only ignorant as respects education of the judgment, but is also ignorant of its ignorance." Summing up the whole province of these faculties in a paragraph, Professor Russell says, "*Reason* comes to the mind laboring under uncertainty, and brings the aid of its discursive processes of ratiocination in the form of dissertation, argument, discussion, and debate. Assuming the seat of judgment, it thus institutes inquiry, conducts examination, prosecutes investigation, discriminates terms, scrutinizes allegations, weighs opposing evidence, judges of facts, rejects assumptions, exposes error, detects truth or falsehood, and pronounces its authoritative and final decision as the inevitable law of intellection."

Now the common-school teacher can hardly be expected to accomplish a great deal with children, in respect to these faculties, when society furnishes so many cases of arrested development of the reason and judgment among adults; but though learning to draw correct conclusions from facts is the hardest thing in the world to do, the teacher must not be deterred from attempting to lay a foundation for the habit of thinking, reflecting, and judging. If the powers of observation, attention, memory, and discrimination are rightly trained in school, the whole after-life of the pupil may become a continuous course of education; for in society, as in school, the sources of knowledge are reading, conversation, observation, and reflection.

It is a common fault in our systems of instruction that the attempt is made to force the reasoning faculties into premature development. At ten years of age, children are set to work on deductive text-books which would be hard for scholars at fifteen. They are overworked, and the result is failure. Huxley, in speaking of the unhappy children forced by the stimulating power of frequent competitive examinations to rise too early in their class, says, "They are conceited all the forenoon of their life, and stupid all the afternoon. The vigor and freshness, which should have been stored up for the purposes of the hard struggle for existence in practical life, have been washed out of them by precocious mental debauchery—by book-gluttony and lesson-bibbing. Their faculties are worn out by the strain upon their callow brains, and they are demoralized by worthless childish triumphs before the real work of life begins."

Chapter V.

SCHOOL GOVERNMENT.

I. CORPORAL PUNISHMENT.

THE foundation of school, as of society, is law and order. The teacher must possess the power of enforcing the regulations which are essential to the existence of the school as a small social organization. School government does not depend wholly upon the teacher; there are two other important factors—home-training and the public opinion of the community of which the school is a part.

The infliction of corporal punishment is one of the questions for the young teacher to meet at the outset of his career. The opinions generally held by practical teachers may be summed up as follows:

1. It should be the *aim* of teachers to govern without resorting to corporal punishment.

2. Teachers should have the right to inflict punishment in extreme cases.

3. In general, it is better to subdue refractory pupils by corporal punishment than to expel them from school.

4. As most parents are compelled, at times, to resort to corporal punishment in the home government of their children, so most teachers must sometimes resort to it in school.

Occasionally there are men of great will-power, women

of great charm of manner, and teachers of long experience, who govern well by moral suasion. Sometimes there are well-bred classes that can easily be controlled without force; but these exceptions afford no basis for the sickly sentimentalism that characterizes *all* corporal punishments in school as barbarous and brutal. Most teachers are averse to whipping; they often fail to inflict it when it is absolutely necessary for the good of the school. The traditional pedagogue, whose chief delight was in the ferule and ratan, is extinct. When all children are well governed at home, when all teachers are professionally trained, when all parents are reasonable, when hereditary tendencies are more in harmony with existing social conditions, corporal punishment in school may safely be abolished. When humanity becomes so highly developed that civil law imposes no severe penalties to hold lawless impulses in check, it will be easy for any teacher to govern any school by moral influences only.

At present, in school as in State, judicious severity is, in the end, the truest kindness. Fear of punishment and physical pain is the only check to the lawlessness of some children as well as of some men. The penalties of crime, which are awarded by the law of the State, are designed, not for the average law-abiding citizen, but for the exceptional savage; and corporal punishment in school is held as a terror only over the exceptional child. In his address before the London School Board, Huxley, with his characteristic pith, sets forth this practical philosophy as follows:

"But your 'street Arabs' and other neglected poor children are rather worse and wilder than colts; for the reason that the horse-colt has only his animal instincts in him, and his mother, the mare, has been always tender over him, and never came home drunk and kicked him in her life; while the man-colt is inspired by that very real devil, perverted manhood, and *his* mother may have done all that and more. So, on the whole, it may probably be even more expedient to begin your attempt to get at the higher nature of the child than at that of the colt from the *physical* side."

II. SELF-CONTROL.

Perhaps the most important object of school discipline is the formation of habits of *self-control;* but upon children whose impulses are strong and whose habits of self-control are weak, the hand of power must be laid, to remind them of duty and compel them to do it.

The power to govern well is an essential quality of every successful teacher. When a new instructor takes charge of a school or a class, there is always a trial of strength between the ruler and the ruled; and woe be to that man or woman who falls a weak prey to young and merciless school tyrants. "A boy," says Plato, "is the most vicious of all wild beasts."

The young are the creatures of impulse, and children seek to gratify their impulses at once, without reflection, and without reference to their moral character. To counteract this tendency, the care and oversight of both parents and teachers are necessary. Get the child to pause—to take time to ask, "Is this right or wrong?"—in other words, *to think*. In all these cases, the old rule for curbing a bad temper is very good—"Count ten slowly before you speak or act." Teachers should strive to strengthen the child's will to do right. And it must be borne in mind that self-control is not learned in a fourteen weeks' course, as some languages and sciences are supposed to be; but that it is acquired only by life-long efforts, and by those alone who *never give up*. " Give self-control," says Charles Buxton, "and you give the essence of all well-doing in mind, body, and estate. Morality, learning, thought, business, success—the master of himself can master these."

III. PUBLIC OPINION OF THE SCHOOL.

The public opinion of the school is an important element in discipline, and the teacher of tact will skilfully direct this power to the side of order and right-doing. Many a boy is influenced by the judgments of his fellows more than by the decisions of his teachers. There are in every school leaders in right-doing and ringleaders in wrong-doing; the teacher who can captivate one set and capture the other will secure good government. Few pupils can resist when they find themselves condemned by the common voice of their companions, whose censure they dread more than that of their superiors. A teacher can easily attach to himself the active, energetic, leading scholars by putting them into places of honor, trust, or duty; and, having done this, it is easy to secure their co-operation in establishing a wholesome and restraining school *influence*.

IV. EMULATION.

Emulation is a powerful agent in school; but it must be kept within bounds. Rank in class is important; but it is not everything. Prizes and gifts cannot be, and ought not to be, much used as stimulants in a public school. "The schoolmaster's means of reward," says Bain, "is chiefly confined to approbation or praise, a great and flexible instrument, yet needing delicate manipulation." A system of ranking pupils according to percentage in recitations and written examinations has, no doubt, its advantages in stimulating pupils to study. But the wise teacher will check the spirit of reckless ambition in the wild race for promotion. In schools for girls, this spirit is often a great evil. Girls are more sensitive and more emotional than boys; and the emotions exhaust health faster than exertions of body or mind. With girls, the eagerness for success is so keen, the dread of failure is so acute, that they are easily injured by appeals to pride and ambition that might benefit boys.

V. SCHOOL DISCIPLINE.

In school discipline, much depends upon making pupils feel that rules and regulations are intended for their own good, not that they are made by the teacher for his own pleasure in exercising arbitrary power. Most pupils prefer order to disorder, firmness to weakness, law to lawlessness. Hence calisthenics and military precision in marching are efficient aids in securing prompt obedience to commands. It is evident enough to pupils themselves that one object of discipline is to secure a sufficient degree of order, quietness, and regularity to enable them to pursue their studies and recite their lessons without interruption; but the higher aim of strict discipline is often lost sight of—namely, to train the will, and to incite scholars to put forth vigorous efforts for self-improvement and self-control.

Eternal vigilance is the price of order in the schoolroom. The teacher must have an eye like a hawk to see what is going on, and a quick ear to detect noise. "Disorder," says Bain, "is the sure sequel of the teacher's failure in sight or hearing; but even with the senses good, there may be absent the watchful employment of them. This is, in itself, a natural incapacity for the work of teaching. A teacher must not merely be sensitive to incipient and masked disorder; he must read the result of his teaching in the pupil's eyes."

VI. OBSTINACY.

It is good policy to avoid driving strong-willed children into obstinacy. It is a sad mistake "to break a child's will" as the foundation of control over him. Respect the personality and individuality of every pupil. By a little patience and forbearance, you may bring to bear on the self-willed child the influence of kindness, sympathy, or reason. Set your own tact against the dull, brutish obstinacy of your pupil. A forced submission often ends in sullen doggedness or a smouldering fire of rebellion. The child must learn obedience; *that* is the first and greatest of lessons. From childhood to old age, all human beings must obey the laws of society and the laws of nature. With the impulsive and inexperienced child, real affection for the teacher will secure implicit obedience, and nothing else will.

VII. SCHOOL DESPOTISM.

The government of a school must be, in many respects, an absolute monarchy, and it will have all the vices of a despotism unless its ruler has a high sense of responsibility, and a knowledge of children based upon a careful study of the nature of body and of mind. The despotism ought to be a modification of patriarchal rule.

"It is in dealing with numbers," says Bain, "that the

teacher stands distinguished from the parent, and allied to the wider authorities of the State; exercising larger control, encountering greater risks, and requiring a more steady hand. With an individual pupil, we need only such motives as are personal to himself; with numbers, we are under the harsh necessity of punishing for example. . . . The stress of the teacher's difficulty lies in the heavings of a mass or multitude. One man against a multitude is always in the post of danger."

VIII. GENERAL PRINCIPLES.

[Selected from Bain's *Science of Education*.]

1. "Restraints should be as few as the situation admits of."

2. "Duties and offences should be definitely expressed, so as to be clearly understood."

3. "Voluntary dispositions are to be trusted as far as they can go."

4. "By organization and arrangement, the *occasions* of disorder are avoided."

5. "The awe and influence of authority are maintained by a certain formality and state."

6. "It is understood that authority, with all its appurtenances, exists for the benefit of the governed, and not as a perquisite of the governor."

7. "The operation of mere vindictiveness should be curtailed to the uttermost."

8. "The reasons for repression and discipline should, as far as possible, be made intelligible to those concerned; and should be referable solely to the general good."

IX. CONDENSED DIRECTIONS.

1. School discipline, like instruction, will take form from the temperament and character of the teacher. A reputation for impartial judgment is the essential requisite of the teacher who governs well.

2. Make but few rules, and do not indulge in much talking about infringements of them. Remember that pupils, as well as teachers, have *rights*, and that both have *duties*.

3. Put yourself in the place of your pupils. Recall your own school experiences, your hopes and fears, your impulses, your notions, and the motives that influenced you. If you do so, you cannot become a tyrant.

4. Secure order, if possible, without corporal punishment; but secure obedience at all hazards. In school, as in an army, discipline is essential to existence.

5. The best way to lead pupils to study is, not by threats and compulsion, but by showing them how to use their text-books, by explaining and illustrating their hard lessons, and by appealing to the higher motives.

6. Do not tempt your pupils to become habitually deceitful and untruthful, by making use of the "self-reporting system" in scholarship and deportment. It is a device worthy of the Inquisition. "It is," says F. S. Jewell, "both stupidly ingenious and transparently vicious."

7. Regard all pupils as truthful until you have positive proof to the contrary. Children with a high sense of honor will never forgive you for doubting their word, or for making an unjust accusation. "The only teacher I ever intensely hated," said a noted instructor, "was a young woman who charged me, unjustly, before the school, with telling a lie, when I was only seven years old." Trust

your pupils if you want them to put their trust in you. "The sweetest praise I ever heard," said a public man, "was the remark made by my father when I was twelve years old: 'My boy never told me a lie in his life.'"

8. Encourage truthfulness by rewarding full and frank confession with a remission of penalties, so far as is consistent with school discipline. Severity is one of the chief causes of lying and deceit. It excites fear, and fear seeks an easy refuge in cunning and evasion.

9. Whispering must be repressed with a firm hand. It cannot be entirely prevented, but it may be checked so as to prevent disturbance and annoyance. One good way of checking it is to allow a short whispering-recess every hour or half-hour.

10. As prevention is better than punishment, children should be trained to a general habit of prompt obedience in minor matters, so that finally they will submit readily to prohibitions which curb their strong inclinations and tendencies.

11. Penalties and punishments must be *certain*, and must seem to be the natural consequences of wrong acts. The child should know *what* he has to expect, and *when* to expect it. There must be no caprice, no variableness, no shadow of turning. The child soon learns to yield to the inevitable.

12. Do not worry; do not be discouraged; think that your agitation, your nervousness, will extend to your pupils. Unite patience with hope, gentleness with firmness, equanimity with force of character. Have a pleasant voice and a cheerful countenance, and show yourself the sincere friend of every pupil; let your school be one that will always have agreeable associations connected with it;

but if an emergency comes, be prompt and resolute to meet it, but *always calm*.

13. Take care of the health of your pupils. See that all exercise during the time assigned for that purpose. Keep the room well ventilated, but expose none to draughts. A strong constitution with fair abilities is better than brilliant talents in a feeble frame. Many a brilliant man has broken down from want of stamina. It is the steady worker that succeeds. Industry, patience, perseverance, energy, endurance, are the keys that unlock the door of success, and these qualities cannot be found in weak and sickly bodies.

14. Be tolerant of thoughtlessness, and severe only in cases of wilful disobedience.

15. Do not assign mental tasks after school hours as a punishment. The practice of compelling children to commit to memory or to translate, as a penalty, is educational barbarism.

16. One of the most effective means of punishment is to deprive the offender of some privilege, or to cut him off from the society of schoolmates at recess or intermission.

17. Among schoolboys, fighting is a constant source of disturbance. It is next to impossible entirely to prevent it; but it may be greatly lessened by cultivating a *true* sense of honor, to take the place of the conventional code prevalent among boys. A little good-natured ridicule will sometimes prove very effective.

18. "Strong terms of reproof," says Bain, "should be sparing, in order to be effective. Still more sparing ought to be the tones of anger. Loss of temper, however excusable, is really victory to wrong-doers, although, for the moment, it may strike terror."

19. Common-sense is in the highest degree requisite for the right administration of school affairs. It is easy enough to sit in judgment on the *black* cases and the *white*, but the *gray* cases are the difficult ones. Nothing but sound judgment can determine a large class of school offences.

20. There is a conventional sense of honor among schoolboys which binds them not to inform the teacher of the misdeeds of their fellows. However false this code may be, he is an unwise teacher who takes ground against the school opinion, and endeavors, by threats of punishment, to compel pupils to become informers. Let him put his tact against the brute power of the school, and he may succeed in modifying the school code so as to draw a line of distinction between the minor matters that belong to the "tattling order" and the graver offences that concern the real welfare of the school.

21. A foundation principle of school government is that every pupil shall be allowed the largest liberty possible, without infringing on the rights, interests, or convenience of others.

22. Do your utmost to *prevent* faults before you think of punishing them. Be patient and forbearing, for obedience is a habit formed only by long-continued training. "Avoid direct collision with children," says Buxton. "Have tact enough to divert the child's attention from its own obstinacy, and in a few moments you will lead it gently round to submission."

23. Do not assume that the parent is your natural enemy, and, above all, do not act as if he were. Parents have rights, and are generally reasonable if those rights are respected.

24. Do not make cast-iron rules with unchangeable penalties. If you fail to enforce fixed penalties, you lose the respect of your pupils; and if you *do* enforce them, you may often be guilty of injustice. Give your verdict and pass sentence after the conviction of the culprit.

X. PUNISHMENT.

1. There can be no government where there is no punishment; but the teacher's aim should be to prevent, as far as practicable, the necessity of punishment.

2. The true object of school punishment is to reform the offender, to deter others from wrong-doing, and to maintain *law*.

3. The chief means of preventing the necessity of punishment are: (1) active and pleasant employment, (2) the personal influence of the teacher, and (3) the public opinion of the school.

4. Punishment must be varied according to the temperament of the child. A frown will act on one; separation from companions, on another; neglect and coldness, on a third; public reprimands, on a fourth; and a whipping, on a fifth. "The first and readiest, and ever the best, form of punishment," says Bain, "is censure, reprobation, dispraise."

5. In general, for younger children, corporal punishment is most effective; for older pupils, isolation, loss of privileges, or appeals to a sense of honor.

6. Do not make threats of punishment in advance of offences; you will only tempt pupils to try you by disobeying, or suggest to them the doing of something they would otherwise never have thought of.

7. It is the *certainty*, not the *severity*, of punishment

that deters pupils from violating regulations. Make your penalties light, but as certain as the rising and setting of the sun.

8. "It is a rule in punishment," says Bain, "to try slight penalties at first; with the better natures, the mere idea of punishment is enough; severity is entirely unnecessary. It is a coarse and blundering system that knows of nothing but the severe and degrading sorts."

9. Do not try to make scholars learn by whipping them for unlearned lessons.

10. *Never strike a child on the head.* Never inflict personal indignities, such as pulling the hair, pulling the ears, slapping the face; for they excite the bitterest resentment, and are seldom forgiven.

11. In extreme cases of wilful and open defiance of authority, punishment may be inflicted publicly and immediately before the school; but, in general, it is better to inflict it in private, not in anger, but coolly and deliberately.

12. Before whipping, be absolutely certain of the guilt of the offender, and then inflict punishment so thoroughly that it will be remembered. Your object is to *inflict pain* so as to deter the culprit from further wrong-doing.

13. It is a good rule to postpone the infliction of punishment to the next day—especially in bad cases. Tell the boy to come to school the next morning half an hour before school-time, and that in the meantime you will think the matter over, and will then let him know what your deliberate decision is in his case. It is surprising what a change a little delay or a night's sleep will make in the feelings of both teacher and pupil—the former losing his irritation, and the latter his stubbornness.

14. If you have a case that calls for some severe punishment of the offender, consult the parents, if possible, before you take action. By doing so you may avoid complaints, irritation, and ill-feeling. But there are cases that demand summary punishment as soon as the offence is committed.

15. "Where a school is well conducted," says Horace Mann, "the *minimum* of punishment is the *maximum* of qualifications."

16. "The sense of honor," says Superintendent Harris, "is developed earlier with each succeeding generation, and corporal punishment should give place to punishments affecting the sense of honor as soon as this sense develops."

"When corporal punishment is kept up," says Bain, "it should be at the far end of the list of penalties; its slightest application should be accounted the worst disgrace."

Chapter VI.
THE SCHOOLROOM.

I. SPECIAL DIRECTIONS AND SUGGESTIONS FOR PRINCIPALS.

1. BEAR in mind that an assemblage of *classes* does not constitute a *school* until a principal has breathed into it a *soul*.

2. Remember that with assistants, as with other people, requests and suggestions are pleasanter and more effective than authoritative directions. Respect the rights and privileges as well as the duties of assistants, and you will, in general, get along pleasantly and peaceably with them, and will secure what is essential to your own success— their hearty co-operation in your plans and methods. One of Thomas Arnold's noblest reforms was to raise the under-masters from being little better than menials to the position of honored and trusted associates and instructors.

3. Be patient with the shortcomings of inexperienced assistants, remembering that you yourself were, once in your life, a young teacher without experience.

4. Do not expect assistants to do everything in exactly your way. Insist upon uniformity only in essentials, allowing the widest possible scope for the exercise of individuality in the details of school-work.

5. Caution young assistants against overwork and worry; against detaining pupils after school; and against expecting to make good scholars out of all their pupils.

6. It is a part of your duty to outline the grade-work of assistants; to see that they make a proper use of globes, maps, charts, and other school appliances; and to order such reviews and general exercises as shall secure attention to the *essential things* of the course of study.

7. Make a systematic use of the school library, and instruct your assistants to keep a close supervision over *what* their pupils read, and *how* they read it. If there is no school library, both principal and assistants should influence their pupils' selection of books from the public library.

8. As far as practicable, arrange your school course so that some studies in the year's work may be completed before others are taken up. In other words, do not crowd the minds of pupils with too many things at once.

9. It is your duty in written examinations to direct the attention of your assistants to the *main points* in each of the studies pursued, not to distract their efforts by dwelling on particulars. Prepare your questions with care and judgment. The art of asking suitable questions is essential to good supervision, for the questions will determine in no small degree the kind of instruction given by assistants. Take your own knowledge of the subject without referring to a text-book; consider a simple fraction of that, and you may succeed in making out a set of questions suited to the capacity of your pupils. When you are preparing questions, think of how little you knew when a pupil, not of what you know now, after years of teaching, or with a book open before you. "How few examiners," says Homer B. Sprague, Principal of the Girls' High School in Boston, "know enough to separate the transient from the permanent, discriminate between knowledge that must be kept in readiness to do service

at any moment and knowledge that, having served its purpose as discipline, may without loss be forgotten!"

10. During the year, prevent "cramming" by never letting your pupils know when an examination is to happen. Hold examinations at irregular intervals, and not too often. Make the percentages obtained subordinate to good standing won by daily attention to school-work. "Like everything else that is good," says Superintendent Eliot, "like exercise, like study, like enthusiasm, examinations can be perverted, and then they turn into evil. Just as any other burdens, these may bend the shoulders and break the spirit, or they may be borne upon uplifted head and with buoyant heart."

11. As the annual examination for promotion or graduation draws near, do not lash your assistants and scholars into a state of feverish excitement. Huxley justly styles the stimulating of pupils to work at high-pressure, by incessant competitive examinations, "the Abomination of Desolation." A principal should be calm; cool, well-balanced, and steady, and should keep his school so. "There is nothing so terrible," says Goethe, "as activity without insight."

12. Do not require assistants to correct an armful of papers every night at home. They need the time for rest, recreation, and reading. This work is a thankless drudgery, and, in most cases, a useless labor. Except in official examinations ordered by superintendents, let your assistants train their pupils to exchange papers, and, under the guidance of the teacher, correct one another's exercises during school hours. On this point Superintendent Eliot says, "While it is wise to test instruction, it is unwise to make as much of testing as of instructing. Yet this is

the natural result of keeping teachers busy as examiners. The preparation and correction of examination papers absorb a large amount of time and force that might be better used."

13. If you are allowed any discretion whatever under the rigid rule of graded-school machinery in cities, classify and promote pupils somewhat according to age, circumstances, and apparent latent capacity, not by "percentage" alone. "The living human being," says Dr. Wiese, in speaking of written examinations, "is not an arithmetical problem."

14. In your higher-grade classes, make frequent oral review examinations on the *essential elements*, so that pupils may not only *know* something, but also may be able to *tell* it. A proper oral examination will show better than a written one what has been acquired.

15. A weekly spelling-match will be found a good general exercise in exciting a lively interest in orthography. A week in advance, send out a list of fifty or one hundred words in current use liable to be misspelled, and let all the grammar-grade classes copy it into blank-books for the next lesson. Or assign a suitable lesson in the spelling-book, if a good one is in use. The match may be conducted in writing, and the percentage reported by each class; or orally, matching classes in pairs, a higher grade against a lower.

16. For a general exercise in composition, assign some suitable topic to all the grammar grades, and another topic to the higher primary grades. Then exchange the compositions by classes, requiring the higher grades to correct the work of the lower, and allowing the lower grades to be benefited by reading the compositions of the higher grades. All children feel a lively interest in anything

written by some one they know. Or give out a subject a week in advance, and tell the pupils to collect all the information about it they please; but require them to write it out in school, so as to prevent the possibility of their copying or receiving outside assistance.

17. If your assistants are inexperienced in graded-school work, mark out month by month what they ought to accomplish in each branch of study.

18. Instruct your assistants to allow regular intervals for study in school. In some branches, such as geography, history, arithmetic, and spelling, the first ten minutes of the half-hour intended for recitation may profitably be given to study, provided the teacher sees that pupils do actually study.

19. Instruct your assistants what lessons to assign for home study, and see to it that the lessons so assigned are of reasonable length. Arithmetic lessons and compositions or exercises which are to be written ought not to be given out for home work. Few of your pupils may have conveniences for writing at home. Only lessons which require mainly an exercise of memory, and which are learned from the book, are suitable for out-of-school study; such as spelling, geography, and history. In order to ascertain if your assistants carry out your instructions, require them at intervals to report to you the exact lessons which they assign, or let them appoint some member of each class to report to you.

20. Do not allow assistants to assign any lessons whatever to pupils in grades below the fourth school-year; except, perhaps, a spelling-lesson, or a reading-lesson to be read aloud to parents.

21. Set apart, every week, half an hour on Monday or

Friday for a lesson in each room on morals and manners. Sometimes assign the same topic for all grades, and sometimes let assistants select their own subject and conduct the exercise in their own way.

22. When you discover pale, weak, sickly, fast-growing boys or girls in any of your classes, advise parents to take them out of school for a season, and turn them loose at work or play.

23. Insist upon neatness of person and dress, propriety of language and deportment, truthfulness and honesty, diligence and obedience.

24. It is a part of your duty as principal to impress upon every pupil in every class the dignity of work, either mental or manual, and the necessity of labor as a means of happiness.

25. Merely looking on and seeing assistants teach is not doing a principal's whole duty in supervision. If you are relieved from teaching a special class, you must teach enough in every class to direct assistants and to give spirit to every pupil.

26. Have no hobby, but give appropriate time and attention to every study laid down in the prescribed course of instruction.

27. Be satisfied to introduce new and improved methods slowly. Assistants, as a general rule, settle into their own ways, and are reluctant to change them. "I came to Rugby," says Arnold, "full of plans for school reform; but I soon found that the reform of a public school was a much more difficult thing than I had imagined."

28. Endeavor to secure from your teachers a wise combination of oral and object teaching after the new style, with the old-fashioned text-book drill. Personal investi-

gation is good, to a certain extent, both for teacher and pupil; but neither that nor lectures can accomplish much compared with the accumulated knowledge of the race crystallized into good books. It is quite as possible for oral instruction to degenerate into idle babble as for textbook study to run into meaningless memorizing.

29. In government, the strongest force is the public opinion of the school. Spare no efforts to turn this opinion in the right direction, so that its rules, customs, judgments, decisions, and unwritten laws shall be inexorably binding on every new-comer, with a force greater than that of master or assistant. When you have breathed the breath of life into your school, when you can feel every beat of its pulse, then you are really its *master*.

30. Do not try to please everybody; do not expect to make your school perfect; do not sacrifice your pupils to your personal ambition for making brilliant scholars. When you get impatient with dulness, remember *that all lasting progress is slow*.

31. Cultivate a habit of cheerfulness that shall shine out from your countenance like the light of the rising sun. Assistants and pupils may take their tone from the manner of the principal. "A teacher has only partially comprehended the familiar powers of his place," says Huntington, "who has left out the lessons of his own countenance. *There* is a perpetual picture which his pupils study as unconsciously as he exhibits it. His plans will miscarry if he expects a genial and nourishing session when he enters with a face blacker than the blackboard."

32. If you stop growing intellectually, if you forget you were once a boy or a girl, if you lose your sympathy with children, *it is time for you to resign*.

33. If you would secure the best results of a good school, keep up your *enthusiasm*, and fire your school with it. "Without enthusiasm," says Chadbourne, "no teacher can have the best success, however learned and faithful and hard-working he may be. Enthusiasm is the heat that softens the iron, that every blow may tell. Enthusiasm, on the part of the teacher, gives life to the student, and an impulse to every mental power. When this is accomplished, there is no more waste in lifting, dragging, or driving. It was the enthusiasm of Agassiz that clothed the commonest things with new life and beauty; that charmed every listener, and transformed the aged and the young, the ignorant and the learned, into joyful learners."

34. In the long summer vacations, flee to the woods or the mountains, where you can rest, think, and absorb vitality from nature. Otherwise there is danger that you may have all your individuality taken out of you by the steady drain of nervous force, and that you may degenerate into a pedagogic machine.

II. SPECIAL DIRECTIONS FOR ASSISTANTS.

1. Carry out, in good faith, the methods and general regulations of your principal.

2. It is not best for you to *say* you know more than the principal, even if you *think* so.

3. Do not expect principals to be absolutely perfect; if they were, they would be unsuited to assistants.

4. As far as possible, govern your class yourself. Every time you refer a case of discipline to the principal, you weaken your own authority in the eyes of your pupils.

5. Do not worry your scholars all the year with the threat that they will probably fail to be promoted.

Your duty is, not to discourage pupils, but to encourage them.

6. Do not make it your chief ambition to promote every member of your class; in every class of fifty there must be a few failures, and there will probably be a few that are too young to be advanced.

7. You have no right to expect that any class just promoted from a lower grade into your room is deficient in nothing; therefore, it is not wise for you to make sharp allusions to the shiftlessness of the previous teacher.

8. Consider your class a part of the school as a whole, not as your exclusive possession.

9. A large school must be conducted on strict business principles, in regard to punctuality and promptness on the part of teachers as well as pupils; but it is not desirable to make a hobby of extremely high reports in respect to attendance. Cheerfully excuse both tardiness and absence occasioned by home duties or by sickness in the family.

10. Be patient and forbearing with your pupils when they take up a new study. It is the first trials that are awkward and hard. When you get impatient at slowness or want of comprehension, sit down at your desk and try to write with your left hand, or to read a page upside down.

11. Remember that what your pupils *do for themselves* makes the strongest impression on their minds.

12. Assign reasonable lessons suited to the capacity, not of the *best*, but of the average scholars. Look out for essentials, and let non-essentials alone.

13. Divide your class into two sections, and match one against the other. Make up a match between your class and another of the same grade. These matches will awaken a generous spirit of class rivalry.

14. Do not allow your pupils to discover that they can annoy you. If they are noisy, you must keep calm, cool, and quiet, and speak in your lowest tone.

15. Seldom detain your scholars after school for discipline, and never detain them long to study unlearned lessons. "No Learning," says Socrates, as translated by Roger Ascham, "ought to be learned with Bondage; for bodily Labours wrought by Compulsion hurt not the Body; but any Learning learned by Compulsion tarrieth not long in the Mind."

16. In some studies, it may be advisable, before each recitation in a graded class, to allow from five to ten minutes for studying the lesson to be recited.

17. If you assign home lessons, show your pupils how to study those lessons, so that they can learn them without calling for assistance from parents. As a general rule, do not require examples in arithmetic, or any other exercises in writing to be done at home.

18. Do not reprove, but encourage, slow, plodding children. Dr. Arnold says he never was so ashamed in his life as when, after a sharp reproof, a boy turned to him and said, "Why do you speak angrily, sir? Indeed, I am doing the best I can."

19. Exercise all your tact to mould the spirit of your class, so that it shall be exerted on your side in favor of good order and right-doing.

20. *Teaching* is the work of the teacher; *learning* is the duty of the pupil. How to rightly combine teaching and learning is the difficult problem that every teacher must try to solve by long-continued study and observation. The scholar's efforts to learn by book-study must be made profitable by good teaching. "Learning without teach-

ing," says Ascham's *Scholemaster*, "makes lubbers, always learning, never profiting."

21. Stand ready to give a fair consideration to new methods in teaching, even if they differ from your preconceived ideas. "The only way in which a human being can make some approach to knowing the whole of a subject," says John Stuart Mill, "is by hearing what can be said about it by persons of every variety of opinion, and studying all modes in which it can be looked at by every character of mind. No wise man ever acquired his wisdom in any mode but this; nor is it in the nature of human intellect to become wise in any other manner."

22. Do not expect, even by the very best teaching, to make good scholars out of all your pupils. "No teacher," says Prof. Raumer, "should ever seek, by excessive stimulation, to spur on his pupils to an unnatural point of attainment which most of them can never reach." "I hate by-roads to education," says Dr. Johnson; "endeavoring to make children prematurely wise is useless labor."

23. "Remember the care of your health," says Carlyle. "You are to regard that as the very highest of all temporal things for you. There is no achievement you could make in the world that is equal to perfect health."

III. MANAGEMENT IN GENERAL.

1. First of all, make your school pleasant. The primary condition of a learner is satisfaction in learning. Spencer says, "to enlist pleasure on the side of intellectual performance is a point of the utmost importance." "The first duty towards children," says Buxton, "is to make them happy. Their school may teach them all learning and all righteousness; but if the pupils are not happy, it is a bad school."

2. Make up your mind that you must leave many things untaught; no man or woman ever yet succeeded in teaching everything. Do not expect your pupils to know as much as you do, and do not call them dull or stupid because they fail in things that seem to you to be simple and easy.

3. The less you threaten, the less you find fault, the less you scold, the more friends you will have among the boys and girls, and the better will be your school.

4. Unless you wish to be hated, beware of sarcasm and ridicule. A cutting remark is never forgotten and seldom forgiven.

5. Consent cordially and gracefully, but let your refusals be firm and absolute.

6. Be courteous and polite; you can more easily win children by kindness than drive them by authority.

7. If everything seems to go wrong in school, it is quite probable that you yourself are out of humor or out of health.

8. You will commit a physical sin if you break down your health and induce nervous exhaustion by overwork, worry, or anxiety about your scholars. Your first and highest duty is to work moderately, sleep long and soundly, and keep yourself in high physical condition in order to do the greatest amount of effective work.

9. Bear in mind that your chief work, beyond imparting a small stock of specific knowledge, is *to teach your pupils the right way to learn for themselves*, just as little children are taught to walk in order that they may go alone.

10. It is only the poorest teachers and the untrained ones that do all the hard work for their pupils. Agassiz

said that the worst service a teacher could render to a pupil was to give him a ready-made answer.

11. The best teachers are those whose pupils are made daily more and more able to pursue their studies without teachers, and whose pupils are awakened to an irresistible desire to *know*. "Instil into the minds of your pupils, if you can," says Arthur Helps, "a love and a desire for knowledge. What a triumph it is for you, if, while he is under your care, you influence him in such a manner that you make study a thing of delight to him! And what a failure it is if he throws you and your books overboard as soon as he leaves you!"

12. Beware of sacrificing children to your personal ambition. "There is no hardness of heart," says the Rev. Dr. Mayo, "like that of the teacher infuriated with ambition for the mental progress of a child." "Our schools," says Eliot, "are for our pupils, not our pupils for our schools."

13. Make use of the stimulus of praise; but use it sparingly, so that it may be of value when bestowed. Given with good judgment, commendation is a powerful agency; but prizes and distinctions often produce the worst effects in school. Generous emulation is good, but the selfish pride of rivalry is bad.

14. While it is your policy to make school pleasant for all, and to make school studies as agreeable as possible, there comes a time when the older pupils must be trained to face drudgery as a duty. Then, in the words of Bain, "Try to measure the child's power to support the strain of forced attention. Begin the discipline of life by inuring gradually to uninviting, to repugnant and severe occupation; but see also that you have at command the alternative of relaxation with enjoyment."

IV. THE CLASS TEACHER.

1. With beginners, in every study, the first processes must be learned slowly and very thoroughly by long-continued iteration. The important point is, not *how much* they learn, but *how well* they learn it.

2. Make the text-book subordinate to skilful teaching. The text-book is designed only as an *aid* both to pupil and teacher, and you must show scholars how to make the best possible use of it. Show them how to find out the meaning of a printed page; but bear in mind the words of Spencer, "that the function of books is supplementary—a means of seeing through other men's eyes what you cannot see for yourself."

3. You can best show your pupils how to study a lesson by going over it with them in advance, calling their attention to the leading facts, and vitalizing dead words by the living voice. In many lessons, pupils do not know *what* to study, nor *how* to study; it is a part of your duty to direct their efforts. "There is no harm, but good," says Bain, "in exacting a certain amount of independent preparation, especially with older pupils; but the teacher's first recitation, and the final iteration during the lessons, are the principal instrumentality whereby the lesson is fixed in the memory; *the learner's own studies are the smallest contribution to the effect.*"

4. If you expect to have lessons learned at all, make them *short*. In the machine-work of graded schools, where text-books are crammed by pages, this principle is habitually violated.

5. As a rule, when conducting a class exercise, *stand*. If you are too weak to stand all the time, *stand* occasion-

ally. Stand where you can see the face of every scholar in your class during a recitation. "In Germany," says Horace Mann, "I never saw a teacher hearing a recitation with a book in his hand, nor a teacher sitting while hearing a recitation."

6. Use your eyes. Look your pupils in the eye when you question them, and make them look you in the eye when they answer.

7. Keep your voice down to the conversational key. A quiet voice is music in the schoolroom.

8. Make up your mind to secure and hold the attention of every member of the class. A lesson has never been given unless it has been received.

9. Lighten up your class with a pleasant countenance. The teacher who cannot occasionally join in a hearty laugh with scholars lacks one element of power. "Whatever temper you have suffered to grow up in the gradual habit of years," says the Rev. F. D. Huntington, "that will get a daily revelation over your desks as visible as any maps on the walls."

10. Have something interesting to say to your scholars at every recitation. If you can keep your pupils busily at work, you will have but little trouble about order. Keep your pupils on the alert by being wide-awake yourself.

11. In general, put your questions to the whole class, in order to make every scholar *think out* the answer; then, after a pause, call upon some one pupil to give it.

12. Seldom repeat a question. Train your pupils to a habit of close attention, so that they can understand what you say the first time you say it.

13. Give your slow scholars time to think and speak. The readiest children are not always the soundest think-

ers. The highest praise given by an English inspector to a teacher was "that he allowed his slow boys time to *wriggle out an answer.*"

14. Never repeat to the class a scholar's half-audible answer. Compel every pupil to speak loud enough to be distinctly understood by every member of the class.

15. Explain when necessary, but make your scholars do a part of the talking. Your talk should consist largely of intelligent questions. "The best instructors," says Diesterweg, an eminent German teacher, "do not *talk* when it is the scholar's business to *work;* therefore the good teacher is neither talkative nor taciturn. *The very worst teachers are those who admire their own talk.*"

16. Encourage scholars to ask questions, but do not answer them yourself until after you have given the class an opportunity to answer.

17. Use the blackboard yourself, and make your class use it. "The best school," says Prof. J. S. Hart, "is founded upon chalk."

18. Train your scholars to recite in good English, but do not worry them by interruptions when they are speaking. Make a note of incorrect or inelegant expressions, and have them corrected afterwards. Do not expect children to speak perfect English, and do not become over-precise and fussy about their expressions.

19. When pupils stand in reciting, insist upon an erect attitude, with the hands clear of the desk. In reading and spelling, call out your classes into line, so as to secure a relief from long-continued sitting at desks.

20. Seldom detain pupils after school to study imperfectly recited lessons. It is a physical impossibility for a tired, fretting, obstinate, hungry child to do good thinking.

21. Assign but few lessons to be learned at home. Children must have time to work, play, eat, sleep, and grow. Children under ten years of age ought not to study at all out of school.

22. Your chief business is, *to make pupils think*, not to think for them; *to make them talk*, not to talk for them; *to draw out their powers*, not to display your own.

23. Point out to your scholars, in advance, the main facts of a lesson, so that they may not fritter away their time upon unimportant details. Continue this until your pupils learn how to discriminate for themselves between chaff and wheat.

24. Before you require *verbatim* definitions or condensed generalizations, make sure that your pupils understand *what the words mean;* in other words, base memorized statements upon a foundation of real conceptions.

25. Train your scholars to hear correctly, and to reproduce accurately in thought and language what has been told to them. "Scholars will learn well only what they are obliged to reproduce and tell," says Diesterweg.

26. Keep your explanations down to the level of your scholars' minds. In order to do this, bear in mind your own feeble powers and limited attainments when you were no older than your pupils. A great deal of teaching flies "over the heads" of the pupils. You must learn to talk in household Anglo-Saxon, such as men use in business and women in the home.

27. Review often and always on *essentials*. However well anything is learned for the time being, it will fade away and pass into oblivion if not called up again and again. *Repetition* is absolutely essential to habit, skill, readiness, thoroughness, and accuracy.

28. Do not become the slave of routine or of one inflexible mechanical system. Stick to some general purpose and plan, but secure the greatest possible variety of ways and means.

V. METHODS IN RECITATIONS.

1. The main objects of the recitation are:
    (1.) Instruction imparted by the teacher.
    (2.) Mental training for the pupil.

The minor objects of the recitation are:
    (1.) To induce study.
    (2.) To test preparation.
    (3.) To cultivate expression.
    (4.) To correct errors or mistakes.
    (5.) To awaken inquiry.
    (6.) To form habits of attention, readiness, and self-possession.

2. Conduct recitations sometimes by questions, and sometimes by topics.

3. Make a judicious combination of oral reciting with written work, but avoid the modern error of making writing-machines out of your pupils. The great advantages of oral over written recitations are, (1) the cultivation of readiness of expression, (2) that pupils learn by hearing one another's answers; and (3) that the teacher becomes a living power in the recitation.

4. Occasionally let your pupils question one another. It will do them as much good to *ask* a question as to answer it.

5. It is a good plan to call for answers by making use of cards having the names of the class members written on them. If you call pupils in regular alphabetical order, or in the order of seats, they are apt to be somewhat inatten-

tive except when their turn comes; if you question at random, you will always have a strong tendency to call on the best and readiest scholars, to the neglect of the poorest and slowest ones.

6. Waste as little time as possible in keeping a daily account of recitation credits. You ought to be a *teacher*, not merely a recording-clerk of text-book questions and answers. No teacher can do his best at instructing when his attention is diverted by jotting down credits. The strong tendency in graded schools to run into excessive dependence upon question and answer from the text-books springs largely from the undue importance attached to credits and rank in marking. Many sensitive girls are kept in a constant worry and fret on account of "checks" in recitations. A "check" is not quite so brutal as a blow; but the effect of its endless dropping is often quite as bad upon the disposition. Besides, if all the half-hour of recitation is spent in putting a question to each pupil in order to "mark" him, there is no time left to explain or to teach. *The most vital work done in a class cannot be reduced to figures.* As far as practicable, substitute the results of weekly or monthly oral reviews or short written examinations. But when pupils have become demoralized by working for credits for several years, it will not do to discontinue the plan suddenly. Continue to mark for some recitations, never letting your pupils know what recitations are to be so marked.

7. Pupils attend school, not merely to recite, but to be instructed and aided by the living teacher. Never stop short with hearing a lesson; add something to it; discuss it; talk about it, even though you cannot reduce the talk to percentage. Go over the ground of the next advance

lesson orally with your pupils, instead of leaving them to master it alone. Tell them enough to get them interested in it, and to lead them to discover the main points. " The moment you drop the thick veil which the text-book interposes between your pupil's mind and yours," says Professor J. H. Allen, " and deal with him face to face, you are right in the line, and are doing the work of the great teachers of the world. It is not merely because Socrates, Plato, and Aristotle were great men themselves, but because they happily lived before text-books were invented, and had to invent their methods as they went along—and test them, too, as they went along, by the responses they got from those who came to learn—that their great original force has so gone out upon the world of thought. It is so, in a modester way and in a lesser degree, as soon as we take the same course with them."

8. Do not confine yourself to the printed questions of the text-book, and do not require your pupils to give their answers in the exact words of the text-book, except in the case of important rules and definitions which cannot be accurately and concisely expressed in other language than that of the text-book. Accept the pupil's own statement if the answer is in good English and is substantially right.

9. Ralph Waldo Emerson once said, in an address to teachers, " If a pupil, in a proper manner, doubt the correctness of your statement or opinion, and a discussion follow, never attempt to silence him by your mere assertion, but hear his reasons patiently and pleasantly. Welcome the doubting spirit and the zeal in arguing that prove the thinker. Encourage his inquiries; and if he convince you that you are wrong and that he is right, acknowledge it cheerfully, and—hug him."

10. Louis Agassiz said, in his opening address to one of his classes,

"I want to make our method so very different that it may appear there is something left to be done in the system adopted in our public schools. I think that pupils are made too much to turn their attention to books, and the teacher is left a simple machine of study. That should be done away with among us. *I shall never make you repeat what you have been told, but constantly ask you what you have seen yourselves.*"

VI. THE MINIMUM OF RULES.

1. *Never attempt to teach what you do not understand.*
2. *Never tell a child what you can make that child tell you.*
3. *Never give a piece of information without asking the children to repeat it.*
4. *Never use a hard word when an easy one will answer.*
5. *Never make a rule you do not rigidly enforce.*
6. *Never give an unnecessary command.*
7. *Never permit a child to remain in the class without something to do.*

VII. SPECIFIC DIRECTIONS FOR PUPILS.

NOTE.—Read these directions to your pupils, and make each direction the topic of a short informal talk.

1. Stand erect when reading or reciting, without touching the desk with your hands.

2. Open your mouth in speaking, and speak clearly, loudly, and distinctly.

3. Answer in full sentences, and try to use good English.

4. In all examinations, whether written or oral, be honest and honorable, never prompting others, nor allowing others to aid you.

5. Study, not so much for credits as for knowledge.

6. Do not study later than eight or nine o'clock, and, when sick, do not study at all.

7. For most scholars, one hour's study in the morning is worth two in the evening.

8. Give your undivided attention to whatever work you try to do.

9. When your eyes ache, stop studying.

10. If you wish to become a good scholar, *take care of your health.* By a judicious interchange of work and play, study and recreation, avoid breaking down.

11. Do your own work, and do not meddle with the affairs of your classmates.

12. Remember that your success in school as well as in life depends mainly upon patient industry and hard work.

13. Remember that you should learn your lessons for your own benefit, not because your teacher requires you to learn them. When you fail to do your work, you cheat, not your teacher, but yourself.

VIII. DIRECTIONS ABOUT WRITTEN EXAMINATIONS.

1. Do not be in a hurry. Take time to read every question carefully, so that you may be sure to answer just what is asked, and nothing else.

2. Work slowly and thoughtfully. *Think out* your answers, and condense them into the fewest words possible.

3. If you come to a puzzling question, pass it by until you have answered the rest, and then turn back to it when you are not pressed for time.

4. Write neatly and legibly, and punctuate as you write. Separate your answers by a space, so that the examiner may distinguish each without confusion.

5. After you have completed a paper, go over it carefully with reference to accuracy, expression, spelling, punctuation, and capitals.

Chapter VII.
THE MANAGEMENT OF UNGRADED COUNTRY SCHOOLS.

I. GENERAL REMARKS.

It requires tact, skill, originality, and common-sense to manage successfully an ungraded country school. In the graded schools of town and city, the course of instruction is definitely laid down in printed manuals; the work of each successive grade is directed by principal and superintendent; the results are tested by written examinations; and each class-teacher is only a cog in a complicated system of wheels. But in the country school the teacher combines the functions of assistant, principal, examiner, and superintendent. He is an autocrat, limited only by custom, precedent, and text-books.

When we consider that about one half of all the school children in our country receive their elementary education in the district schools, their importance as a part of our school system is obvious. Many of these schools in the sparsely settled districts are kept open only from three to six months in the year, and even then the attendance is irregular. The whole schooling of many children, from the age of five to fifteen, hardly amounts to four years of unbroken school attendance. In such schools and for such pupils, what instruction will best fit the children for their life-duties? What knowledge is of most worth to them? What things are essential?

Now a man or woman gifted with sound common-sense will look at the work somewhat in this way: These boys are the sons of farmers, mechanics, miners, and workingmen; most of them will follow the occupations of their fathers. The girls—most of them—will become the wives of farmers, mechanics, miners, and workingmen, and will "keep house." What are the essential things that these boys and girls need to learn in order to aid them to become industrious and intelligent men and women, fitted for their sphere in life? The prodigies and geniuses and exceptional cases are not to be taken into account at all.

It requires decisive firmness to clear away the rubbish of a superficial education and get down to a solid basis. There is no mistaking the fact that a great deal of our current school education, like the ornamental tattooing of the South Sea Islanders, is only skin-deep, and is valuable only as fashionable ornamental work. To a certain extent, every teacher must perhaps yield to the prevailing customs, and decorate his pupils with educational paints and feathers; but there is still some room left for the exercise of sound judgment. As an axiom, we may safely take this statement of John Stuart Mill: THE AIM OF ALL INTELLECTUAL TRAINING FOR THE MASS OF THE PEOPLE SHOULD BE TO CULTIVATE COMMON-SENSE.

In the country school leave untouched the things you have not time to teach nor your pupils the talents to learn. Leave out a smattering of non-essentials, in order that your scholars may be thorough in essentials.

"There can be no other curricular arrangement," says Bain, "even for the laboring population, than to give them as much methodized knowledge of the physical and the moral world, and as much literary training, as their time will allow. About two thirds of the day, as a rule, might be given to knowledge, and one third to literature —music, drill, and gymnastics being counted apart from both."

II. THINGS ESSENTIAL.

1. *Pupils must be trained to read and write their mother-tongue correctly.*

Teach them to do this so that every scholar, at fifteen years of age, shall be able to read a newspaper readily; shall be able to spell common words correctly; shall be able to converse free from provincialisms in pronunciation; shall be able to write a legible letter in correct English. In reading, teach them not merely to pronounce words, but to get at the meaning of what they read. There must be no sham scholarship here. Good spelling is a conventional test of education, and even a spelling-lesson may be made the means of valuable mental training.

2. *They must be trained, in arithmetic, to work, accurately and readily, examples in the "four rules;" to work business examples in common and decimal fractions; to reckon simple interest; and to write bills, receipts, and promissory notes.*

In most country schools the pupils throw away a great deal of time in "going through," term after term, bulky text-books on arithmetic, filled to repletion with schoolmasters' puzzles about things unknown in real life, and crammed with technical "rules," which are learned only to be forgotten. Concentrate your drill upon the four rules, fractions, the tables, and interest, and thus give your pupils the mental training which will enable them to do a few essential things skilfully, accurately, and readily.

None of your pupils need to study such schoolmasterisms as "allegation," "duodecimals," "circulating decimals," "permutation," "single and double position;" and few except the big boys who have nothing else to do need waste time upon "compound proportion," "reduction ascending and descending," "true discount," "bonds," "exchange," "insurance," "equation of payments," "partnership," "arithmetical progression," "geometrical progression," "custom-house business," "annuities," etc. Omit these, and you may find time to give short lessons in the elements of natural science, and to open the eyes of your pupils to the wonders of the world around them.

It is true that many country schoolmasters still contend that the reasoning faculties of a pupil cannot be properly disciplined unless he devotes half his school-days to abstruse logical analysis, as they choose to call it, of useless problems, worse than Chinese puzzles, involving only blind adherence to rule, or still blinder imitation; but the real truth is that mental discipline in the study of arithmetic is not one whit more valuable than is hard thinking upon other school studies.

No mental work of any kind, rightly done, is utterly useless; but the real question is, not what is *good*, but what, under the circumstances, is *best*, and *how much*, and *when*. "Get your discipline," says Chadbourne, "by doing a greater amount of work, and doing it in better style." A wealthy merchant once set his son to wheeling stones from one corner of his garden to the other, in order to train him to work. He was wiser than the man who never makes his boy work at all; but he would have been wiser still had he kept his son at work sawing wood or laying out a garden, or weeding the onion-bed or hoeing potatoes.

Now in country schools, a great many boys and girls are kept at wheeling educational stones. A teacher who keeps young pupils at work, term after term, upon complex or puzzling problems in mental arithmetic, repeating long-drawn-out formulas in logical analysis, including statement, solution, and conclusion, before they have acquired readiness and accuracy in addition and multiplication, is only making them wheel stones. A country teacher who neglects "the four rules" and "the tables" in order to train big country boys upon a normal-school analytical demonstration of the reason for inverting the divisor in division of fractions is wheeling stones; and if, added to this, he requires allegation, exchange, and progression, he is wheeling glacial boulders. Avoid making a hobby of arithmetic and algebra. Two hundred years ago, Roger Ascham, in *The Scholemaster*, wrote as follows: "Mark all Mathematical heads, which be only and wholly bent to those Sciences, how solitary they be themselves, how unfit to live with others, and how unapt to serve in the world." And a modern educator, Superintendent Eliot, of Boston, says now, "A faculty to be called out by the knowledge of numbers and their relations is too often stupefied by the drugs substituted for them."

In his unsurpassed paper on *Waste of Labor in the Work of Education*, President Chadbourne truthfully says,

"The principle of dealing with essentials mainly should prevail in all the work of education. We have too much to do to spend time fooling over complicated arithmetical puzzles which abound in some books—questions which no one should undertake to solve till well versed in algebra and geometry. At the proper stage of education, such puzzles, which are a discouragement to the young scholar, because he thinks them essential to the subject, will be solved in the natural progress of his work. They are an annoyance and discouragement simply because they are introduced before their time, before the study of the principles on which their solution depends."

3. *They should acquire a good general knowledge of geography.*

In order to do this, it is not at all necessary that boys and girls should be compelled, day after day, and term after term, and year after year, to memorize the dreary pages of "map questions" that crowd the three padded books in a series of geographies. If any teachers of country schools, or indeed of *any* schools anywhere on this planet, require their pupils to learn by heart one tenth of the boundaries, cities, towns, villages, rivers, mountains, capes, bays, and microscopic bits of topography included under the head of "Map Lessons" in the books; or to learn by rote one twentieth of the stereotyped descriptions of countries and their inhabitants; or one hundredth of the dry census statistics of the States even of our own country about bushels of corn, wheat, rye, barley, oats, beans, pease, and potatoes; or the value of the annual crops of cotton, tobacco, sugar, rice, hemp, and hay; or the value of manufactured articles, such as boots and shoes, cotton cloth, hardware; or the annual catch of mackerel and codfish—statistics in which text-books abound—such teachers ought to be indicted for a lack of common-sense. No reasonable human being expects even a schoolmaster, who has studied and taught geography half a lifetime, to know, without looking on the book, the entire returns of the last census, or the exact population of every city in the world, or the length of every river, or the height in feet of every mountain-peak, or the boundary-line of every State in the Union and every country in the world, or the exact distance in miles from Ujiji to Walla-Walla. Is it reasonable, then, to attempt to make boys and girls master this chaos of facts? The plain truth is that no small part of what children are forced to cram at school, not only in geography, but also in other branches, might appropriately be labelled THINGS WORTH FORGETTING! Nature is wiser than teachers and text-book-makers; she casts off the dead and waste matter and saves the child.

Cut out of your text-book on geography, then, all but essentials. Cross out all local State geography except that of the pupil's own State.

Read the descriptive text, and mark, now and then, something to be put away in the storehouse of memory. Use the scalpel with merciless severity. "It takes a brave man," says President Chadbourne, "one merciless to himself, to make a small, simple, but thorough text-book; but such text-books we must have, if we use them at all."

4. *They should be trained in writing and in speaking good English, and should learn the elements of grammar.*

The technical study of grammar should be preceded by a course of elementary exercises in "Language Lessons," such as are found in modern text-books, notably in Swinton's *Language Primer.* Children learn to swim by trying to swim, to skate by skating, to talk by talking, and to write by writing. They cannot be trained to speak or to write correctly by parsing according to Latinized formulas. They will never learn to construct a good sentence by analyzing complex or compound sentences, or by memorizing and repeating the rules of syntax, though this method be followed until they grow gray.

Require at least two short composition exercises a week, on slates or paper, upon subjects about which the pupils *know something*.

Let them write about farming, about animals, birds, fishes, flowers, trees. Read them short stories, and require them to be reproduced in writing. Let them write short biographical sketches of great men. Let them make compositions about their history and geography lessons; and then let the older pupils correct the compositions of the younger ones, and the younger ones read those of the older ones as models.

"Nothing is of more value in education," says Buxton, "than this, to make a point of opening the child's eyes to take an interest in the world around him. Teach him, if a country boy, to know the birds, their nests, eggs, and notes; the wild animals, their haunts and habits; the domestic animals, their nature, peculiarities, and various breeds; the flowers; the trees; the insects; the different soils. You can do this at mere odds and ends of time, and you have opened springs of pure enjoyment in his soul."

Require all pupils over eight years of age to write at least one short letter a week, until they can write it in due form, punctuate it, capitalize it, spell correctly every word they use in it, fold it neatly, and direct it. In addition to this, pupils over twelve years of age ought to be able to express their thoughts in well-constructed sentences. After this is done, let the big boys and girls take to parsing and analysis, which are good enough exercises at the right time. From a text-book let them learn the chief "rules of syntax" and the technical distinctions of etymology. If the text-book in use is a good one, omit two thirds of it, and give out the remainder in substantial lessons to be learned by heart; if it be a poor one, of the antique Latinized type, deal it out in homœopathic doses.

5. *They should have a good general knowledge of the leading events in the history of our own country.*

But do not compel the memorizing of three or four hundred pages of dates and details which no teacher living could stow into his head in a lifetime, and which, if learned, would be next to worthless. Let your pupils read the text-book aloud in the class; then it is your business to winnow out the three grains of wheat from the bushel of chaff, and tell them what to mark as fit to be learned. You must supplement the text-book with stories, anecdotes, incidents, and well-selected extracts. Make use of the school library as an assistant. The real spirit of history does not consist in dates and details. "My grandfather's stories about his service as a private in the Revolutionary war," said a noted teacher, "made history a living reality to me."

Narrative and biography make the life of history to the young.

6. *They ought to be trained to habits of careful observation; or, in other words, they ought to acquire some knowledge of common things in the phenomena of nature.*

And right here the good teacher will do his best work, drawing out of his young pupils all they know of the world around them, directing their attention, indicating relations and harmonies, and encouraging every effort to increase their knowledge. Here the teacher is everything, books nothing. "We teach too much by manuals; too little by direct intercourse with the pupil's mind; we have too much of words, too little of things," said Daniel Webster, who, though but a short time a teacher, well understood the American school system. Excite in your pupils a burning desire to learn; inspire them with *motives*. "The primary principle of education," says Sir William Hamilton, "is the determination of the pupil to self-activity."

7. *They must learn to practise the principles and precepts of morality.*

It is not necessary that they study ethics as a science, or religion as theology. What they most need is that plain preceptive morality which is diffused among the people as their best rules of action in their daily life. You cannot mould character or form good habits by dealing out hackneyed commonplaces, or by merely repeating maxims. The art cannot be conveyed to you in condensed directions or taught in twelve easy lessons. It must be an outgrowth of your own life and character, your own observation and experience combined with the best thoughts you glean from books and men.

III. MISCELLANEOUS THINGS.

Physiology is not an essential text-book study, but it is necessary that your pupils should know something about the laws of health in relation to diet, sleep, air, exercise, work, play, and rest. Teach your pupils that sickness is the penalty of violated laws; that bad habits are physical sins; that bad health, unless hereditary, is the result of carelessness or ignorance. All this you can do without a text-book.

For the right training of the perceptive faculties, you must give elementary lessons in physics, botany, and other natural sciences. Country boys and girls generally have a considerable stock of crude knowledge, picked up empirically by their own observation, about animals, plants, and the phenomena of every-day life. Draw out this fragmentary store of facts, and supplement it by the facts of science. Set the girls to collecting and pressing flowers. Let the boys bring in specimens of minerals, shells, woods, and grains for a school cabinet. Open their eyes to the harmonies of nature. Teachers are apt to deal too much with books and too little with things; they mistake shadow for substance. Do not depend too much on mechanical "mental discipline," or too little on direct information. A great part of teaching is avowedly empirical, desultory, utilitarian. To acquire information is a mental exercise of no mean order. If you can only find out the secret, you can make your whole school alive to *know;* but the secret cannot be conveyed in set rules. If you are nothing but a bookworm, you will never learn the art.

If possible, have some singing, and drawing for those who have any taste for it. If there is a school library, make good use of it by selecting suitable books for your pupils to read, and by questioning them about *what* they read. Many a dull boy, lazy and listless over his lessons, has been made alive by good story-books. If you have tact, good-nature, and firmness, you need not have much trouble about order, discipline, or government. Win the good-will of the older scholars, and they will become your assistants in governing.

Keep in mind this central fact, that in country schools certain leading results must be obtained, even at the sacrifice of ornament and system. Only concentration can give strength. Make your pupils learn well the things they most need in the common walks of life, without regard to changes in educational fashions. Feathers and finery you do not need. Do not waste your time in striving after the impossible. You cannot, however hard you may try, educate beyond the barriers fixed by nature and surrounding circumstances. You will find some slow scholars, and some dull ones; some with strong latent powers, and others the reverse; some stubborn and others pliant, some good and others bad. If you are gifted with sound judgment and good common-sense, you will work on calmly, faithfully, hopefully, good-naturedly, disciplining the troublesome, taming the savage, bearing in mind that all the dull boys and careless girls will, somehow or other, grow up into better men and women than you dare hope for. Take comfort from the words that quaint old Thomas Fuller wrote two centuries ago:

"Wines, the stronger they be, the more lees they have when they are new. Many boys are muddy-headed till they be clarified with age; and such afterwards proved the best. Bristol diamonds are both bright and squared and pointed by nature, and yet are soft and worthless; whereas Orient ones in India are rough and rugged naturally. Hard, rugged, and dull natures in youth acquit themselves afterwards the jewels of the country; and therefore their dulness at first is to be borne with, if they be diligent. The schoolmaster deserves to be beaten himself who beats nature in a boy for a fault. And I question whether all the whipping in the world can make their parts who are naturally sluggish rise one minute before the hour nature hath appointed. All the whetting in the world can never set a razor's edge on that which hath no steel in it."

Add this consolatory statement by Emerson: "Nature makes fifty poor melons for one that is good, and shakes down a tree-full of gnarled, wormy, unripe crabs, before you can find a dozen dessert apples."

IV. MINOR MATTERS.

The arrangement and length of recitations are matters of judgment to be modified according to conditions. When one class is reciting, set the others about some specific piece of work at their desks. The very youngest children should have two short reading and spelling lessons daily; the middle classes one lesson, and the highest class two lessons, a week. It is poor economy to hear your advanced classes recite daily lessons in all their studies. The few advanced pupils ought not to monopolize your attention. Assign all your older pupils good solid lessons to be learned at home; for children who attend school only a part of the year cannot easily be overtaxed with brain-work. Train them to depend upon themselves, and to find out things by hard thinking. In recitations, your explanations and illustrations must be condensed, for your time is limited. It is one of the defects of graded city schools that teachers talk too much and do most of the thinking for their pupils. Country scholars who enter the city high-school generally come out ahead because they have habits of self-reliance, and know how to learn from books.

Give the children under eight years of age long recesses for play; they ought not to be shut up in school more than two or three hours a day. In pleasant weather, after they read and spell, turn them out of doors.

When you take charge of a new school, adopt, at first,

the classification and order of exercises of your predecessor; if changes are needed, make them by degrees after you know the needs of the school. Beware of turning your pupils back to the "beginning of the book," as if you took it for granted they knew nothing at all. Rather, let them go on, and review when necessary. Still, if you happen to find a set of scholars taught by unskilled "school-keepers," you must act on this axiom from the great German educator Niemeyer, "Pupils who have been injured by wrong modes of instruction, and by an injurious multiplicity of studies, must be taught in almost all the elementary branches *as if they were beginners*."

On the morning of the first day, that crucial test of the teacher, introduce yourself by a few good-natured remarks, distribute slips of paper on which the scholars are to write their names, age, class, and studies, and, having collected these, proceed at once to business by giving out a sheet of paper to all who can use a pen, and requiring them to write a composition about their last vacation. This will keep them at work an hour at least, during which time you can attend to the little ones, and make out your rough programme. The art of the first day is to keep your scholars busy. You will avoid much mischief by getting everybody hard at work in ten minutes after school opens. If you know how to tell a good story, close school with one; if not, read one from some book.

Make no reflections on the former teacher, and allow none to be made by your scholars. If the people of your district are old-fashioned, introduce normal-school methods by degrees after you have won over your pupils. Be careful of what you say; any inadvertent remark made in a moment of passion will be taken home by twenty tongues, and discussed in cold blood at twenty family supper-tables. A short call at the homes of your pupils will convince the old folks that the young teacher "isn't stuck up," will disarm prejudice, and conciliate the young folks.

Find out the two or three ruling families of the neighborhood, and make friends of them. Attend social gatherings whenever you are invited; the young folks like a *human* teacher. Bring the public opinion of the district over to your side, and you cannot make a failure in school.

V. ADVANTAGES OF COUNTRY SCHOOLS.

For a young teacher, whether man or woman, there is no better school of practice than an ungraded country school. Nor should its educational advantages for pupils be underrated. In the long race of life, boys educated in country schools do actually come out ahead of those ground out by the graded machinery of the city school. Perhaps one reason for this is that the country boy combines physical training with mental. During a part of the year, he works on the farm, and gets, not only muscular strength, *but a habit of work.* He goes back to school with a keen relish for study, and a habit of steady application. One day of hard work at ditching in his father's meadow made John Adams begin to be a good student of Latin. Hard work on his father's farm, from sunrise to sunset, hoeing corn, or haying, or digging potatoes, has made school-life seem a play-spell to many a boy, and has laid the foundation of habits that have led to brilliant success in mental work. The trouble with most city boys is that they have no work to do out of school, and they never learn what labor means until school life is over. My observation as principal of an evening school of a thousand boys, for three years, convinced me that many of the boys made quite as rapid progress in the essential branches as did the boys of the day schools. The evening-school boys had a steadiness of purpose unknown to boys untrained to labor. Professor Runkle, of Boston, says, "So far from interfering with intellectual culture, industrial culture really lends to it a powerful support by strengthening the character and developing the moral energies. It is upon these moral energies that the entire value of human character depends."

"It takes more than a mere knowledge of books," says Superintendent Wickersham, "to make a useful member of society. We must so modify our system of instruction as to send out, instead, large classes of young people fitted for trades, and *willing and able to work.*

Herein lies the great advantage of the country school: both boys and girls have a combination of mental and physical exercise. The morning and evening "chores" on the farm and in the household prevent undue mental exertion. They are not surfeited with school and books; school, indeed, is a relief from hard labor. Better six months' schooling in earnest than ten months of unwilling dawdling. For one, I am thankful that I was trained to habits of hard work in my boyhood, and went to a country school where I was not crammed with studies or worried with credits, or made wretched with written examinations.

If, for the teacher, the country school has its dark side in low wages or lack of society, it has also its bright side in contrast with the great schools of the towns and cities.

To show this, let me give you an encouraging thought from Professor William Russell, whose words, after a lapse of thirty years, still linger lovingly in my ears:

"A mind accustomed to large views, and working on broad principles, will, unconsciously and necessarily, adopt methods correspondent, and will radiate, from its own action, light and truth throughout the sphere of its influence. Nowhere is this statement more strikingly verified than in the case of an intelligent teacher, in the direction and instruction of an elementary school. It is in this sphere that ingenuity and tact, and originality and skill, are most needed, in endeavors to develop intellectual capabilities and build up the great fabric of mental power. Nowhere else, in the whole field of education, is the demand so urgent for a thorough insight into the nature and working of the mind, for the light to guide its advances, or the power to mould its expanding character."

VI. CONDENSED DIRECTIONS.

1. The true economy of teaching an ungraded school is to make the fewest possible number of classes, and to consider both age and capacity in making your classification.

2. If your school is a large one, do not attempt to hear daily recitations in everything, but alternate the studies of the more advanced pupils.

3. When they are not reciting, assign your classes text-book lessons or some piece of definite work on slates or blackboards.

4. Economize time and instruction by means of as many general exercises as possible, in which all except the youngest pupils can join; such as drill exercises in the four rules of arithmetic, mental-arithmetic examples, the

spelling of common words, abstracts in composition, review questions on the leading facts of geography, etc. To do this will require tact and forethought; but when well done, it is invaluable.

5. Take an hour, weekly, for select readings, dialogues, and lessons on morals and manners. You can fire a whole school with enthusiasm for good by reading the right kind of stories.

6. Occasionally give your classes a written examination. In most city schools, written examinations are carried to great extremes; but in most country schools there is not enough of written work to give readiness and exactness in the written expression of thought.

7. Train your older pupils to correct and credit the papers of the younger ones, and let the oldest girls play teacher occasionally.

8. If you are a woman, give your girls occasional talks on domestic economy. Buy some sensible book on the subject and lend it to them. A great many homes are poorly kept on account of ignorance. Huxley says, "I put instruction in the elements of household work and of domestic economy next in order to physical training." "Knowledge of domestic economy," says Kingsley, "saves income."

9. If you are a man, take some interest in the home-work of your boys. Instil into their minds the necessity of labor for every human being. Point out to them the life-long value of being trained in boyhood to habits of regular employment in useful labor. Many a boy on a farm complains of his hard lot when he is really being blessed by hard labor. A wise teacher can often set him right in his notions.

10. Endeavor to make your school the district centre of civility, politeness, and good manners. If they learn good-breeding at all, many pupils must learn it at school. There is no limit to the civilizing influence of a gentle woman or a gentlemanly man in a country school. Send out your pupils with the seal of honor and truthfulness.

11. Persuade the parents to visit your school even if you have to do so by means of exhibitions in which their children take a part.

12. Remember that school trustees are your legal superiors in office. Argue with them, persuade and convince them if you can, but *do not contradict them.*

13. Bear in mind that though you may have more "book-learning" than most of the men and women in a country district, there are sure to be many parents who are your superiors in sound sense, in judgment, and in a knowledge of the solid facts of human life.

14. Before you begin school, if possible, call a meeting of the "trustees," or "committee." Talk over matters with them, ask their advice, and tell them your plans. It is well to go into a new school backed by the weight of official power.

15. Whenever you have any unusual cases of discipline, consult the trustees or the parents *before* you take action.

16. The following may be taken for practical guidance in your course of instruction:

A child of average mental powers ought to be able, on leaving school at fifteen years of age—

1. To read well and spell well.
2. To write a neat and legible hand.
3. To know the main points in the geography of the world, and the leading events in our country's history.

4. To speak correct English and to write readily a well-expressed letter of business or friendship.

5. To work accurately any plain business questions involving the four rules, common and decimal fractions, and simple interest.

PART II.

CONDENSED DIRECTIONS FOR TEACHING COMMON-SCHOOL ESSENTIALS.

Chapter I.

GENERAL PRINCIPLES.

I. "The aim of all intellectual training for the mass of the people should be to cultivate common-sense, to qualify them for forming a sound practical judgment of the circumstances by which they are surrounded." — *John Stuart Mill.*

II. "The intellectual training to be given in the elementary schools must, of course, in the first place, consist in learning to use the means of acquiring knowledge, or reading, writing, and arithmetic; and it will be a great matter to teach reading so completely that the act shall have become easy and pleasant.

"But along with a due proficiency in the use of the means of learning, a certain amount of knowledge, of intellectual discipline, and of artistic training should be conveyed in the elementary schools; and in this direction I can conceive no subject-matter of education so appropriate and so important as the rudiments of physical science, with drawing, modelling, and singing."—*Huxley.*

III. "An educational course may be packed so full of work that one piece crushes out another; so many books to be gone over, so many pages to be taken at a lesson, so many exercises of all sorts to be attempted, if not accomplished; and then the pressure is the obstacle against which both teachers and taught beat until they are often pitifully bruised."—*Superintendent Eliot.*

IV. "Worth belongs to any subject of study if it conveys methods that are useful far beyond itself. The sciences that embody an organization for aiding the mind —whether in deductive method, such as geometry and physico-mathematical science; in observation and induction, as the physical sciences; or in classification, as in the natural-history sciences — would on these grounds alone be admitted to the higher circle of mental discipline or training, irrespective of the value of the facts and principles viewed separately or in detail. It depends partly on the teacher and partly on the scholar whether the element of method shall stand forth and extend itself, or whether the subjects shall only yield their own quantum of matter or information. . . . In estimating the value of a branch of study, we must consider not merely what it gives us, but what, through engrossment of our time, it deprives us of."—*Bain's Education as a Science.*

Chapter II.

CONDENSED DIRECTIONS FOR TEACHING READING.

1. Teach beginners by a judicious combination of the word method, phonic method, and spelling method. After learning to call a limited number of words at sight, the methods practically run together, and the difference is so little apparent that no one method need be made a hobby of.

2. Make use of the school chart, the Primer, or First Reader, and the blackboard: best of all is the blackboard. Make the letters, and let your pupils try to imitate you. Write or print words, and let your scholars do the same.

3. Lessons for beginners should be very short, not exceeding ten minutes in length.

4. Give patient and long-continued attention to the correction of slovenly and incorrect pronunciation, both in spoken language and in reading from the book.

5. Give special attention to drill on the elementary sounds, both vowel and consonant. The *sounds* of the letters must be taught with their *names*. Take frequent concert exercises in vocal culture, including drill on force, pitch, movement, and inflection, in order to bring out the voices of timid pupils, and to secure flexibility of the organs of speech.

6. Call out your reading classes into line. Train pupils to stand erect, and to hold the book in the left hand.

7. Train pupils to open the mouth freely. This may be done by long-continued concert drill on the vowel sounds, such as *a* in *arm*, or *a* in *all*. There can be no good reading with the teeth and lips half closed.

8. Train pupils, not only to call words, but also to think about the meaning of what they read. "The great and almost universal fault in teaching reading," says Superintendent Philbrick, "is the too great neglect of attention to the sense of what is read." "Even long after a child can read," says Bain, "it is unable to extract much information from books." Hence the need of the teacher's assistance.

9. Question pupils upon what they read. By conversation with them upon the subject of the lesson, endeavor to make it interesting and instructive. When they thoroughly understand what they read, and have a real appreciation of the subject, they will read naturally and with correct emphasis and inflection. The teacher may read a piece to let his pupils perceive how, by a natural tone and correct emphasis and inflection, he brings out the meaning; but he must carefully avoid training his pupils to imitate him. They must read well of themselves, because they understand and appreciate the subject; they must never read as parrots.

10. In order to secure close attention to the reading-lesson, require pupils to copy one paragraph, at least, of every lesson. Continue this even in the higher grades, as an aid in punctuation and spelling as well as in reading.

11. When the lesson is a suitable one, let pupils close their books, and tell from memory, in their own words, the substance of the piece. Occasionally require a written abstract of some suitable story.

12. Read aloud to younger classes every advance lesson. Explain the meaning of difficult or unusual words. In this way, it is possible for pupils *to get the sense of what they read.*

13. Make a list of words that pupils most frequently mispronounce, and drill your pupils in the correct pronunciation of these words. It is not enough to tell a pupil of a fault he commits; make him correct it himself. Put an instant stop to screaming, shouting, or drawling.

14. Occasionally take a spelling-lesson from the reading-lesson, but do not mix up spelling and reading together. "To make the child spell all the time he is reading," says Superintendent Eliot, "is like tripping him when we would have him walk. Spelling is to be practised at the outset only so far as it is a help to reading; but it never should have the lion's share it has long claimed in our teaching."

15. Train your classes daily, the higher grade as well as the lower, in some one of the following exercises in vocal culture:

1. Attitude.   4. Articulation.
2. Breathing.   5. Enunciation.
3. Vowel sounds.   6. Pronunciation.

16. Breathing exercises are of great value as an aid in securing an erect attitude and the free use of the vocal organs. Introduce every lesson with a short drill. Train your pupils to keep their lungs well filled with air, and to breathe often while reading.

17. In all classes, from the highest to the lowest, give frequent and thorough drill upon words containing the vowel sounds, properly grouped and arranged. Pay special attention to those sounds which children in some parts of

our country are apt to give incorrectly : such as *a* in hälf, cälf, läugh, etc.; intermediate *a*, as in ȧsk, lȧst, pȧst, ȧfter, etc.; *u* after *r*, as in true, rude, fruit, etc.; *u* as in tube, tune, etc.; *o* as in do, two, etc.; *o* as in road, coat, etc. The school is the proper place for correcting provincialisms in pronunciation.

18. Do not allow children to pronounce the words one by one, slowly and monotonously. From the first, pay particular attention to the much-abused articles *a* and *the*. These should be read as if they formed a syllable of the following word: as, *a-book'*, *a-hat'*, just as *a* is sounded in *around'*, *along'* — the sound of *a* slightly obscured and shortened, not the sound of *u* in *bŭt*. So, also, "the book" is sounded *thŭ-book'*, not "thē' book'" nor "*thur'-book'*." Pupils from the outset should be taught to read in *phrases :* as, The-poor-man, had-on-his-head, a-white-hat.

19. In the primary classes, teach pupils at least the dictionary notation of the long and the short vowel sounds; and, in the grammar grades, explain, by blackboard drill, the entire notation of the school dictionary in use, so that pupils may be able to find out for themselves the correct pronunciation of words. Train your pupils to refer to the dictionary for definitions as well as pronunciation.

20. Avoid the extreme of a high-pitched, sharp, piercing, unnatural school-tone, as well as the other extreme of feebleness and indistinctness. The following will indicate a good standard of force and loudness in school reading:

Every scholar must read so that every other member of the class can easily hear every word without looking at the book.

In order to determine this standard, listen to the reading without a book in your hands, and occasionally let your pupils close their books while one of their number is reading.

21. In a graded class of fifty pupils, it is desirable to train the whole class together a part of the time; but sometimes it is best to divide the class into sections of ten each, taking one section at a time, and allowing the others to study a spelling-lesson or to write a composition.

22. In grammar-grade classes, make reading-lessons the basis of exercises in grammar and composition, but take them as exercises distinct from the mere act of reading aloud. [See Part III., "Reading."] In one lesson let the pupils find out all the nouns, in another the verbs, and in a third every pronoun, etc. In one lesson confine the attention of pupils to *phrases*, in one to *clauses*, and in another to simple, complex, or compound sentences. In one lesson call attention to nothing but the use of capitals, in one to the use of the period, and in another of the comma. The interest and success of these lessons depend on the principle *of taking one thing* at a time. Then let your pupils copy the whole or a part of a lesson from the open book, and, next, require them to write what they can of it from memory.

23. In order to prevent monotony, occasionally carry into school a good story book or paper, such as *The Nursery, Harper's Young People, Æsop's Fables, St. Nicholas, Robinson Crusoe*, etc., and from that let each pupil, in turn, read a paragraph or page while the others listen. Such an exercise, rightly managed, will kindle an interest in the deadest class ever fossilized under the steady dropping of the old-style reading-lesson.

24. Let the older scholars occasionally read something from their scrap-books. When you find an exceedingly

interesting story or anecdote in the newspaper suitable for school use, clip it out, cut it up into short paragraphs; paste these upon card-board slips, number them, distribute them to your class, and let each pupil read one slip.

25. The speaking of dialogues is a material aid in securing naturalness in reading. The reading or recitation of short selections of poetry also forms a part of reading culture.

26. In order to fix and hold the attention, occasionally let each pupil read only one line of poetry or prose, around the class, until the lesson is finished. Again, let each scholar read only one word.

27. For concert reading, sometimes divide your class into small sections of four, six, or ten pupils each, and then match one against another to see which reads the best.

28. Do not allow a scholar, when reading, to be interrupted by corrections, or made nervous by upraised hands. Let the corrections be made after the reading.

29. Do not be too critical yourself, and do not allow class criticism to run into needless fault-finding. Be more watchful to commend good reading than to criticise poor reading.

30. Once in a while, let the scholars choose sides and make up a reading-match, every one who makes any mistake to be seated.

31. The pupils of all the higher-grade classes should be trained to lift their eyes from the book and look at the teacher or the class. In order to do this, the eye must anticipate the voice, taking in the last part of the sentence, so that it can be uttered while the reader is looking at his listeners.

32. "The investigation of the reading-lesson," says Currie, "forms the highest exercise of connected thinking in the common-school, and, if judiciously conducted, ought to contribute very much to the habit of reflective reading in after-life."

33. As ninety-nine hundredths of all the reading done by men and women is done *silently* and *mentally*, it is evident that the main purpose of the teacher, in all the higher-grade classes, should be to train pupils to *think* when reading, *and to gather up all the thoughts of the writer from the printed page.*

34. "*Systematic reading*," says Russell, "is a valued means for cultivating reflective habits of mind; reading which is *study*, not *perusal;* reading which is attentively done, carefully reviewed, exactly recorded, or orally recounted. Memory, under such discipline, becomes thoroughly retentive, information exact, judgment correct, conception clear, thought copious, and expression ready and appropriate."

35. Every school library ought to contain several sets of school Readers, to supplement those in the hands of the pupils. When scholars have read through their own books, the new ones will excite a fresh interest. Besides, in all except the lowest classes, an intelligent child will extract most of the information worth anything, from an ordinary class-book, in less than sixty days. "No one thing," says Horace Mann, "will contribute more to intelligent reading than a well-selected school library."

II. QUOTATIONS FROM EDUCATORS.

I. "If teachers will cease to require little children to 'read over' and to 'study' beforehand their reading exercise—a task entirely unsuitable at their age—and will also put an end to the absurd practice of allowing pupils to keep up, during the reading exercise, a running criticism upon each other by irritating and aggravating remarks, thus mortifying their more timid companions, and sometimes paying off old grudges; and will then confine their labors mainly to two points— to making the child realize the thought of the sentence to be read, and to showing him, by example and good vocal drill, how to give a pleasant and natural expression to that thought—the best part of the victory will be won."—*Superintendent A. P. Stone.*

II. "A part of the time saved by judicious management should be given to reading; not to the mere calling of words, nor to premature lessons in elocution, but to plain reading in good books for the sake of the information they contain. It is not creditable to our efforts as educators that so large a proportion of pupils passes from us without having acquired a taste for the reading of good books. If our system confers the ability to read without creating a desire for the right kind of reading, it surely stands in need of reformation. . . . Very little of the arithmetic which children learn at school can be made available in after-life. Their feats of analysis and parsing are never to be repeated in the actual contests of actual life. Nine tenths of what they have learned as geography will pass away as the morning cloud and the early dew. But a taste for good reading will last for life; will be available every day and almost every hour, and will grow by what it feeds on; will so occupy the time of the young as to rob temptation of half its power by stealing more than half its opportunities; and will be a refuge and a solace in adversity."—*Superintendent Newell.*

III. "We not only want more reading-books, but different ones; not Readers, not fragments of writings, but writings, however brief—a story or a history, a book of travels or a poem—associated as vividly as possible with the author who wrote them, not a mere book-maker who has patched together pieces of them. With such reading-books, intelligently used, the inability of our children to read at sight and with expression would become less common and less painful. As for grammar, it would almost develop itself from such reading as this. Familiarity with the best thoughts and expressions would lead children, with comparatively little effort, to think and express themselves in good language."—*Superintendent Eliot.*

IV. "I do not hesitate to declare my conviction that if half the school-time were devoted to reading, *solely for the sake of reading;* if books were put into the scholars' hands all that while, under wise direction, divested of every shadow of association with text-book work, to be perused with interest and delight inspired by their attractive contents—choice volumes of history, biography, travels, poetry, fiction—there would be a far more profitable disposal of it than marks its lapse in many a schoolroom now. The ordinary reading of the schools is a pointless, starveling performance, so far as language-teaching is concerned."—*Superintendent Harrington.*

V. "Good reading is an art so difficult that not one in a hundred educated persons is found to possess it to the satisfaction of others, although ninety-nine in a hundred would be offended were they told that they did not know how to read. The essential requisites are, perfect mastery of pronunciation, and the power of seizing instantaneously the sense and spirit of an author."—*Marcel.*

Chapter III.

CONDENSED DIRECTIONS FOR TEACHING SPELLING, WORD ANALYSIS, AND DEFINING.

I. SPELLING.

1. MAKE a judicious combination of oral spelling with written exercises. Oral spelling secures correct pronunciation, and awakens a keener interest in pupils; written spelling is the more practical, but is apt to become wearisome if carried on exclusively.

2. Train primary pupils on short lists of the names of common things.

3. Require them to copy at least one paragraph from each reading-lesson.

4. In oral spelling, excite a spirit of emulation by allowing pupils to win their rank in line by "going up" when they spell a word that has been missed.

5. Allow pupils, at least once a week, to "choose sides" and have a spelling-match.

6. If a spelling-book is in the hands of your pupils, when you assign a lesson pronounce every word, and require the class to pronounce in concert after you, in order to secure correct pronunciation. Then let each scholar in turn pronounce one word, going over the lesson a second time. Call special attention to words of difficult spelling, and to those containing silent letters. Occasionally call upon some pupil to dictate the spelling-lesson. Require

pupils to study their lessons, both oral and written, by copying the words on their slates; the act of writing will secure some attention to the lesson.

7. If a spelling-book is not used, you must supply, in some measure, the lack of one by grouping words into short lessons and dictating them to your pupils, to be copied into blank-books. There is a great waste of labor in taking up words heterogeneously, instead of by groups.

8. In written exercises, after the papers or slates are corrected, require pupils to rewrite their misspelled words.

9. Do not require pupils to commit to memory and repeat all the words of the spelling-lesson. "How such an absurdity," says Superintendent Philbrick, "could ever enter the head of a sane teacher, it is difficult to conceive."

10. Require pupils to pronounce each word before spelling it.

11. In oral spelling, require pupils to divide words into syllables; but, in long words, do not require the syllables to be pronounced or repronounced.

12. In all grades above the lowest, make out carefully arranged lists of words which pupils are liable to misspell; let the pupils copy the words into blank-books, and study the lessons until they are thoroughly learned.

13. Let pupils exchange papers and correct the spelling in one another's exercises. This of itself is one of the most profitable of spelling-lessons.

14. In oral spelling, require pupils occasionally to define words, and to construct sentences showing the meaning and use of the words.

15. Give early and continued attention to the practical application of a few of the important rules of spelling,

such as doubling the final consonant before -*ing* and -*ed*, dropping final *e*, etc. By this means, pupils will learn to spell correctly a large class of words in current use.

16. The teaching of spelling should be so conducted as to unfold something of the meaning of words, and something of the formation of derivative from primitive words and roots. The exercise then becomes a part of good intellectual training, instead of a blind effort of memory.

17. Correct spelling is a conventional test of accurate scholarship. The teacher should endeavor to secure the best results by stimulating the interest of pupils by the charm of novelty, variety, emulation, and amusement.

II. SPELLING-GAMES.

Let the whole class stand in line. Require pupils to sit down if they fail to give a word or to spell it, or if they repeat a word given before by some other scholar. Continue until all but one are seated.

1. Give and spell the name of some article of food.
2. Give and spell the name of some animal.
3. Give and spell the name of some city.
4. Give and spell the name of some article manufactured of iron; of wood.
5. Give and spell the given name of some boy; of some girl.

Other Topics for Lists.

1. Trees.   3. Countries.   5. Fishes.
2. Rivers. 4. States of the U. S. 6. Birds, etc.

6. Take long words, like *incomprehensibility*, and let each scholar in the line name, in order, one letter.

7. Take a similar method by letting each pupil spell *one* syllable.

8. Let each pupil dictate to the next scholar a word of two syllables.

9. Require each scholar to name and spell a word having the sound of long *a* in the first syllable. Also of
    1. Italian ä.   4. ȧ in ȧsk.   7. e in hẽr.
    2. Broad ạ.   5. â in câre.   8. Long ī.
    3. Short ă.   6. Long ē.   9. Etc.

10. Give and spell a word of three syllables.

11. Give and spell a word of four syllables; of five syllables.

12. Let the first pupil name and spell some monosyllable; the next scholar, name and spell one beginning with the last letter of the previous word, and so on.

Note. — *Words ending in* x *must be ruled out.*

13. Let the first pupil give and spell a word of one syllable, and the second scholar name and spell a word that *rhymes* with it; the second scholar then to name a new word, and the third to give a *rhyme* for it, etc. In the same way, take words of two and three syllables.

III. WRITTEN EXERCISES FOR PRIMARY CLASSES.

Note.—Take one of the following exercises at a lesson. Let pupils exchange slates or papers, and correct one another's exercises.

1. Write the names of five articles of dress.
2. Of five wild animals; five domestic animals.
3. Of five garden flowers; five wild flowers.
4. Of five species of birds; five fishes.
5. Write ten given or Christian names.
6. Write the full names of ten of your schoolmates.
7. Write the names of five great men.
8. Of five of your uncles, aunts, or cousins.

9. Write the names of five cities; five rivers.

10. The names of five States; five countries.

11. The names of ten articles kept for sale in a grocery-store.

12. The names of twenty articles of food.

IV. WRITTEN EXERCISES FOR GRAMMAR GRADES.

1. Bring in a list of twenty words of one syllable, to illustrate the rule for doubling the final consonant before *-ing* or *-ed*.

2. Of twenty words that do not double the final consonant before *-ing* or *-ed*.

3. Of twenty words of two syllables that double the final consonant before *-ing* and *-ed;* of twenty that do not.

4. Of twenty words in which final *e* is dropped on adding a suffix beginning with a vowel.

5. Of twenty words in which final *y* of the primitive word is changed into *i* before a suffix.

V. ORAL EXERCISE FOR GRAMMAR GRADES.

1. Name and spell a derivative word, to illustrate the rule for doubling the final consonant of the primitive word.

2. Ditto, the rule for not doubling it.

3. Ditto, the rule for dropping final *e*.

4. Ditto, the rule for changing *y* into *i*.

5. Ditto, the rule for not changing *y* before a suffix.

VI. WORD-ANALYSIS.

If you teach word-analysis in classes where pupils have no text-book on this subject, taking it up as an occasional exercise,

1. Take the suffix *-er*, and ask each pupil in the class to give and define some word which contains it as a suffix; as, teach*er*, *one who* teaches, etc.

2. Next require each pupil to bring in a list of all such words that he can think of.

3. Take a similar exercise with the suffix *-or*, meaning *one who*.

4. Then take up in a similar way each of the Anglo-Saxon, or Teutonic, prefixes and suffixes.

5. Take the leading Romanic prefixes and suffixes in a similar manner.

6. Take a few of the leading Latin roots, such as *facere, ducere, tendere*, etc., and make out lists of words derived from them.

7. Give from time to time lists of interesting words, and let pupils find out their origin and history from the dictionary; as, for example, *Bible, heaven, pagan, daisy, fuchsia, agate, calico, tariff, crusade, candidate*, etc.

8. "The first decided exemplification of language-lessons on the great scale," says Bain, "is the teaching of synonymous words. The best example of this is the perpetual passing to and fro between our two vocabularies— Saxon and Classical. The pupils bring with them the homely names for what they know, and the master translates these into the more dignified and accurate names; or, in reading, he makes the learned names intelligible by referring to the more familiar."

9. A thorough knowledge of words gained by a careful study of roots, definitions, and synonyms is the only solid basis for an appreciative study of the masterpieces of literature, or for the formation of a good style in writing. It is said that Daniel Webster acquired his remarkably

accurate use of words by studying synonyms half an hour daily for ten years.

10. "The study of English words," says Russell, " if faithfully pursued, in the daily lessons of our schools, with anything like the application exhibited in the examination and classifying and arranging and labelling of the specimens of even a very ordinary cabinet, would enrich the intellectual stores of the young, and even of the mature, mind to an extent of which we can at present hardly form a conception. Nothing, however, short of such diligence will serve any effectual purpose."

VII. WORD-MATCHES.

Let the pupils choose sides and stand in line. Those who fail to give a word will be seated. A word repeated is counted as a failure.

1. Require each pupil in turn to give a word having the prefix *out-*.
2. Give a word with the prefix *un-*.
3. A word with the suffix *-er*.
4. A word with the prefix *in-*.
5. A word with the suffix *-ness; -ion*.
6. Extend the exercises by taking any *suffix* that is in common use.
7. Give a word derived from the Latin verb-root *facere*.
8. Continue the exercise with other Latin roots.
9. Let one side give out a word, and require the other side to give a synonym.
10. Let one side give a word, and require the other side to give a word of *opposite* meaning.
11. Give a Romanic suffix, state its force, and give a word to illustrate.

12. Give a word containing the Greek root *graphein*, to write.

13. Give and define a word containing the Greek root *logos*.

14. Give and spell a word derived from the Greek.

15. Give and spell a word derived from the French.

16. Spell a word of Latin derivation.

17. Name and spell a word of Teutonic, or Anglo-Saxon, derivation.

18. Name a Teutonic word, and give a synonymous word of Latin origin; as *brotherly, fraternal.*

VIII. DEFINING.

1. Never require a scholar to give formal definitions of simple words whose meaning is already well enough known.

2. Train your pupils at an early age to the habit of referring to the school dictionary for definitions.

3. Mark any difficult words in the advance reading-lesson, and require pupils to find out the dictionary definitions.

4. Give out, once or twice a week, a list of five words to be defined at the next lesson.

5. Require each pupil to bring into the class one word, define it orally, and use it in a sentence.

6. If a spelling-book is in use, call attention in every lesson to the meaning of every word not likely to be fully understood by the class. Call for volunteer definitions by the pupils; and if they fail, give a definition yourself. Then require the word to be used in a sentence.

7. Exact and full definitions should be required, in general, only from advanced pupils when they have gained

the knowledge necessary to frame definitions, or to understand *why* they are so framed.

8. A simple explanation by a pupil of the *use* of a word is often better than a formal dictionary definition.

9. Beware of defining a word by means of a synonym equally incomprehensible. The profound scholar who, in addressing a class of little children, made use of the word *abridgment*, and then explained its meaning by using *epitome*, was a poor teacher, though a classical scholar.

10. The following hints about definitions in general, in the various school studies, are taken from Currie's *Common-school Education:*

"Elementary instruction should therefore not *begin*, but *end*, with definitions. But, on the other hand, since the definition of a thing is that conception of it with which alone the mind can go forward to any higher knowledge regarding it, the teacher must contemplate its use in due time. He may introduce it almost from the first, if he keep it in its proper place and within proper limits. As the pupil advances, his training should make him more and more capable of forming definitions."

Chapter IV.
CONDENSED DIRECTIONS FOR TEACHING ARITHMETIC.

1. Train beginners from four to six years of age on combinations of numbers, not exceeding 10, in addition, subtraction, multiplication, and division. Begin with *counters*, such as small blocks of wood, shells, corn, beans, or pebbles, and use them for two or three months, until the pupils can make the combinations without the aid of objects. [See Grube's Method in Part III.]

2. After these combinations are thoroughly learned, whether in three months or in a year, extend the combinations to 20; then to 50; next, 100.

3. In connection with object-work and mental operations, teach pupils how to make figures on the blackboard, and how to express operations according to the forms of written arithmetic. [See Part III., "Arithmetic."] In the beginning, proceed slowly, allow no hesitation, pass no error. Aim here, as afterwards, to form the habit of accurate and ready calculation, and of using rightly the reasoning powers.

4. After the first year, teach decimals in connection with whole numbers, at least to the extent of adding and subtracting; and of multiplying and dividing them by whole numbers. Limit: first step, *tenths;* second, *hundredths;* third, *thousandths.* [See Part III., "Arithmetic."] In the second and third years, teach common fractions, limited mainly to *halves, thirds, fourths,* etc., to

twelfths. Illustrate simple operations by means of apples, crayons, or lines upon the blackboard. [See Part III., "Arithmetic."]

5. Children under ten or twelve years of age should be limited mainly to operations in addition, subtraction, multiplication, and division, in order to secure accuracy and readiness. Problems, analyses, and demonstrations come properly when the reasoning faculties are more fully developed. "In certain respects," says Bain, "this knowledge [empirical] is highly scientific; the terms are clearly conceived, the directions precisely followed, and the results accurately arrived at. There is nothing slipshod, no vagueness to be corrected, nothing to be unlearned. The theory, rationale, or demonstrative connection of the steps is alone wanting; and that is a later acquirement."

6. Let beginners in the four rules, fractions, and table-work learn first the mechanical process of doing things. Work an example on the blackboard before their eyes, and let them learn by imitation. Of course, in some cases, you make the reason plain by suitable explanations; *but do not require your pupils to explain at this stage.* Keep your long-drawn-out demonstrations, and your normal-school "analyses" for pupils nearer your own age. For some parts of arithmetical work, there are no patent devices for escaping from downright memory and hard practice-work. The learning of the multiplication-table, however introduced by object-lessons, must mainly be an affair of memory and the result of long-continued repetition, even when pupils have reached the proper age. Hence the necessity of giving pupils a much greater number of drill exercises in the four rules than it is possible to put into a small text-book on arithmetic.

7. Do not try to make pupils understand demonstrations and analyses which are beyond the comprehension of young children, though easily perceived when they are older. There are some things in arithmetic that must be learned practically as an art before the scientific principles are understood. Thomas Hill, ex-President of Harvard University, very truly says, "The great reform needed in our public schools is to postpone reasoning to the higher grammar classes and to the high-schools, and give attention to the powers of perception and imagination and the acquisition of skill. It is worse than useless for a child to explain his arithmetic until he has acquired rapidity and certainty in ciphering; it is worse than useless to study spelling and grammar before the child can read fluently and intelligently."

8. If a text-book is used by the pupils, omit complicated problems, and all questions involving very large numbers. On this point Superintendent Stone, of Springfield, remarks, "Improbable examples, such as never occur in business, and fractional expressions of large and unusual terms, which require much time and wear of brain to handle, are not profitable work for children. It is said that in ordinary business computations, four fifths of all the fractions used, aside from decimals, are halves, fourths, eighths, thirds, and sixths. If, therefore, such examples only are given as will admit of rapid solution, time will be gained for practice greater in amount and variety." Superintendent Eliot, of Boston, remarks, "Instead of some conception of the simpler laws of mathematics, our scholars are misled with rules, or bewildered with puzzles, until they know neither what they are trying to learn, nor what powers they are trying to use."

9. Instead of teaching the tables by merely requiring pupils to memorize and recite them, put the *real measures* of every kind before them, until hand and eye are familiar with their use. Train your scholars in actual measurements in long, square, and cubic measure; borrow from some shop the ounce, half-ounce, and pound weights; the pint and quart measures; the peck, bushel, and half-bushel; and experiment with them until your children know the reality as well as the words and numbers. By all means, teach what you can of the metric system in the same way. [See Part III., "Arithmetic."]

10. It is highly desirable that scholars above the primary grades should thoroughly understand all operations in common fractions. Proceed slowly, step by step, limiting all operations to small numbers. [For appropriate models, see Part III., "Arithmetic," sec. v.] But do not crowd analytical explanations upon children at too early an age. "Children," says Bain, "can with difficulty rationalize common and decimal fractions. The memory for the tables and for the manipulating of fractions advances much faster than the comprehension of the reasons; and it is not desirable to face these at the age when they are not readily intelligible. There is plenty of interest in the operations without the comprehending of the scheme of mathematical demonstration; the ability to work the prescribed exercises brings its own reward."

11. Use the blackboard yourself, for the purpose of giving explanations or models. Drill your pupils at the blackboards, sending up one half the class while the other half is engaged in slate-work. Give both divisions the same examples, and insist on good figures and neat work in addition to accuracy. Give frequent drill exercises

in addition—the operation in which more mistakes are made than in any other. Train pupils to consider *accuracy* as vastly more important than rapidity. Train pupils to exchange slates and correct one another's work.

12. Carry on mental and written arithmetic together. Introduce principles by mental operations with small numbers; then, having fixed the principle, apply the rule to larger numbers on the slate or blackboard.

13. An excellent class drill in mental arithmetic is to take a five-minute exercise as follows: Make up a set of ten practical business questions; read a question and allow from a quarter to a half minute for the mental solution, and require the *answers* to be written on slates or paper; so continue with the set. Then let pupils exchange slates, and credit the correct answers as given by the teacher. Aside from its practical business training, the disciplinary value of this exercise is *that it trains to a habit of fixed attention*. [For models, see Part III., "Arithmetic."]

14. A good method of oral drill is as follows: Let the pupils stand in line around the room, requiring any one who fails to give a correct answer to go to his seat. "Count by 2's to 50, and then backwards." The first scholar counts 2, the second 4, and so on. Continue this drill with the numbers 3, 4, 5, 6, 7, 8, 9, and 10, according to the advancement of the class. The value of this exercise as a mental discipline is that it requires the fixed attention of every member of the class, and leads to a habit of readiness and promptness. The same exercise may be taken as a concert drill.

15. Let the pupils stand and allow each scholar to give the next in line some short business example.

16. Occasionally match one class against another, or one division against another, by submitting five business questions to be worked in a given time on the slate. Then compare the percentage obtained.

17. Do not take more than one hour a day for arithmetic. Depend mainly upon slate and blackboard drill in school. It is a bad plan to give out long lists of examples to be solved at home.

18. The essential parts of arithmetic which all pupils should understand are the four rules, common and decimal fractions, the tables of money, weights and measures, and their application, percentage, and the principles of proportion. All the rest of the text-book may be omitted, without much loss, by all except high-school pupils. A great deal that passes in school-books under the name of arithmetic consists largely of conventional exercises, of no practical and of little disciplinary value. If you are allowed any discretion in the matter, cut out half of the text-book; but make up and give to your class numberless sets of simple, practical, business questions, both mental and written.

19. One marked defect in most of the modern school arithmetics is that they are filled up with long "explanations" and "analyses," to the exclusion of drill examples. The explanations, if given at all, should be given orally by the teacher; they do not belong to a pupil's book, unless it is assumed that the teacher knows nothing whatever about the subject. Another marked defect, arising from limited space, is the stepping from very simple questions to complex ones, and a too rapid transition from one topic to another. As a teacher, it is your business to remedy, in some degree, these defects by adding here and

cutting out there. Difficult problems, requiring sustained processes of reasoning, or complicated forms of analytical explanations, should be given only to the more advanced pupils whose reflective faculties are somewhat developed. In fact, what are termed "hard questions" do not come within the province of the common school at all, if, indeed, of any school.

"For the large majority," says Bain, "the solution of problems is not the highest end. Nine tenths of the pupils derive their chief benefit from the ideas and forms of thinking which they can transfer to other regions of knowledge."

20. Review frequently by giving out short, simple problems that involve a knowledge of all that the pupil has gone over in any preceding grade. Repetition will fix principles. What pupils can *do* they *know*, and they know little else.

21. Take especial pains to make the pupils familiar with common business forms. See that they thoroughly understand the ordinary phraseology used in mercantile transactions.

22. Train the pupils to reason for themselves, to state not only what they do, but why they do it. Let them test the truth and accuracy of their processes by *proof*, the only test they will have to rely upon in real business transactions. Endeavor to form in them habits of patient investigation and self-reliance, so that they will be able to *know for themselves* whether their work is correct or not.

23. Arithmetic is a means of promoting sustained attention; of rendering the memory more tenacious by retaining the conditions of a question in mind during the solution; and of cultivating, to some extent, the reasoning

powers. It trains to habits of accuracy. It teaches the pupil how to proceed from the known to the unknown, the simple to the complex, the particular to the general, example to rule. More than any other elementary study, it enables the teacher to estimate the exact amount of work actually done by pupils. The teacher must keep clearly in mind the two leading objects of the study of arithmetic : (1) for practical business in life; (2) for mental discipline in habits of attention, and in simple processes of reasoning.

24. Teachers should bear in mind that for many pupils arithmetic is a difficult study, especially at an early age. It is not wise to assume that pupils who are dull in arithmetic are obtuse in all other studies. Benjamin Franklin, at school, was a dullard in arithmetic, but he managed to get on in the world nevertheless.

"It is a very common notion," says De Morgan, "that arithmetic is easy; and a child is called stupid who does not receive his first ideas of number with facility; but this is a mistake. Were it otherwise, savage nations would acquire a numeration, and a power of using it, at least proportional to their actual wants."

25. While arithmetic is a very important study, the young teacher should avoid making it a hobby. It is well to bear in mind the caution of Bain as to what mathematics does not do: "It does not teach us how to observe, how to generalize, how to classify. It does not teach us the prime art of defining by the examination of particular things. It guards us against some of the snares of language, but not all; it is no aid when statements and arguments are perplexed by verbiage, contortions, inversions, and ellipses. The too exclusive devotion to it gives a wrong bias of mind respecting truth generally; and, his-

torically, it has introduced serious errors into philosophy and general thinking."

"Life is not long enough," says Thomas Hill, "to spend so large a proportion of it on arithmetic as is spent in the modern system of teaching it; and arithmetic is too valuable an art to have our children neglect to acquire facility in it, while they are being stupefied and disgusted with premature attempts to understand it as a science."

Chapter V.
LANGUAGE-LESSONS, GRAMMAR, AND COMPOSITION.
I. LANGUAGE-LESSONS AND GRAMMAR.

1. In considering this branch of school studies, it is well to bear in mind the following axioms:
(1.) "*Speech is acquired mainly by imitation.*"
(2.) *Imitation precedes originality.*
(3.) Language precedes arithmetic.
(4.) Grammar comes, not before language, but after it.

2. In the primary grades, teachers must give patient and persistent attention to the correction of vulgarisms, provincialisms, and current blunders in speech, without waiting for any grammatical knowledge whatever.

3. Oral and written language-lessons should precede the use of a text-book on grammar. Begin written exercises by requiring pupils to construct short simple sentences that begin with a capital and end with a period. [See Part III., Chapter IV., I.]

"Teachers who take the pains to observe well," says Professor Russell, "know that there is a stage in the life of childhood when expression is a spontaneous tendency and a delight; when to construct a sentence on his slate, or pencil a note on paper, is to the miniature ambitious student a conscious achievement, and a triumph of power."

4. For beginners in composition, after the prerequisite

exercises in sentence-making, write a very short, simple story on the blackboard, and let them copy it on their slates, or on paper. Continue this for a time, and then let them copy short reading-lessons from the book, or interesting paragraphs from the longer lessons. A few exercises of this kind, taken at long intervals, are not enough; they must be continued daily for several years of school life. "The necessity of a progressive and graduated course of training in the mother tongue," says Professor Swinton, author of "Language Lessons," etc., "extending over some years, and beginning in practice and ending in theory, is now generally recognized and acted upon."

5. One of the very best of exercises is to let children reproduce from memory, in their own words, stories told them by the teacher, or which they themselves have read or heard out of school. In this way writing becomes a pleasure instead of a task. Originality in thought must not be expected of children.

"Stories," says Miss Keeler, "offer the best opportunity to improve the child's language and culture. You can do almost anything with children if you will only tell them stories. You can refine their feelings, touch their emotions, rouse their enthusiasm, awaken their ambition, enkindle their devotion. There is nothing in the broad sweep of noble living or noble thinking that you cannot bring to their consciousness by means of a story. As for language, the story is the very royal road to its acquisition. Tell a group of children a story which awakens their interest and enchains their fancy, and then ask for it back again, and notice how accurately it will come."

6. If pupils are kept busy upon sentence-making and composition exercises up to the age of twelve, it will not

be necessary to waste much time in "parsing" or sentence-analysis. On this point Superintendent Newell remarks, "Being an art, grammar must be learned in the beginning, as all other arts are learned, by the practice of it. We learn to draw by drawing, we learn to paint by painting, we learn to dance by dancing, and we must learn 'the art of speaking and writing the English language' by writing and speaking it, not by parsing and analyzing it."

7. In all grammar grades except the highest class, language-lessons and actual composition work constitute the best means of acquiring a ready and correct use of language, which, in its turn, becomes a sound basis for the study of technical grammar. "It is constant use and practice, under never-failing watch and correction," says Whitney, "that makes good writers and speakers." "As grammar was made *after* language," says Spencer, "so it ought to be *taught* after language."

8. One of the most practical of all exercises is letter-writing. As soon as a child can write at all, it ought to be trained to write a short letter. In every grade during the whole course, repeated exercises in letter-writing should be given, so that on leaving school, at any age from ten to fifteen years, every scholar should be able to write a letter neatly and correctly, to fold it, direct it properly, and to put on a postage-stamp. [For suggestions in this exercise, see Part III., Chapter IV.]

9. Require pupils to memorize a part or the whole of a short poem, and then to write it out from memory, punctuate, and capitalize it.

10. Require pupils to write compositions drawn from their lessons in history and geography, thus utilizing their knowledge on those subjects.

11. Require only brief and reasonable forms of parsing, limited mainly to the *construction* of the word, or its office in the sentence, and its relation to some other word. The Latinized "models for parsing" in many text-books involve a great waste of time.

"It makes one shudder," says President Chadbourne, "to think of the trash which scholars have been compelled to learn in connection with the simple studies of grammar, arithmetic, and geography."

12. Require a few essential definitions to be thoroughly learned, but first show your scholars *how a definition is made up, and why it must be expressed in the words which are used, so that it may be remembered by meaning as well as in words.* A comparison of the different ways of expressing the same definition is an excellent class exercise for discussion and criticism.

13. Explain clearly the meaning and use of the ten leading rules of syntax, and then require your pupils to get them by heart. *But make sure that they first understand what the rules mean, and how they are practically applied.* Thousands of pupils have repeated hundreds of times Rule I., "A verb must agree with its subject in number and person," without the slightest notion of its real meaning or practical application.

14. Give your older pupils some training in the analysis of sentences, but make use of brief and simple forms. Sentential analysis has its uses, but it must not be made a hobby of. Sentence-making is a more profitable exercise than complicated metaphysical sentence-analysis with a long array of minor modifiers.

15. Grammar is one of the most difficult of the common-school studies. To teach it successfully requires the

highest degree of skill on the part of the teacher. "It is more difficult than arithmetic," says Bain, "and is probably on a par with the beginnings of algebra and geometry. It cannot be effectively taught to the mass before ten years of age." "To teach grammar without a printed text is like teaching religion without a manual or catechism: either the teacher still uses the catechism without the print, or he makes a catechism for himself. There can be no teaching except on a definite plan and sequence, and good instead of harm arises from putting the plan in print. The grammar-teacher working without books either tacitly uses some actual grammar, or else works upon a crude, untested, irresponsible grammar of his own making."

16. Bear in mind that the main object of the study of grammar is not so much to enable pupils to speak and write correctly as *to enable them better to understand what they read.* A knowledge of grammar is essential to a right appreciation of the masterpieces of literature. With more advanced pupils, the right study of grammar is a means of mental discipline fully equal to that of mathematics.

"I hold," says Tyndall, "that the proper study of language is an intellectual discipline of the highest kind. The piercing through the involved and inverted sentences of *Paradise Lost;* the linking of the verb to its often distant nominative, of the relative to its distant antecedent, of the agent to the object of the transitive verb, of the preposition to the noun or pronoun which it governed; the study of variations in mood and tense; the transformations often necessary to bring out the true grammatical structure of a sentence—all this was to my young mind a discipline of the highest value, and, indeed, a source of unflagging delight."

II. COMPOSITION.

1. DIRECTIONS FOR TEACHERS.

1. When you take charge of a class not previously trained in composition writing, set the pupils to copying short reading-lessons. Let them exchange papers, and, with open book, correct one another's exercises with reference to spelling, punctuation, capitals, and paragraphs.

2. Next, let them write out an abstract of some familiar story, told or read to the class.

3. When you require a formal composition, select a subject for the entire class, and give the necessary directions, explanations, and suggestions. Select subjects about which your pupils know something—never abstract subjects, such as happiness, or knowledge, or virtue.

4. Train your pupils to correct one another's compositions, and *require them to rewrite corrected exercises.*

5. "I call that the best theme," says Thomas Arnold, "which shows that the boy has read and thought for himself; that the next best which shows that he has read several books and digested what he has read; and that the worst which shows that he has followed but one book, and followed that without reflection."

6. "Training in the appropriate use of the English language ought not to be limited to the mere grammatical exercise of composing sentences. Even in our common-schools, it should extend to the cultivation of taste by which neat as well as correct expression is acquired as a habit."—*Russell.*

7. "I hold it as a great point in self-education that the student should be continually engaged in forming exact ideas, and in expressing them clearly by language. Such

practice insensibly opposes any tendency to exaggeration or mistake, and increases the sense and love of truth in every part of life. Those who reflect upon how many hours and days are devoted by a lover of sweet sounds to gain a moderate facility upon a mere mechanical instrument ought to feel the blush of shame if convicted of neglecting the beautiful living instrument wherein play all powers of the mind."—*Professor Faraday.*

8. "The study of rhetoric in high-schools ought not to be completed in fourteen weeks. It should be continued through the entire course, at the rate of one lesson a week, because it relates to language, which is the instrument used by teacher and pupil throughout the course. This method will give time to write the exercises assigned in works on rhetoric, and will not interfere with other studies relating to the English language. — *George W. Minns.*

2. DIRECTIONS TO BE GIVEN TO PUPILS.

1. Think about the subject, and make some plan of arrangement.

2. Do not run together a long string of statements connected by *ands, buts,* or *ifs;* but make short sentences.

3. After writing the first draft, examine it critically, cross out superfluous words or phrases, interline, correct, and then rewrite.

4. In correcting, examine with reference to—1. Spelling; 2. Capitals; 3. Punctuation; 4. Use of words; 5. Construction of sentences.

5. Acquire the habit of crossing *t*'s, dotting *i*'s, and punctuating as you write.

6. Do not put off writing until the day before you must hand in your composition.

Chapter VI.

CONDENSED DIRECTIONS FOR TEACHING GEOGRAPHY.

1. MAKE beginners familiar with the local geography of the place where they live. Lay some kind of a basis for conception by calling attention to whatever natural features of land and water are within the limited field of the pupil's observation; such as hill, mountain, valley, plain, spring, brook, river, pond, lake, village, city, etc. Then extend these lessons to the surrounding country, questioning pupils about all the places that they have ever seen in their short journeys. Next, connect this knowledge with the elementary lessons in the text-book, or with an outline map. [For first lessons, see Part III., Chapter III., sec. iii.] "In geography," says Agassiz, "let us not, at first, resort to books, but let us take a class into the fields, point out the hills, valleys, rivers, and lakes, and let the pupils learn out-of-doors the points of the compass; and then, having shown them these things, let them compare the representations with the realities, and the maps will have a meaning to them. Then you can go on with the books, and they will understand what these things mean, and will know what is North and East and South; and will not merely read the letters N., E., S., W. on a square piece of paper, and perhaps think that the United States are about as large as the paper they learn from. When I was in the College of Neufchâtel, I desired to

introduce such a method of teaching geography. I was told it could not be done, and my request to be allowed to instruct the youngest children in the institution was refused. I resorted to another means, and took my own children—my oldest a boy of six years, and my girls, four and a half and two and a half years old—and invited the children of my neighbors. Some came upon the arms of their mothers; others could already walk without assistance. These children, the oldest only six years old, I took upon a hill above the city of Neufchâtel, and there showed the magnificent peaks of the Alps, and told them the names of those mountains and of the beautiful lakes opposite. I then showed them the same things on a raised map, and they immediately recognized the localities, and were soon able to do the same on an ordinary map. From that day geography was no longer a dry study, but a desirable part of their education."

2. Use the school globe daily for several weeks, showing your pupils the grand divisions, the oceans, the equator, the poles, etc. Send every pupil by turns to the globe. [See Part III., " Geography," sec. i.]

3. The method of beginning with outlines and afterwards filling in with details must, to a certain extent, be carried on *pari passu* with that of laying a foundation of correct notions based upon a knowledge of local geography. The extent of local lessons, however, is limited; and, beyond the limit of personal observation by pupils, it seems to be the better plan to begin with the grand outlines of geography. Unless children have travelled a great deal, they can no more form a correct notion of the size of their native State than they can of the United States or of Asia. A great deal of elementary work nec-

essarily consists in getting familiar with names and maps. It must be borne in mind, too, that generalizations, in order to be of any value, must be based on a knowledge of particulars.

4. In using the school text-book, let the advance lesson be read over aloud in the class, and then direct your scholars to mark with a pencil a few leading points to be committed to memory, certainly not more than from one tenth to one fourth of an ordinary lesson of descriptive text. The following direction from the Massachusetts State Course of Instruction embodies a valuable general rule for guidance:

"As travel broadens ideas, so will the study of geography, if rightly pursued; and pupils may increase the value of their lessons by reading books of travel and stories of great explorers. The teacher can afford to deal sparingly in statistics, latitudes, longitudes, areas, and heights, and to avoid dry definitions and detailed map questions that lead only to a recital of names of places destitute of associations. Such knowledge is not worth the time it takes to acquire it, though it may secure rapid and accurate recitations."

5. In the lower grades, let the "map lessons" be read aloud in the class, and answered with open book in the hands of the pupils; then select a few of the leading questions, mark them, and let the class recite them from memory at the next lesson. Supplement these lessons by short oral descriptions of places mentioned, or by some interesting facts connected with them, so that they may be remembered by the aid of *association*.

6. Train pupils in detail on the geography of their own State; then, in a more general way, on their section; and,

finally, on a few main points on the United States as a whole. Do not attempt to overload the memory with the local geography of all the States, as given in most of the text-books. As the school geographies are designed for use in all parts of our country, they are necessarily crowded with details to meet the wants of each State or locality. The sensible teacher will omit all that properly belongs to the local geography of States other than that in which the pupil resides.

"Most of the geographies," says Superintendent Eliot, "contain an extraordinary amount of matter, not only useless to the few who can master it, but injurious to the many who cannot."

7. Do not expect your pupils to know more of a lesson than you remember without referring to the text-book. If you forget details, it is a sure sign that your pupils will, and therefore it is best not to require such details to be learned at all.

8. Having fixed on the main outlines to be learned, take frequent reviews upon them in order to fix them firmly in the memory. [See Part III., "Geography," sec. vii.]

9. It is almost impossible for children to remember the name and location of a place unless some association is connected with it. You must illuminate geography by means of history and descriptions.

10. If you have a good relief globe, make use of it regularly, even in your higher grades. Use the outline maps also. Secure, if possible, a set of cheap German *papier-maché* relief maps of the grand divisions. The cost is trifling, and the value great. From these maps, the pupil will be able, in a few hours, to form an idea of plateaus, mountain-ranges, plains, and general configuration

that an ordinary map fails to give, and which no verbal descriptions can convey.

11. It will be a pleasant variation from routine work to let your pupils write short compositions about the countries included in their regular text-book descriptions, or about imaginary voyages or travels.

12. In general, blackboard map-drawing in the rough is better than labored drawings with pen or pencil. Map-drawing should not be made a hobby of; kept within due limits, the exercise is good, but it often runs into a waste of time and labor.

13. Let beginners draw first a map of the schoolroom, then of the schoolhouse and grounds. As they advance, let them draw upon the blackboard, from the open book, on a large scale, an outline map of their own State, and, if possible, of their own county. Then let them outline the grand divisions, etc. Finally, require them to outline off-hand, from memory.

14. Require every class to draw on the blackboards, at least once a year, an outline map of their own State and of the United States.

15. Relieve the monotony of daily lessons by exercises intended to stimulate and amuse. Show pupils the pictures, from illustrated magazines or papers, of beautiful or grand scenery, or of great natural curiosities, and read any short, vivid description of them by travellers.

I. GEOGRAPHY MATCHES.

Every pupil that fails, or repeats a name given before, must sit down. Continue until all but one are seated.

1. Name a city in the United States, and tell in what State it is.

2. Name a river in the United States, and tell into what it flows.

3. Name a city anywhere on the globe, and tell in what country it is.

4. Name any river on the globe, and tell into what it flows.

5. Name a sea, and tell where it is.

6. Name some useful vegetable production, and tell where it grows.

7. Name some manufactured article, and tell where it is made.

8. Name some *cabinet* curiosity, and tell where it may be found.

9. Name a town or city in our country beginning with the letter B, C, etc.

10. Name a country or a state; and give its capital city.

11. Let the first pupil name a city or town, and tell in what country or state it is; the next in order must name another beginning with the last letter of the town or city previously named; and so on.

II. CLASS EXERCISES IN GEOGRAPHY.

I. Let one pupil describe some city, and the others guess the name of it.

II. Let one pupil think of some city in the United States, and the others guess its name by questioning as follows:

1. Is it in the Northern, Southern, Middle, or Western States? *Ans.* Northern.

2. Is it a seaport, or an inland city? *Ans.* A seaport.

3. Is it a large city, or a small one? *Ans.* A large city.

4. Is it New York? *Ans.* No.
5. Was a battle ever fought there? *Ans.* Yes.
6. Is it Boston? *Ans.* Yes.

III. Let one scholar describe some river, and the others guess its name.

IV. Let one pupil name some city situated on a river, and the others tell the name of the river.

V. Let the teacher take an imaginary voyage, exchanging products at various ports—the pupils to guess the ports.

Chapter VII.
HISTORY OF THE UNITED STATES.

1. "Whoever undertakes to instruct youth in history," says the German educator Niemeyer, "as the value of that science requires, must regard equally the memory, the understanding, and the feelings."

2. There is no "patent method" for teaching history. In this study, more than in most other elementary school branches, the teacher, by his skill, tact, and stores of information, must clothe the skeleton of facts with the flesh of imagination, and breathe into it the breath of life. But, rightly pursued, it has the two characteristics of a useful study—namely, good mental exercise and useful information.

3. Let the advance lesson in the text-book be read aloud in the class. Call attention to the leading facts to be memorized, and let the pupils mark them with a pencil. A considerable part of the history is intended, not to be memorized, but merely to be read.

4. Of the early discoveries treated of so fully in the text-book, single out three or four to be learned, and let the remainder alone. In the period of settlements, select the four great centres—namely, Virginia, Massachusetts, New York, and Pennsylvania; the remaining settlements belong properly to *local State history*. Out of the numberless details of Indian and colonial wars, select only

half a dozen important points; let the rest go as local State history. So in the Revolutionary War, single out a very few marked events, and have them learned so that they cannot be forgotten. Dwell at length on events that happened in the pupil's own State.

5. Do not attach much importance to chronological tables except for reference. Fix in the minds of your pupils the dates of a few great events, and fasten them there by frequent reviews. A multitude of minor dates may be temporarily learned for to-day's lesson, only to be crowded into oblivion by to-morrow's recitation. "By means of history," says Montaigne, "the pupil enjoys intercourse with the great men of the best periods; but he must learn, not so much the year and the day of the destruction of a city, as noble traits of character; not so much occurrences, as to form a correct judgment upon them." Examination questions, unfortunately, too often run to dates, because such questions are easiest to be asked from the book, and easiest to be credited.

6. Require pupils to become familiar with the details of the history of the State in which they live.

7. Fix in the memory the *causes* and the *results* of the War of the Revolution and of 1812, of the Mexican War and the War of Secession; but do not attempt to make pupils remember the dates of many battles.

8. Short biographical sketches of the great men in our history are both interesting and valuable, if they show how, by their character and abilities, they improved the condition of their nation and of the world.

9. In written exercises, train pupils to correct one another's work.

10. A comprehension of the great facts of history, of

their causes, results, and relations, is more important than the verbatim memorizing of pages of text-books.

11. In questions for written examinations, confine yourself strictly to leading events. Include as few dates as possible. Teaching chronological tables is not teaching history.

12. As much as possible assign lessons by *topics*, and require pupils to recite in their own language. Close the text-book yourself, and you will be better satisfied with your scholars' answers.

13. Supplement the dry, condensed statements of the text-book by anecdotes, incidents, stories, and biographical sketches of noted men, drawn from your own memory or from good books. If you are a good story-teller, you will thus make history charming to your pupils. Under the dead mass of dates and political events, you must kindle the fire of enthusiasm by familiar narrative. "If you tell a boy," said a famous teacher, "that in a certain battle General Smith had his horse's tail shot off, he will never forget *that*, though all else soon becomes a blank."

14. Call the attention of pupils to the progress of the nation in the arts and sciences; to the great inventions and discoveries that have been made; to everything that has improved the condition of the people. Lead them to perceive that, though history is hardly anything but a record of wars and conquerors, yet "Peace hath her victories no less renowned than those of war," and that the most glorious victory of war is that which establishes an honorable peace.

15. "To the youthful spirit," says Russell, "the great attraction of history lies in its pictures of life and action, and in the sympathies which these evoke. To the juvenile reader all history is biography." "All history," says

Emerson, "resolves itself very easily into the biography of a few stout and earnest persons."

16. "Of all departments of early teaching," says Bain, "none is so unmanageable as history. Its protean phases of information and of interest, its constant mixture of what attracts the youngest with what is intelligible only to the maturest minds, renders it especially troublesome in early teaching. Nothing comes sooner home to the child than narratives of human beings — their pursuits, their passions, their successes and their disasters, their virtues and their vices, their rewards and their punishments, their enmities and their friendships, their failures and their triumphs."

CLASS EXERCISES IN HISTORY.

1. Call upon each pupil in turn to name some person distinguished in the history of our country, and to state something that he did.

2. To name some important battle, and tell something about it.

3. To name some settlement, and tell who made it.

4. Let one pupil describe some noted person, and allow the class to guess the name.

5. Describe some important event, and let the class tell when and where it happened.

6. Give one or more facts as a *cause*, and let the class state one or more facts as a result.

7. Let one pupil *think* of some noted historical person, place, or event, and the others ask questions to ascertain what is *thought of* by that pupil. [See "Geography."]

8. Let one pupil *think* of some historical character, and then give to the class circumstance after circumstance, until some one is able to guess the name.

Chapter VIII.

OBJECT-LESSONS AND THE ELEMENTS OF NATURAL SCIENCE.

I. HINTS ON OBJECT-LESSONS.

1. "The first teaching a child wants," says Huxley, "is an object-lesson of one sort or another; and as soon as it is fit for systematic instruction, it is fit for a modicum of science."

2. The main purpose of object-lessons is, not to crowd the memory with facts and names, but to train children to *observe*, and to tell what they are able to find out about things.

"Observation," says Pestalozzi, "is the absolute basis of all knowledge. The first object, then, in education must be to lead a child to observe with accuracy; the second, to express with correctness the result of his observations."

3. Begin with things that most of your pupils already know something about, adhering strictly to the principle of examining real objects, when they are procurable; and, when not, of using pictures. Agassiz, having been asked to give some instruction on insects at a teacher's institute, says, "I thought the best way to proceed would be to place the objects in the hands of the teachers, for I knew that mere verbal instruction would not be transformed into actual knowledge. I therefore went out and collected several hundred grasshoppers, brought them in, and

gave one into the hands of every one present. It created universal laughter; yet the examination of these objects had not been carried on long before every one was interested, and, instead of looking at me, looked at the thing. And they began to examine, and to appreciate what it was to see, and see carefully. At first I pointed out the things which no one could see. 'We can't see them,' they said. 'But look again,' said I, 'for I can see things ten times smaller than these;' and they finally discerned them."

This, which is the true kind of object-teaching, is worth introducing into the schools, if for no other purpose than the training of the eye. There is an old proverb, "Seeing is believing," which cannot be said of the other senses. Also, "What is seen is easily remembered;" but "what goes in at one ear generally goes out at the other."

4. Do not be over-scientific. Avoid technical terms when common names will serve your purpose. "It is not science that we want here," says Superintendent Eliot; "much less is it the lion's skin sometimes wrapped round the pretence of science, but the simple truth."

5. Endeavor to train your scholars to observe accurately, to be sure of facts, to think for themselves, to reason correctly, and not to make up their minds until they have reflected carefully upon all the facts.

6. Train your pupils to write out on slates or paper what they can remember about their oral lessons. Writing leads to habits of attention, serves to fix ideas in the memory, and leads to a ready and correct use of language.

7. The *uses* of the object-lesson may be summed up as follows:

(1.) They constitute the first efforts in gaining an empirical knowledge of *things*.

(2.) They train the mind to habits of connected thought.

(3.) They stimulate *curiosity*, the motive power of the youthful mind.

8. "The teacher," says Bain, "can make anything he pleases out of the object-lesson; it may aid the *conceiving* faculty, or it may not. The first good effect of it is to waken up observation to things within the pupil's ken; by asking such questions as will send them back to re-examine what they have been in the habit of slurring over, or by questioning them on objects actually present."

9. "The predominant aspect of the object-lesson," says Currie, "is the mental exercises it gives; it is meant to awaken the intelligence, and to cultivate the different phases of observation, conception, and taste, without which little satisfactory progress can be made in education. It is a disciplining, not a utilitarian process; the information it gives is a means, not an end.

"The range of this department of instruction is exceedingly comprehensive. It draws its materials from all the branches of knowledge, dealing with things which can interest the child or exercise his mind. Thus, it is natural history for children; for it directs their attention to animals of all classes, domestic and others, their qualities, habits, and uses; to trees and plants and flowers; to the metals, and other minerals which, from their properties, are in constant use. It is physical science for children; for it leads them to observe the phenomena of the heavens —sun, moon, and stars; the seasons, with the light and heat which make the changes of the weather; and the properties of the bodies which form the mass of matter around us. It is domestic economy for children; for it exhibits to them the things and processes daily used in their homes, and the way to use them rightly. It is industrial and social economy for children; for it describes the various trades, processes in different walks of art, and the arrangements as to the division of labor which society has sanctioned for carrying these on in harmony and mutual dependence. It is physiology for children; for it tells them of their own bodies, and the uses of the various members for physical and mental ends, with the way to use them best and to avoid their abuse. It is the science of common things for children; for it disregards nothing which can come under their notice in their intercourse with their fellows or their superiors. And, finally, it is geography for children; since it has favorite subjects of illustration in mountain and river, forest, plain, and desert, the different climates of the earth, with their productions and the habits of their people, the populous city, and the scattered wigwams of the savage."

II. THE ELEMENTS OF NATURAL SCIENCE.

1. In most of the common-schools, instruction in the elements of natural science, if given at all, must be given in the form of oral lessons, without a text-book in the hands of pupils. Hence teachers must select for their own use the best possible science primers in the different branches of natural science, and from those, or from their own knowledge, outline their own course of instruction.

2. At the outset, train your pupils to use their eyes, to examine *things*, to observe phenomena, and to make experiments. "Experiment," says Huxley, "is the great instrument for the ascertainment of truth in physical science. Mere book learning in physical science is a sham and a delusion; what you teach you must first *know*, and

real knowledge in science means personal acquaintance with facts, be they few or many."

3. Begin at once the collection of a school cabinet, and invite your pupils to bring in specimens. Encourage them to make collections for a home-cabinet, of minerals, shells, woods, etc. Take them on collecting tours into the fields and forests. "The elements of botany, zoology, and mineralogy," says Russell, "afford a delightful and effective means of training to habits of observing, comparing, and classifying."

4. By wisely put questions, set your pupils to observing the habits of animals and birds, of ants, bees, wasps, flies, and butterflies. Encourage them to make collections of butterflies and beetles. Let the older boys try their hand at stuffing birds. Persuade your pupils to buy a magnifying-glass or a cheap microscope, and begin examining things for themselves. "For many years," says Carlyle, "it has been one of my constant regrets that no schoolmaster of mine had a knowledge of natural history, so far, at least, as to have taught me the grasses that grow by the wayside, and the little winged and wingless neighbors that are continually meeting me with a salutation which I cannot answer as things are. Why didn't somebody teach me the constellations, too, and make me at home in the starry heavens which are always overhead, and which I don't half know to this day."

5. If you wish to succeed, you must do the actual work of the naturalist, and must make your pupils do it. You must fit yourself to do this work by taking an interest in it. It is not at all necessary that you should be a specialist in botany, zoology, or natural philosophy; but it *is* necessary that you should know something about the

true methods of the specialist. Taken up in the right spirit, instruction in the natural sciences can be made one of the most effective means of education. "No subjects," says Professor Barnard, "are better suited than botany, zoology, and mineralogy to gratify the eager curiosity of the growing mind; to satisfy its cravings after positive knowledge; to keep alive the activity of the perceptive powers; to illustrate the beauty and value of method, and to lead to the formation of methodical habits of thought."

6. In physics, make your experiments with the simplest kind of improvised apparatus. Whenever you make an experiment, however simple, make it with great care and exactness, telling your pupils in advance what to expect and what to observe. Encourage them to make simple experiments at home by themselves. Set them to observing natural phenomena, such as rain, hail, snow, dew, frost, changes of seasons, etc. "The elements of physics," says Hotze, "are no more difficult for pupils than are the elements of arithmetic." "As a means of intellectual culture," says Tyndall, "the study of physics exercises and sharpens observation."

7. In giving the outlines of physiology, make use of real objects as far as practicable. The heart and lungs of a sheep or an ox can easily be obtained, and are always better than models or charts or pictures. If human bones cannot be obtained, take the bones of animals and make a lesson in comparative anatomy. Dissect the eye of an ox, the brain of a sheep or calf or rabbit, and exhibit the skull of any domestic or wild animal. The chief object of lessons in anatomy and physiology is to make them the means of imparting a knowledge of the laws of health. Reiterate practical directions about cleanliness, ventila-

tion, food, work, rest, play, sleep, and regular habits. Preach short sermons against idleness, gluttony, intemperance, and impurity. Teach your pupils that without health life is a failure, and make them realize as fully as possible that they must themselves take care of their own health.

8. In botany, begin with collecting and examining plants, and end in classifying and naming them by referring to text-books. "Now, to learn to classify," says Bain, "is itself an education. In these natural-history branches the art has been of necessity attended to, and is shown in the highest state of advancement. Botany is the most complete in its method, which is one of the recommendations of the science in early education. Mineralogy and zoology have greater difficulties to contend with; so that where they succeed, their success is all the greater."

9. First in the order of nature comes empirical knowledge; afterwards, scientific knowledge. Therefore, the younger the children, the less methodical should be their instruction. Beginners store up facts by items, often in an indirect and desultory manner.

10. Mere text-book study of natural science, without observation and experiment by the pupil, is *not* knowledge. The real guide to true knowledge is *a habit of observing*. "Learn to make a right use of your eyes," says Hugh Miller; "the commonest things are worth looking at, even stones, and weeds, and the most familiar animals." Agassiz says, "The difficult art of thinking, of comparing, of discriminating, can be more readily acquired by examining natural objects for ourselves than in any other way."

11. Skilful questioning by the teacher is the chief means of awakening thought, and of inducing pupils to

observe for themselves. Superintendent Eliot says, "We teach best when we seem to teach least. Tell the child a fact, and it is all your telling. Lead him to find it himself, and it seems to him all his finding. Because it seems so, he is interested in it, and his interest secures his mastery of it."

12. Stimulate and encourage curiosity. Faraday says, "I am indebted to curiosity for whatever progress I have made in science. There are common experiments which I perform now with as much glee at the result as when I was a boy." Lead your pupils into the practice of proposing questions in the class. "If not snubbed and stunted," says Huxley, "by being told not to ask foolish questions, there is no limit to the intellectual craving of a young child, nor any bounds to the slow but solid accretion of knowledge, and the development of the thinking faculty in this way."

13. As to methods in specific lessons, the following directions by Superintendent Harris are to the point: "Prepare yourself beforehand on the subject of the lesson of the week, fixing in your mind exactly what subjects you will bring up, just what definitions and illustrations you will give or draw out of the class. All must be marked and written down in the form of a synopsis. The blackboard is the most valuable appliance in oral lessons: on it should be written the technical words discussed, the classification of the knowledge brought out in the recitation, and, whenever possible, illustrative drawings. Pains should be taken to select passages from the reference books, or from other books illustrative of the subject under discussion, to be read to the class with explanation and conversation. Wherever the subject is of such a nat

ure as to allow of it, the teacher should bring in real objects illustrative of it, and encourage the children to do the same. But more stress should be laid on a direct appeal to their experience, encouraging them to describe what they have seen and heard, and arousing habits of reflection, and enabling the pupil to acquire a good command of language. Great care must be taken by the teacher not to burden the pupil with too many new technical phrases at a time, nor to fall into the opposite error of using only the loose, common vocabulary of ordinary life, which lacks scientific precision."

III. QUOTATIONS FROM EDUCATORS.

I. "For discipline as well as for guidance, science is of the chiefest value. In all its effects, learning the value of *things* is better than learning the meaning of *words*. Whether for intellectual, moral, or religious training, the study of surrounding phenomena is immensely superior to the study of grammars and lexicons."—*Spencer*.

II. "The processes by which truth is attained—reasoning and observation—have been carried to their greatest known perfection in the physical sciences. As classical literature furnishes the most perfect types of the art of expression, so do the physical sciences those of the art of thinking. Mathematics, and its application to astronomy and natural philosophy, are the most complete example of the discovery of truths by reasoning; experimental science, of their discovery by direct observation."—*John Stuart Mill*.

III. "In childhood there is a vast capability of accumulating simple facts. The higher forms of mental activity not having come into exercise, the whole plastic power of the brain is devoted to the storing-up of perceptions, while the vigor of cerebral growth insures the highest intensity of mental adhesiveness. When curiosity is freshest and the perceptions keenest, and the memory most impressible, before the maturity of the reflective powers, the opening mind should be led to the art of noticing the aspects, properties, and simple relations of the surrounding objects of nature."—*Youmans.*

IV. "But if scientific training is to yield its most eminent results, it must, I repeat, be made practical. That is to say, in explaining to a child the general phenomena of nature, you must, as far as possible, give reality to your teaching by object-lessons. In teaching him botany, he must handle the plants and dissect the flowers for himself; in teaching him physics and chemistry, you must not be solicitous to fill him with information, but you must be careful that what he learns, he knows of his own knowledge. Don't be satisfied with telling him that a magnet attracts iron. Let him see that it does; let him feel the pull of the one upon the other for himself. And, especially, tell him that it is his duty to doubt, until he is compelled by the absolute authority of nature to believe, that which is written in books. Pursue this discipline carefully and conscientiously, and you may make sure that, however scanty may be the measure of information which you have poured into the boy's mind, you have created an intellectual habit of priceless value in practical life."—*Huxley.*

Chapter IX.

WRITING AND DRAWING.

I. HINTS ON WRITING.

1. MAKE a judicious use of whatever series of copy-books is officially adopted for your school. Penmanship is essential as a mechanical means for acquiring and conveying information. But do not make your pupils slaves to "elements," "analysis," "proportion," "harmonies," and an endless series of engraved lessons. Penmanship is learned, in the main, by imitation and practice.

2. With beginners, during the first school year, put your copies on the blackboard, and let your pupils imitate them on the blackboard. Little children like writing with chalk in large-hand, because the teacher and the class see their work. Follow these lessons by slate-work.

3. Do not drill beginners on elements, principles, or analysis, but put them at once to writing short words, and then short sentences, as in reading. In fact, reading and writing ought to be carried along *pari passu*.

4. Bear in mind that many of the capital letters are no harder to make than are the small letters.

5. In blackboard lessons, see that your pupils form tne habit of holding a crayon properly, and give a drill lesson occasionally on large ovals to secure freedom of arm-movement.

6. In slate writing, use only long pencils, and train

your children to hold them as a pen is held. Give frequent drill movements in making ovals, running m's, etc., in order to secure freedom of arm-movements and an easy way of holding the pencil.

7. Give attention at every lesson to the manner of placing the slate upon the desk, and to the position of the pupil in writing. It is exceedingly difficult to break up bad habits of holding a pencil, when the pencil is followed by a pen.

8. Do not sit down in a chair behind your table, as some teachers do, but go about among your scholars, place their slates or books properly, take hold of their rigid fingers, and show them how to hold a pen easily and properly. It is not enough to do this *once*, it must be continued for years.

9. Train pupils from the beginning to write with a free and ready movement, not the slow, constrained, rigid, snail-like tracing that is often current in school.

10. The use of engraved copy-books is indispensable in school, but they must not be relied on exclusively. Let copy-books alternate with blank-books in which to write maxims, rules of health, choice selections of prose and poetry, compositions, etc. When pupils are able to write a fair business hand, drop all copy-books, and rely on the written school exercises. Require weekly or monthly specimens from every pupil.

11. Upon the lowest line of each page of the copy-book, require the pupil to write his name and age, the name of the school and class, and the date when the page was finished.

12. Train your more advanced classes on the elements, and the analysis of forms. Point out the defects of bad

forms and the merits of good forms. Require your pupils to make on the blackboards the capital letters on a large scale, and let them criticise one another.

13. Do not attempt to make the older scholars write a uniform "copy-book hand," but let them form their own characteristic style. The main thing is *to make every letter legible.*

14. "Writing, like spelling and grammar, is capable of self-development, but not unless many of the books prepared upon purely mechanical principles give way to blank books or sheets, which our children may use with greater freedom of hand and of the will that guides it. The days of copy-setting were better than those of copy-engraving, for this reason, if for no other, that the teacher wrote for the pupils, as well as the pupils for him. If he went further, and encouraged them to write out passages in prose or verse, perhaps helping them a little in their choice, then those days were a great deal better, and we had better revive their practices."—*Superintendent Eliot.*

15. "A corrupt taste in regard to writing has been for several years gradually creeping into our schools. This corruption consists in the substitution of a slender, faint, and weak kind of writing, with certain outlandish and fanciful capitals, for a good, honest, plain, neat, firm, clear, legible, strong, and regular hand."—*John D. Philbrick.*

II. HINTS ON DRAWING.

1. In schools where a series of text-books on drawing is adopted, teachers must master the instructions, require their pupils to fill out the drawing-books, and teach according to the system.

2. But there is no good reason why the "book-work,"

often a piece of drudgery, should not be supplemented or introduced by exercises in harmony with the child's taste. "Send the primary children to the blackboards, and let them learn to handle a crayon by drawing anything they choose. A rude outline of a ship delights the miniature man more than a geometrical figure does. The little girl draws a rough house, but she invests it with wondrous beauties. Allow full play for what most drawing teachers are pleased to term 'barbaric art.' The child is a young savage; let him pass through the barbarian stage before entering upon the scientific and artistic."

In country schools, where no regular course of drawing is adopted, the teacher has a wide field for the exercise of tact, skill, and judgment. In addition to elementary exercises previously mentioned, the first four books of Krusi's *Drawing Series* will furnish excellent copies which can be put upon the blackboard.

Speaking of the Prussian schools, Horace Mann says, "The child is taught to draw things with which he is familiar, which have some significance, and which give him pleasing ideas. The practice of beginning with making inexpressive marks bears some resemblance, in its lifelessness, to that of learning the alphabet. Each exhales torpor and stupidity to deaden the vivacity of the work."

3. Supply the little ones with a "Kindergarten slate," ruled in small squares. The directions for its use are so simple that any teacher can understand them in an hour. "The simpler lessons of drawing," says Bain, "are obviously easier than writing; while the making of symmetrical shapes is more agreeable than forming letters. Probably the natural course to follow would be the method of the Kindergarten, which is to train the hand upon mould-

ing objects in clay, followed by cutting out paper figures, and gradually leading up to elementary drawing; after which writing would come with comparative ease, but would still be a considerable step in advance, like beginning a trade."

4. Children prefer blackboard drawing to exercises on slates or paper, because their drawings are on a larger scale, and because their work can be seen by the other children. Direct their feeble efforts, but leave full play to individuality. One may take to ships, another to dogs, a third to horses, a fourth to flowers.

5. Violate all laws of the old-type drawing by encouraging the children to bring in a box of paints, and then set them to work at coloring all the old picture-books and wood-cuts that you can collect.

III. QUOTATIONS FROM EDUCATORS.

I. "The spreading recognition of drawing as an element of education is one among many signs of the more rational views on mental culture now beginning to prevail." —*Spencer*.

II. "I look to music, drawing, natural-history lessons, elementary science, and object-lessons, to protect our children from over-education, and to make them love their childish work; and were there no other reason for the introduction of such subjects into our common-schools than that, it seems to me that it would be reason sufficient."— *Professor Walter Smith*, State Director of Art Education for State of Massachusetts.

III. "It is now understood by well-informed persons that drawing is an essential branch of education, and that it should be taught to every child who is taught the three

R's. It is indispensable as an element of general education, and it lies at the very foundation of all technical education. It is difficult to conceive of any human occupation to which education in this branch would not prove beneficial. Everybody needs a well-trained eye and a well-trained hand. Drawing is the proper means of imparting this needed training. Drawing, properly taught, is calculated, even more than vocal music, perhaps, to facilitate instruction in all other branches of education."— *John D. Philbrick.*

IV. " Commercially speaking, the power to draw well is worth more in the market to-day than anything else taught in the public schools; and education in industrial art is of more importance to the development of this country, and the increase of her wealth and reputation, than any other subject of common-school education. The intelligent, well-educated draughtsman is prepared for work in the great majority of industrial occupations, and in every country of the civilized world, wherever a workshop exists."— *Walter Smith.*

V. "Drawing," says Superintendent Dickinson, "has for its object that training of the hand and eye which lays a foundation for skill in the arts. Such training leads to that appreciation of art necessary to create a demand for its products; it leads the mind to make a more careful examination of objects of study; it furnishes the best method of describing those objects that have form and size; it has a refining influence by cultivating the taste; and it improves morals by exciting a love for the beautiful."—*John W. Dickinson.*

Chapter X.

MISCELLANEOUS MATTERS.

I. MUSIC.

1. "Of all the fine arts," says Bain, "the most available and influential is music. This is perhaps the most unexceptionable as well as the cheapest of human pleasures."

2. Open and close your school with singing. If you cannot sing yourself, make up a small singing club, and let the leader conduct the exercises.

3. Train your pupils carefully in respect to the following points:

I. The proper position in singing.
II. The right management of the breath.
III. Singing with open mouth.
IV. Melody.

II. MANNERS.

I. Children are supposed to learn manners at home, or to take them on unconsciously from intercourse with their schoolmates; but it is exceedingly desirable that manners should be made the subject of definite instruction in every school. It is said that the winning manners of Henry Clay were owing, in no small degree, to the careful training of one of his early teachers.

II. "A beautiful behavior is the finest of the fine arts." —*Emerson.*

III. "Give a boy address and accomplishments, and you

give him the mastery of palaces and fortunes where he goes."—*Emerson.*

IV. "A noble and attractive every-day bearing comes of goodness, of sincerity, of refinement; and these are bred in years, not moments. The principle that rules your life is the sure posture-master."—*Huntington.*

V. "I wish good behavior might enter into the curriculum of every school in our country. Under this head should be taught such things as how to gracefully enter a room, meet with the person upon whom the pupil is supposed to be calling, pass the compliments of the day, and peacefully and politely leave the room; and to introduce parties in a proper manner; and also under this head you may teach how to write notes of invitation and acceptance."—*J. H. French,* Principal of the State Normal School, Indiana, Pennsylvania.

RULES OF POLITENESS.

Note.—Let your pupils copy the following rules into their blank-books. Add other directions as circumstances may require, those given here being merely a suggestive model. Make each direction the subject of a conversation with your pupils.

1. True politeness consists in having and showing due regard for the feelings, comfort, and convenience of others.
2. Avoid giggling or tittering in school or in company.
3. Avoid loud talking or laughing in school or in company.
4. Avoid the use of slang.
5. Be particularly courteous to new scholars.
6. Never laugh at the mistakes or blunders of other scholars or other persons.

7. Look persons in the eye when they speak to you, or when you speak to them.

8. Whispering at lectures, places of amusement, or in public is both rude and vulgar.

9. Be respectful to your elders in tone, look, and manner.

10. Be as polite to your father and mother, and your brothers and sisters, as you are to strangers.

PART III.

WORKING MODELS IN ESSENTIALS.

INTRODUCTORY NOTE.

It is by no means to be understood that the following "working models" in the essential school studies are the only methods by which good teachers can produce good results. The competent teacher who makes use of them will, of course, modify them to suit his own views, and use them as he may see fit to supplement the text-books in use in his school. It is hoped that they will be directly useful to inexperienced teachers by serving as model lessons until they themselves form the habit of preparing and arranging at least a part of their work independent of the school text-book. In country schools, where the teacher is allowed a wide range of discretion in methods and matter, these lessons may be available to a considerable extent. All of the following exercises are the result of the needs of a large city grammar and primary school, in which, on account of unsuitable text-books, or a lack of books altogether, such lessons seemed essential in order to secure practical work. They have all been tested by use in the hands of a large number of assistants; and, while few teachers will find time to use them all, it is hoped that every teacher will find some of them available for his own use. "It is a defect pertaining to all models," says Bain, "that they contain individual peculiarities mixed up with the ideal intention."

Chapter I.
WORKING MODELS FOR READING-LESSONS.

Note.—Suggestions for teaching beginners during their first year at school will be found in Sheldon's *Manual of Reading*, Calkins's *Manual*, or in any modern Primer, or First Reader. The following exercises are general in their character, and are only suggestive of what may be done by any thoughtful teacher. Whatever method teachers begin with, after a limited number of words or sentences are learned by sight, children must learn the letters and their powers, and must be trained in forming, writing, and spelling words.

I. LESSONS IN WORD-MAKING.

1. Write or print on the blackboard the vowels *a, e, i, o, u,* giving their *name* sounds. Then to each of these add the letter *t;* thus, *ăt, ĕt, ĭt, ŏt, ŭt.* Next, form such words as can be made by prefixing a letter; thus, *bat, cat, fat, hat, mat,* etc., and so on with each vowel.

2. Take the letter *b,* combine it with each of the vowels, and then make words by prefixing letters, thus, *cab, tub,* etc.

3. In a similar way, take *ad, ag, am, an, ap, ar, ed, id, od,* etc.; *ack, eck, ick, ock; ass, ess, iss, uss; all, ell, ill.*

4. Continue similar construction lessons, as a relief from book or chart work.

II. LESSONS FOR PRIMARY GRADES.

[Second and third school years.]

I. *Read the lesson to the class.*
II. *Allow five minutes for pupils to study it.*
III. *Explain any difficult words.*
IV. *Require pupils to read singly.*

QUESTIONING.

After the lesson is read, question the pupils about every sentence, making use of the following interrogatives:

Who?	*What?*	*Why?*
Whose?	*Where?*	*How?*
Whom?	*When?*	

MODEL.

Sentence.—"The merry boys skated on the pond in winter."

[Note.—*Require the answers to be in complete sentences.*]

1. *Who* skated on the pond in winter? *Ans.* The merry boys, etc.
2. *What kind* of boys skated, etc.? *Ans.* The merry boys skated, etc.
3. *What* did the boys *do?*
4. *Where* did the boys skate?
5. *When* did the boys skate?

REPRODUCING THE LESSON.

After answering such questions as these, applied to every sentence, require pupils to write out the paragraph on slates, exchange slates with each other, and correct by comparing with the book.

III. MISCELLANEOUS EXERCISES.

Apply one to each reading-lesson.
1. Copy the title or heading, and the first paragraph or stanza.
2. Write the names of the things you can see in this picture.
3. Learn the first stanza by heart.
4. How many periods in this lesson? How many question-marks?
5. Count all the commas in this lesson.
6. How many words of one syllable in the first paragraph? Of two syllables?

IV. LESSONS FOR LOWER GRAMMAR GRADES.

LESSON I.—OCCUPATIONS.

The farmer and gardener raise grain, vegetables, and fruit for our use. The farmer also supplies the market with milk, butter, cheese, cattle, sheep, wool, horses, poultry, and eggs. The miller grinds wheat and corn, and the baker makes bread. The butcher kills live-stock and sends to market beef, mutton, and pork.

Our clothes are made by the labor of many hands. Men, women, and children in China, Italy, and France are kept busy in rearing silk-worms and reeling silk. Thousands of men are hard at work in our own country raising and picking cotton, and thousands of farmers and sheep-raisers are shearing the wool from herds of sheep. Then there is the weaver, who makes the cloth; and the tailor or dressmaker, who makes it into clothing.

The tanner makes leather for us, and the shoemaker makes our boots and shoes. The carpenter and mason build us a house, the painter paints it, and the cabinet-maker makes the furniture. The bookseller supplies us with books, and the printers sell us the newspaper. The tea which we drink at supper has been picked by busy hands in China. The coffee that we use at breakfast comes from the plantations of Brazil or Java, and the sugar with which we sweeten it was made from the sugar-cane of Louisiana. It is wonderful to think how many trades there are, and how many busy hands are at work for our comfort or convenience.

QUESTIONS ON THE PRECEDING LESSON.
PUNCTUATION AND CAPITALS.

1. Call attention to the use of the comma in the numerous series of nouns, and then make up a rule.
2. How many commas in the whole lesson?
3. Call attention to the proper nouns beginning with a capital. How many are there in all?
4. How many periods in this lesson? How many sentences? With what does each begin and end?

PARTS OF SPEECH.

1. Write in columns all the nouns. How many are there?
2. How many nouns are plural? How many are singular?
3. Write in columns all the verbs. How many?
4. How many times is the article *the* used in this lesson? The article *a* or *an?*
5. How many times is the preposition *of* used? The preposition *in?*
6. How many times is the conjunction *and* used?
7. How many times is the relative pronoun *who* used? How many times is *which* used?
8. How many full sentences in this piece? How many paragraphs?
9. Reproduce from memory the first paragraph; the second.
10. Compare with the original, and correct the punctuation.

LESSON II.—A STORY.

There was once a prince who wished to marry a princess. He travelled all the world over in hopes of finding one. There were plenty of princesses, but he could not be certain that they were real ones. At last he gave up the search and went home quite cast down.

One stormy evening there was a knock, and, on opening the door, a princess asked for shelter. The prince's mother went into the bedroom, took off all the bedclothes from the bed, and put three little peas on the bedstead. She then laid twenty mattresses over the three peas, and put twenty feather beds over the mattresses. Then she put the princess to bed and tucked up the bedclothes.

In the morning the queen asked her how she had slept. "Oh! very badly indeed!" she replied; "I hardly closed my eyes all night. There was something hard in my bed, and I am black and blue all over."

It was now plain to the queen that this was a real princess, because she was so delicate. So the prince married her, and put the three peas in a cabinet of curiosities, where they are still to be seen, if they have not been lost.—*Adapted from Hans Andersen.*

EXERCISES ON THE PRECEDING STORY.

SENTENCES.

1. How many sentences?
2. How many paragraphs?

PARTS OF SPEECH.

1. Make a list of the proper nouns.
2. Make a list of the common nouns.
3. How many verbs?
4. How many times is the verb *is*, or some form of it, used?
5. Make a list of the transitive verbs.
6. How many nouns are in the nominative case? In the objective case? The possessive case?
7. Make a list of the personal pronouns. How many?
8. Make a list of the adjectives.
9. *Exchange slates, and correct under the direction of the teacher.*

PUNCTUATION.

1. How many commas are used in this lesson?
2. The teacher will give the reason for the use of each comma, if the pupil is unable to do so.
3. Reason for the use of quotation-marks.

ORAL EXERCISE.

Require several pupils to *tell* the story in their own language.

Reproduce the story from memory, exchange slates, and correct errors by comparing with the printed copy.

V. LESSONS FOR HIGHER GRAMMAR GRADES.
INVENTIONS AND INVENTORS.

The mariner's compass and the galvanic battery were invented in Italy.

Germany claims the honor of inventing printing, and Holland of inventing the microscope.

France has contributed to the world photography, the Jacquard loom, the electro-magnet, and iron armor for ships.

Great Britain has enriched the world with the steam-engine, the spinning-jenny, weaving-machines, the chronometer, the rolling-mill, the screw-propeller, iron ships, and the steam-plough.

The United States has contributed the steamboat, the cotton-gin, the electric telegraph, the sewing-machine, vulcanized rubber, the steam fire-engine, revolving fire-arms, street-cars, reaping-machines, pin-machines, cut-nail machines, and a great number of minor but very useful inventions.

EXERCISES.
GRAMMAR.

1. Make a list of the proper nouns in the above lesson.
2. Make a list of the simple subjects, and of the verbs.
3. How many simple sentences?
4. How many complex sentences?
5. How many compound sentences?
6. Parse each word in the first sentence.
7. How many phrases beginning with *of?*

GENERAL.

[Questions to be copied by a class, with directions to learn the answers.]

1. Tell the situation of each country named.
2. Who invented the galvanic battery?
3. Who invented photography?

4. Who invented or improved the steam-engine? When?
5. When and by whom was the cotton-gin invented?
6. The sewing-machine? Steamboats? The electric telegraph? Vulcanized rubber?

COMPOSITION.

Reproduce from memory, exchange and correct.

PUNCTUATION.

Give the reasons for the use of each comma.

Chapter II.
Working Models in Arithmetic.

Section I. — Lesson for Beginners; an Adaptation of the Grube System.

Grube's method consists in teaching beginners from four to six years of age, during the first year, all possible combinations and comparisons of numbers from 1 to 10. He gives, in substance, the following

Principles.

1. "Each lesson in arithmetic must be also a lesson in language. The teacher must insist on readiness and correctness of expression. As long as the language for the number is imperfect, the idea of the number will be defective."
2. "The teacher must require the scholar to speak as much as possible."
3. "Answers should be given, sometimes by the class in concert, and sometimes by the scholar individually."
4. "Every process must be illustrated by means of objects."
5. "Measure each new number with the preceding ones."
6. "Teachers must insist on neatness in making figures."

Order of Steps.

First Step. — Illustrate the required combinations by means of *counters* in the hands of the children themselves, and by other objects in the hands of the teacher. Each child must be supplied with ten small square wooden blocks, like the blocks of a checkerboard. If the blocks cannot be had, use shells, corn, pebbles, pins, sticks, buttons, etc. Make use of a numeral frame, if there is one in school.

Second Step.—Express the same combinations on the blackboard or on slates, both with *marks* and with figures.

Third Step.—Take the same combinations mentally with abstract numbers.

Fourth Step.—Practical problems in applied numbers.

HOW TO BEGIN.
FIRST TERM OR YEAR.

The time required for this work will depend upon the age of the children, as also upon their natural ability. Children from four to five years of age may require a year to complete it, while those of six years may master it in from three to five months.

I. THE NUMBER ONE.

1. Hold up one counter, one hand, one finger, one slate, etc.
    On your slates make one straight mark, one dot, one cross, etc.
    On the blackboards make one mark, one dot, one cross, etc.
2. Place one counter on the middle of your desk; take it away; how many have you left?
    Make one mark on your slate; rub it out; how many marks are left?
3. Send the class to the blackboards and let them make the mark for one—thus, |—and also the figure—thus, 1.

II. THE NUMBER TWO.

1. Each of you take one counter and place it by itself on your desk; now take another and place close to it; how many counters have you? (Require the answer in a full sentence.)
    Make one straight mark on your slate; make another close to it; how many have you now?
    Go to the blackboards; make one mark; another close to it; how many now?

Clap your hands once; again; how many claps?
Rap on your desks once; again; how many raps?

2. *Counting.*—Place one counter on your desk; a little way off from the first one, place two counters close together; thus, * **

Count, *one, two; two, one.*

On your slates make marks — thus, |, | |, and count forwards and backwards.

3. *Addition.*—(*a.*) Place one counter on the desk; place another counter close to it; how many have you now? *Ans.* I have two counters. How many counters are one counter and one counter? *Ans.* One counter and one counter are two counters.

[The teacher will further illustrate with books, pencils, crayons, etc.]

(*b.*) *Slate and Blackboard.*—Make one mark; another one near it. How many marks have you made?

[Continue with rings, dots, crosses, etc.]

4. *Subtraction.*—(*a.*) Place two counters together on your desk; take one away; how many have you left? *Ans.* I have one left. One counter from two counters leaves how many? *Ans.* One counter from two counters leaves one counter.

[Teacher will continue with fingers, hands, books, and other objects.]

(*b.*) *Slate and Blackboard.*—Make two marks; rub out one; how many are left? Make two marks; rub them out; how many are left? *Ans.* None are left. Two taken away from two leaves how many?

5. *Multiplication.*—(*a.*) Each of you put one counter on the desk; now put another one with it; how many times have you taken one counter? *Ans.* I have taken one counter twice.

Two times one counter are how many counters? *Ans.* Twice one counter are two counters.

(*b.*) *Slate and Blackboard.*—Make one mark; now another. How many times have you made one mark? *Ans.* I have made one mark twice. Then two times one mark are how many marks? *Ans.* Two times one mark are two marks.

6. *Division.*—Place two counters on the desk. Call up two boys and give one counter to each. Question thus: How many counters has John? How many has Frank? If two boys divide two counters between them, how many has each boy? Show the similarity of the expressions $2 \div 2 = 1$, and $\frac{1}{2}$ of $2 = 1$.

7. *Comparison.*—Give one counter to John and two to Frank. How many counters has John? Frank? How many has Frank more than John? How many more is two than one? How many counters has John less than Frank? Then one is one less than two. *Blackboard.*—Illustrate the same with marks.

8. *Applied Numbers.*—(*a.*) *Addition.*
  1. John ate one apple at recess, and another apple at noon; how many apples did he eat?
  2. Frank had one dime, and his father gave him one more; how many dimes did he have?
  3. The teacher will make up ten similar questions.

(*b.*) *Multiplication.*—1. John went a-fishing, and twice he caught one fish; how many fishes did he catch?
The teacher will make up ten similar questions.

(*c.*) *Division.*—1. If two boys divide two marbles between them, how many will each have?
Dictate ten similar questions.

9. *Figures and Signs.* — Teach the use of the five signs $+$, $-$, $\times$, $\div$, $=$. Tell them that $+$ means "and" or "added to," and that it is read "*plus;*" that $-$ means "taking away" or "less," and that it is read "*minus;*" that $\times$ means "times," and is read "*multiplied by;*" that $\div$ means "contains," and that it is read "*divided by;*" that $=$ means *equal to, equals.*

$+$	is called the sign of		addition.
$-$	"	"	subtraction.
$\times$	"	"	multiplication.
$\div$	"	"	division.
$=$	"	"	equality.

ILLUSTRATIONS OF THE USE OF SIGNS.

Let the children make each combination first with the counters.

a. By Marks.

$| + | = ||$
$|| - | = |$
$| \times || = ||$
$|| \div || = |$

b. By Figures.

$1 + 1 = 2$
$2 - 1 = 1$
$1 \times 2 = 2$
$2 \div 1 = 2$
$2 \div 2 = 1$
$\frac{1}{2}$ of $2 = 1$

10. *Table to be Taught.*

2 pints make 1 quart.
1 quart equals 2 pints.

III. THE NUMBER THREE.

1. *Measuring.*

First illustrate by using counters.

By One.

$1 + 1 + 1 = 3$
$3 - 1 - 1 - 1 = 0$
$3 - 1 - 1 = 1$
$3 - 2 = 1$
$1 \times 3 = 3$
$3 \times 1 = 3$
$3 \div 1 = 3$

By Two.

$2 + 1 = 3$
$1 + 2 = 3$
$1 \times 2 + 1 = 3$
$3 - 2 = 1$
$3 \div 2 = 1$ and 1 remainder, or
$\frac{1}{2}$ of $3 = 1$ and $\frac{1}{2}$

2. *Second Form of Expressing.*

Add.	Subt.	Subt.	Mult.	Div.	Div.
1	3	3	1	$1\overline{)3}$	$2\overline{)3}$
1	-1	-2	$\times 3$	$\overline{3}$	$\overline{1\frac{1}{2}}$
$\underline{1}$	$\underline{-1}$	$\overline{1}$	$\overline{3}$		
3	1				

WORKING MODELS IN ARITHMETIC. 201

Note.—Read $3 \div 1$, at first, thus: "1 is contained in 3 three times;" 1×3 thus: "3 times 1 equals three." The idea of "to be contained" must precede the higher and more difficult conception of "dividing."

3. *Practice.*

1. How many are $3 - 1 - 1 + 2$ divided by 1?
2. $1 + 1 + 1 - 2 + 1 + 1 - 2 + 1 + 1 = $ how many?

4. *Applied Numbers.*

The teacher will make up ten questions.

IV. THE NUMBER FOUR.

1. *Measuring.*

First illustrate by using counters.

By One.
$1 + 1 + 1 + 1 = 4$
$4 - 1 - 1 - 1 - 1 = 0$
$4 - 1 - 1 - 1 = 1$
$1 \times 4 = 4$
$4 \times 1 = 4$
$4 \div 1 = 4$

By Two.
$2 + 2 = 4$
$4 - 2 = 2$
$2 \times 2 = 4$
$4 \div 2 = 2$, or
$\frac{1}{2}$ of $4 = 2$

By Three.

$3 + 1 = 4$
$1 + 3 = 4$
$1 \times 3 + 1 = 4$
$3 \times 1 + 1 = 4$

$4 - 3 = 1$
$4 - 1 = 3$
$4 \div 3 = 1$ and 1 r., or
$\frac{1}{3}$ of $4 = 1\frac{1}{3}$

2. *Second Form of Writing.*

Add.	Add.	Subt.	Subt.	Mult.	Mult.	Div.
2	3	4	4	2	1	2)4
+2	+1	−2	−3	×2	×4	2
4	4	2	1	4	4	

3. *Practice.*

1. $2 \times 2 - 3 + 2 \times 1 + 1 - 2 \times 2 =$ how many?

The teacher will give ten similar questions.

4. *Combinations.*

1. What number must we double to get 4?
2. 2 is one half of what number?
3. 1 is the fourth part of what number?

Give similar questions.

5. *Practical Illustrations.*

1. Name 4 animals that have only 2 legs.
2. Name 4 animals that have 4 legs each.
3. Name a *thing* that has 4 legs.
4. Name a *thing* that has 3 legs.

6. *Table to be Learned.*

4 gills make 1 pint.
2 pints make 1 quart.
4 quarts make 1 gallon.

Pass around the class a pint measure and a quart measure, and then make up numberless practical examples.

V. THE NUMBER FIVE.

First, combinations with counters.

1. *Measuring.*

By One.	By Two.
$1+1+1+1+1=5$	$2+2+1=5$
$5-1-1-1-1-1=0$	$5-2-2=1$
$5-1-1-1-1=1$	$2 \times 2 + 1 = 5$
$1 \times 5 = 5$	$5 \div 2 = 2$ and 1 r.
$5 \times 1 = 5$	$\frac{1}{2}$ of $5 = 2\frac{1}{2}$
$5 \div 1 = 5$	

WORKING MODELS IN ARITHMETIC. 203

By Three.	By Four.
$3 + 2 = 5$	$4 + 1 = 5$
$2 + 3 = 5$	$1 + 4 = 5$
$5 - 2 = 3$	$5 - 4 = 1$
$5 - 3 = 2$	$5 - 1 = 4$
$1 \times 3 + 2 = 5$	$1 \times 4 + 1 = 5$
$5 \div 3 = 1, 2$ r.	$5 \div 4 = 1, 1$ r.
$\frac{1}{3}$ of $5 = 1\frac{2}{3}$	$\frac{1}{4}$ of $5 = 1\frac{1}{4}$

2. *Practice.*

1. $5 - 2 - 3 + 2 \times 2 =$ how many?
2. $2 \times 2 + 1 - 3 \times 1 + 2 \div 4 = ?$

3. *Applied Numbers.*

The teacher will make up at least ten simple questions.

VI. THE NUMBER SIX.

1. *Illustration.*

(*a.*) Place six counters in a row, count forwards and backwards.

(*b.*) Make six marks on slates—thus, | | | | | |. Count forwards and backwards.

(*c.*) Make figures—thus, 1, 2, 3, 4, 5, 6. Count forwards and backwards.

2. *Addition.*

Illustrate the following combinations first with counters, next with marks:

$1 + 1$	$1 + 2$	$1 + 3$	$1 + 4$	$1 + 5$
$2 + 1$	$2 + 2$	$2 + 3$	$2 + 4$	
$3 + 1$	$3 + 2$	$3 + 3$		
$4 + 1$	$4 + 2$			
$5 + 1$				

3. *Subtraction.*

Illustrate as in addition.

1 — 1	2 — 2	3 — 3	4 — 4	6 — 6
2 — 1	3 — 2	4 — 3	5 — 4	
3 — 1	4 — 2	5 — 3	6 — 4	
4 — 1	5 — 2	6 — 3		
5 — 1	6 — 2			
6 — 1				

4. *Analysis.*

$6 = 1+1+1+1+1+1$	$6 = 3+2+1$
$6 = 2+1+1+1+1$	$6 = 3+3$
$6 = 2+2+1+1$	$6 = 4+1+1$
$6 = 2+2+2$	$6 = 4+2$
$6 = 3+1+1+1$	$6 = 5+1$

Write the preceding in the second form.

5. *Multiplication.*

$1 \times 1 = ?$	$2 \times 1 = ?$	$3 \times 1 = ?$	$1 \times 4 = ?$
$1 \times 2 = ?$	$2 \times 2 = ?$	$3 \times 2 = ?$	$1 \times 5 = ?$
$1 \times 3 = ?$	$2 \times 3 = ?$		$1 \times 6 = ?$
$1 \times 4 = ?$			
$1 \times 5 = ?$			
$1 \times 6 = ?$			

Write the preceding in the second form.

6. *Division.*

$2 \div 2$	$3 \div 3$	$4 \div 4$	$5 \div 5$	$6 \div 6$
$3 \div 2$	$4 \div 3$	$5 \div 4$	$6 \div 5$	
$4 \div 2$	$5 \div 3$	$6 \div 4$		
$5 \div 2$	$6 \div 3$			
$6 \div 2$				

7. *Exercise with Counters.*

1. Place two counters together; two more; two more; how many counters?
2. How many times two counters?
3. How many times are two counters contained in six counters?
4. Place three counters together; three more; how many?
5. How many times three counters?
6. Etc.

8. *Division.—Another Form.*

$\frac{1}{2}$ of $2 = 1$	$\frac{1}{3}$ of $3 = 1$	$\frac{1}{4}$ of $4 = 1$
$\frac{1}{2}$ of $3 = 1\frac{1}{2}$	$\frac{1}{3}$ of $4 = 1, 1$ r.	$\frac{1}{4}$ of $5 = 1\frac{1}{4}$
$\frac{1}{2}$ of $4 = 2$	$\frac{1}{3}$ of $5 = 1, 2$ r.	$\frac{1}{4}$ of $6 = 1\frac{2}{4}$
$\frac{1}{2}$ of $5 = 2\frac{1}{2}$	$\frac{1}{3}$ of $6 = 2$	
$\frac{1}{2}$ of $6 = 3$		

9. *Division.—Regular Form.*

Write thus: $\quad 2\overline{)2} \atop 1 \qquad 2\overline{)3} \atop 1\frac{1}{2} \qquad 2\overline{)4} \atop 2 \qquad$ etc.

10. *Comparison.*

6 is 1 more than 5	1 is 5 less than 6
6 is 2 more than 4	2 is 4 less than 6
6 is 3 more than 3	3 is 3 less than 6
6 is 4 more than 2	4 is 2 less than 6
6 is 5 more than 1	5 is 1 less than 6

All these examples are to be given promiscuously as well as in regular order.

[Proceed in a similar manner with the numbers seven, eight, and nine.]

VII. THE NUMBER TEN.

1. *Illustration.*

(*a.*) Place ten counters on the desk.
(*b.*) Make ten marks on the slate or board.

(c.) Make the figures 1, 2, 3, 4, 5, 6, 7, 8, 9, 10.
(d.) Count forwards and backwards.

2. *Measurement.*

Measuring by counters.

1. How many *twos* in ten?
2. How many *threes* in ten?
3. How many *fours, fives, sixes,* etc.?

3. *Combinations.*

Let pupils make all the combinations they can that shall equal ten—thus:

$$2+2+2+2+2=10$$
$$3+3+3+1=10$$
$$5+5=10$$
$$4+4+2=10, \text{ etc.}$$

4. *Second Form of Expressing.*

Put the same into the regular form of addition—thus:

$$\begin{array}{r} 3 \\ 3 \\ 3 \\ 1 \\ \hline 10 \end{array}$$

Correct Way.—One, four, seven, ten.
Incorrect Way.—One and three are four, and three are seven, and three are ten.

5. *Multiplication.*

$1 \times 1 = 1$	$2 \times 1 = 2$	$3 \times 1 = 3$	$4 \times 1 = 4$
$1 \times 2 = 2$	$2 \times 2 = 4$	$3 \times 2 = 6$	$4 \times 2 = 8$
$1 \times 3 = 3$	$2 \times 3 = 6$	$3 \times 3 = 9$	
$1 \times 4 = 4$	$2 \times 4 = 8$		
$1 \times 5 = 5$	$2 \times 5 = 10$		
etc. to 10			

6. *Division.*

$2 \div 2 = ?$	$3 \div 3 = ?$	$4 \div 4 = ?$	$5 \div 5 = ?$
$3 \div 2 = ?$	$4 \div 3 = ?$	$5 \div 4 = ?$	$6 \div 5 = ?$
$4 \div 2 = ?$	$5 \div 3 = ?$	$6 \div 4 = ?$	$7 \div 5 = ?$
etc. to 10	etc. to 10	etc. to 10	etc. to 10

7. *Another Form of Division.*

$\frac{1}{2}$ of 2 = ?	$\frac{1}{3}$ of 3 = ?	$\frac{1}{4}$ of 4 = ?
$\frac{1}{2}$ of 3 = ?	$\frac{1}{3}$ of 4 = ?	$\frac{1}{4}$ of 5 = ?
$\frac{1}{2}$ of 4 = ?	$\frac{1}{3}$ of 5 = ?	$\frac{1}{4}$ of 6 = ?
etc. to 10	etc. to 10	etc. to 10

8. *Another Form of Division.*

$2)\overline{2}2)\overline{3}2)\overline{4}2)\overline{5}$ etc. to 10
$11\tfrac{1}{2}22\tfrac{1}{2}$

In the same way divide by three, four, and five.

9. *Comparison.*

10 is 1 more than 9	1 is 9 less than 10
10 is 2 more than 8	2 is 8 less than 10
10 is 3 more than 7	3 is 7 less than 10
10 is 4 more than 6	4 is 6 less than 10
10 is 5 more than 5	5 is 5 less than 10
etc. to 10	etc. to 10

All these comparisons are to be given promiscuously as well as in regular order.

10. *Concrete Examples.*

Teachers will make up from ten to twenty concrete examples.

SECTION II.—SECOND TERM OR YEAR.

I. NUMBERS FROM TEN TO TWENTY.

1. Illustration with the number nineteen.
    1. Place the counters on the desk.
    2. Make marks on the slate or board.
    3. Make the figures from one to nineteen.
    4. Count forwards and backwards.

METHODS OF TEACHING.

2. Measuring by counters.
    1. How many *twos* in nineteen?
    2. How many *threes*, etc., to *nines*?

3. *Addition Table.*

$1+2+2$, etc., to 19 $5+5+5+4=19$ $9+9+1=19$
$2+2+2$, etc., $+1$ to 19 $6+6+6+1=19$
$3+3+3$, etc., to 19 $7+7+5=19$
$4+4+4+4+3=19$ $8+8+3=19$

Put the preceding also into vertical columns.

4. Let scholars make as many combinations as possible equal to nineteen.

5. *Subtraction.* — Reverse the tables for addition.

6. *Multiplication.*

1×2	1×2	1×3	1×4	1×5
1×3 to 19	2×2 to 9	2×3 to 6	2×4 to 4	2×5 to 3

7. *Division.*
    $19 \div 1, 19 \div 2, 19 \div 3$, up to 19.

8. *Miscellaneous Exercises.*

$8+4=12$	$3+3+3-8=1$	$2 \times 3 \times 3 = 18$
$7+5+6=18$	$12 \div 6 = 2$	$4 \times 3 \times 1 = 12$
$19-4=15$	$17 \div 4 = 4, 1$ r.	$16 \div 8 = 2$
$19-9=10$	$16-12=4$	$18 \div 9 = 2$
$3 \times 6 = 18$	$2 \times 2 \times 2 = 8$	$18 \div 5 = 3, 3$ r.
$16 \div 4 = 4$	$17-9+9=17$	$19 \div 4 = 4, 3$ r.
$5+9-7=7$	$9+9-11=7$	

Table to be Learned.

12 inches = 1 foot.   16 ounces = 1 pound.
3 feet = 1 yard.

Note.—The inch, foot, and yard to be drawn repeatedly on the board by pupils. An ounce weight and a pound weight must be passed around in the class.

II. FRACTIONS.

Directions.—Illustrate halves, thirds, etc., by breaking up crayons, cutting up apples, or by breaking slips of wood. Having shown your pupils how *one half* is made and how one half is written, send them to the blackboards, saying nothing whatever about *numerator* or *denominator*, and drill them on numberless examples like the following:

1. *One Half.*

1. $\frac{1}{2} + \frac{1}{2} = \frac{2}{2} = 1$.
2. $\frac{1}{2} + \frac{1}{2} + \frac{1}{2} + \frac{1}{2} + \frac{1}{2} + \frac{1}{2} = \frac{6}{2} = 3$; etc.

2. *Mixed Numbers.*

$$2\tfrac{1}{2} \qquad 6 = 5\tfrac{2}{2} \qquad 1\tfrac{1}{2} \qquad 4$$
$$3\tfrac{1}{2} \qquad -3\tfrac{1}{2} = 3\tfrac{1}{2} \qquad 2\tfrac{1}{2} \qquad -1\tfrac{1}{2} \qquad \text{etc.}$$
$$\overline{6} \qquad \overline{2\tfrac{1}{2} = 2\tfrac{1}{2}} \qquad \overline{4} \qquad \overline{2\tfrac{1}{2}}$$

Note.—Give a great many drill examples like the preceding, and keep your little scholars busy on such simple questions until they become expert in their work. Do not be in a hurry to proceed immediately, after the manner of text-books, to crowd a dozen new things upon them.

3. *Combinations.*

$\frac{1}{2} + \frac{1}{2} = \frac{2}{2} = 1 \qquad \frac{1}{3} + \frac{1}{3} = \frac{2}{3} \qquad \frac{1}{4} + \frac{1}{4} = \frac{2}{4} = \frac{1}{2}$

$\frac{2}{2} - \frac{1}{2} = \frac{1}{2}$, or $\qquad \frac{2}{3} - \frac{1}{3} = \frac{1}{3} \qquad \frac{2}{4} - \frac{1}{4} = \frac{1}{4}$, or

$1 - \frac{1}{2} = \frac{1}{2} \qquad \frac{1}{2} \times \frac{1}{3} = \frac{1}{6} \qquad \frac{1}{2} - \frac{1}{4} = \frac{1}{4}$

$\frac{1}{2} \times \frac{1}{2} = \frac{1}{4} \qquad \frac{1}{3} \div \frac{1}{3} = 1 \qquad \frac{1}{2} \times \frac{1}{8} = \frac{1}{16}$

$\frac{1}{2} \div \frac{1}{2} = 1 \qquad\qquad\qquad \frac{1}{4} \div \frac{1}{4} = 1$

4. *Addition.*

$\frac{1}{3} + \frac{1}{3} + \frac{1}{3} + \frac{1}{3} + \frac{1}{3} + \frac{1}{3} + \frac{1}{3} + \frac{1}{3} + \frac{1}{3} = \frac{9}{3} = 3$

$\frac{1}{4} + \frac{1}{4} + \frac{1}{4} + \frac{1}{4} + \frac{1}{4} + \frac{1}{4} + \frac{1}{4} + \frac{1}{4} + \frac{1}{4} + \frac{1}{4} + \frac{1}{4} + \frac{1}{4} = \frac{12}{4} = 3$

$\frac{1}{5} + \frac{1}{5} + \frac{1}{5} + \frac{1}{5} + \frac{1}{5} + \frac{1}{5} + \frac{1}{5} + \frac{1}{5} + \frac{1}{5} + \frac{1}{5} = \frac{10}{5} = 2$

Note.—Send the class to the boards and give twenty similar examples.

5. Addition.

$3\frac{1}{2}$	$3\frac{1}{3}$	$1\frac{1}{4}$	$6\frac{1}{8}$	$5\frac{1}{6}$
$2\frac{1}{2}$	$2\frac{1}{3}$	$3\frac{1}{4}$	$2\frac{1}{8}$	$2\frac{1}{6}$
$4\frac{1}{2}$	$4\frac{1}{3}$	$5\frac{1}{4}$	$4\frac{1}{8}$	$3\frac{1}{6}$
$1\frac{1}{2}$	$1\frac{1}{3}$	$2\frac{1}{4}$	$5\frac{1}{8}$	$4\frac{1}{6}$
12	$11\frac{1}{3}$	12	$17\frac{4}{8}$	$14\frac{4}{6} = 14\frac{2}{3}$

Note.—Give at least one hundred similar drill examples, in ten successive lessons.

6. Multiplication.

$\frac{1}{2} \times 1 = \frac{1}{2}$
$\frac{1}{2} \times 2 = \frac{2}{2} = 1$
$\frac{1}{2} \times 3 = \frac{3}{2} = 1\frac{1}{2}$
$\frac{1}{2} \times 4 = \frac{4}{2} = 2$
etc.

$\frac{1}{3} \times 1 = \frac{1}{3}$
$\frac{1}{3} \times 2 = \frac{2}{3}$
$\frac{1}{3} \times 3 = \frac{3}{3} = 1$
$\frac{1}{3} \times 4 = \frac{4}{3} = 1\frac{1}{3}$
etc.

$\frac{1}{4} \times 1 = \frac{1}{4}$
$\frac{1}{4} \times 2 = \frac{2}{4} = \frac{1}{2}$
$\frac{1}{4} \times 3 = \frac{3}{4}$
$\frac{1}{4} \times 4 = \frac{4}{4} = 1$
etc.

Second Form.—Mixed Numbers.

$2\frac{1}{2}$	$4\frac{1}{3}$	$2\frac{1}{3}$	$5\frac{1}{3}$	$3\frac{1}{4}$	$2\frac{1}{4}$
2	3	2	3	3	4
5	$13\frac{1}{2}$	$4\frac{2}{3}$	16	$9\frac{3}{4}$	9

7. Division and Multiplication.

Division.

$1 \div 2 = \frac{1}{2}$
$1 \div 3 = \frac{1}{3}$
$1 \div 4 = \frac{1}{4}$
etc., to tenths.

Multiplication.

$\frac{1}{2} \times 2 = \frac{2}{2} = 1$
$\frac{1}{3} \times 3 = \frac{3}{3} = 1$
$\frac{1}{4} \times 4 = \frac{4}{4} = 1$
etc., to tenths.

8. Decimal Fractions. [*Tenths.*]

Directions.—Send your pupils to the blackboards, and let them write and read examples like the following, without going into any philosophical explanation whatever. At this stage, the point is to *do* something.

WORKING MODELS IN ARITHMETIC. 211

Addition.	Subtraction.
(1.) .2 + .2 = .4	(2.) .4 − .2 = .2
(3.) .3 + .3 = .6	(4.) .6 − .3 = .3
(5.) .4 + .3 = .7	(6.) .7 − .4 = .3

Give at least ten lessons, each containing from ten to twenty similar examples.

Second Form.

(1.)	(2.)	(3.)	(4.)	(5.)	(6.)
.2	.3	.4	.4	.6	.7
.2	.3	.3	− .2	− .3	− .4
.4	.6	.7	.2	.3	.3

9. *Addition.*

.2	.5	1.2	1.3	2.2
.3	.6	1.3	1.4	3.3
.2	.4	1.5	1.5	4.4
.7	1.5	4.0	4.2	9.9

Send the class to the boards and give similar examples.

10. *Multiplication.*

.2 × 1 = .2	.2 × 4 = .8	.2 × 7 = 1.4
.2 × 2 = .4	.2 × 5 = 1.0	.2 × 8 = 1.6
.2 × 3 = .6	.2 × 6 = 1.2	.2 × 9 = 1.8

In the same way take .3, .4, .5.

11. *Addition of Common and Decimal Fractions.*

(1.)	(2.)	(3.)
$\frac{1}{2}$ = .5	$2\frac{1}{2}$ = 2.5	$1\frac{1}{2}$ = 1.5
$\frac{1}{2}$ = .5	$3\frac{1}{2}$ = 3.5	$1\frac{1}{2}$ = 1.5
$\frac{1}{2}$ = .5	$4\frac{1}{2}$ = 4.5	$1\frac{1}{2}$ = 1.5
$1\frac{1}{2}$ = 1.5	$10\frac{1}{2}$ = 10.5	$4\frac{1}{2}$ = 4.5

12. *Table.*

10 cents 1 dime.
10 dimes 1 dollar.

Pass a dollar, a dime, and a cent around the class, and give easy practical questions. Make the sign of dollars, and give simple questions in adding dollars.

13. *Decimals.*

Multiplication.
1. $.2 \times 4 = .8$
3. $.3 \times 3 = .9$
5. $.4 \times 4 = 1.6$
7. $.7 \times 2 = 1.4$, etc.

Division.
2. $.8 \div 4 = .2$
4. $.9 \div 3 = .3$
6. $1.6 \div 4 = .4$
8. $1.4 \div 2 = .7$

14. *Multiplication.*

.2	.3	.4	.7	.7	.6	.5
4	3	4	2	3	2	2
.8	.9	1.6	1.4	2.1	1.2	1.0

The teacher will give five lessons of five examples each, similar to the above.

SECTION III.—THIRD YEAR OR TERM.

1. *Adding by tens, twenties, thirties, forties, etc.*

Models.

(1.)	(2.)	(3.)	(4.)	(5.)	(6.)
10	20	30	40	50	90
10	20	30	40	50	90
10	20	30	40	50	90
30	60	90	120	150	270

Divide each amount in the preceding examples by 3—thus:

$$3 \overline{)30} \qquad 3 \overline{)150}$$
$$10 \qquad 50 \qquad \text{etc.}$$

The teacher will give five similar lessons of ten examples each.

2. *Multiplying and dividing tens, twenties, thirties, forties, etc., by one, two, three, etc., to ten.*

Model of Blackboard Work.

Mult.	Div.	Mult.	Div.
$10 \times 2 = 20$	$20 \div 2 = 10$	$50 \times 2 = 100$	$100 \div 2 = 50$
$10 \times 3 = 30$	$30 \div 3 = 10$	$50 \times 3 = 150$	$150 \div 3 = 50$
$10 \times 4 = 40$	$40 \div 4 = 10$	$50 \times 4 = 200$	$200 \div 4 = 50$
etc.	etc.	etc.	etc.

WORKING MODELS IN ARITHMETIC. 213

3. *Decimals.—Dollars and Cents.*

Dictate hundreds of simple examples like the following:

(1.)	(2.)	(3.)	(4.)	(5.)
$10	$25	$1.25	$4.40	$0.10
$12	$25	$2.25	$4.50	$0.25
$13	$50	$3.25	$4.60	$0.50

(1.)	(2.)	(3.)	(4.)
$\$\tfrac{1}{2} = .50$	$\$\tfrac{1}{4} = .25$	$\$\tfrac{1}{10} = .10$	$\$\tfrac{3}{4} = .75$
$\$\tfrac{1}{2} = .50$	$\$\tfrac{1}{4} = .25$	$\$\tfrac{1}{10} = .10$	$\$\tfrac{3}{4} = .75$
$\$\tfrac{1}{2} = .50$	$\$\tfrac{1}{4} = .25$	$\$\tfrac{1}{10} = .10$	$\$\tfrac{3}{4} = .75$
$\$1\tfrac{1}{2} = \$1.50$	$\$\tfrac{3}{4} = .75$	$\$\tfrac{3}{10} = .30$	$\$2\tfrac{1}{4} = \$2.25$

4. *Slate and Blackboard Drill.*

Multiplication.
1. $1.25 × 3 = ?
3. $2.75 × 4 = ?
5. $1.12½ × 2 = ?
7. $2.37½ × 4 = ?
9. $1.05 × 3 = ?

Division.
2. $ 3.75 ÷ 3 = ?
4. $11.00 ÷ 4 = ?
6. $ 2.25 ÷ 2 = ?
8. $ 9.50 ÷ 4 = ?
10. $ 3.15 ÷ 3 = ?

The teacher will dictate five similar lessons of ten examples each.

5. *Table of Federal Money to be Learned.*

SECTION IV.—DRILL EXERCISES IN THE FOUR RULES.

I. ADDITION.

Direction.—Put this table on the blackboard; with a pointer, point out successively different numbers to be combined with the number at the head of the column. As, pointing to 11, the combination will be 5 + 11 = 16, etc. Let the class answer in concert and singly.

Add the first column under "5" downwards and upwards, until the scholar has thoroughly mastered it. Do not allow pupils to repeat five and ten are fifteen, five and six are eleven, five and eleven are sixteen, etc., but require them to point on the blackboard to each figure in the column, and give only results; downwards thus: 15, 11, 16, 10, 9, 6, 8, 12, 17, 14, 7, 13; upwards, 13, 7, 14, 17, 12, 8, 6, 9, 10, 16, 11, 15.

Add the other columns in the same manner.

5	2	3	4	6	7	8	9	10
10	12	7	5	4	12	3	9	11
6	3	9	3	9	9	2	6	4
11	6	4	6	6	11	7	12	6
5	4	8	10	10	5	8	7	10
4	9	6	4	12	10	12	11	5
1	7	12	1	7	4	10	4	3
3	2	3	11	11	6	9	10	7
7	11	5	9	3	3	11	3	12
12	5	10	12	8	2	6	1	9
9	1	1	7	5	7	5	5	2
2	8	11	2	2	1	4	8	8
8	10	2	8	1	8	1	2	1

II. SUBTRACTION.

6	2	3	4	8	5	10	7	9
15	12	9	13	14	11	10	17	12
10	9	11	10	18	15	15	13	9
9	7	5	14	12	13	20	8	19
16	11	12	12	16	9	14	7	17
14	8	10	4	13	5	16	10	14
12	6	8	6	11	8	11	14	18
8	10	6	9	9	6	17	11	15
11	5	4	5	15	10	13	16	10
6	3	7	8	8	7	12	12	13
13	2	3	7	10	12	19	9	11

WORKING MODELS IN ARITHMETIC. 215

III. MULTIPLICATION.

4	3	6	9	2	5	7	8	10	11	12
9	3	6	11	8	10	8	3	10	12	12
12	4	12	10	11	12	12	6	8	1	6
10	8	7	1	10	1	10	12	12	11	1
2	12	11	4	6	4	9	9	6	4	2
11	10	9	12	5	8	4	5	1	8	4
8	5	4	2	4	9	1	4	2	6	8
7	6	10	6	1	3	3	1	4	4	3
4	11	8	8	3	7	6	8	3	5	11
6	9	3	5	9	5	5	7	9	7	7
3	7	1	7	2	2	11	10	5	10	10
5	2	5	9	7	6	2	2	11	2	5
1	1	2	3	12	11	7	11	2	4	9

IV. DIVISION.

Under the head of "7," giving only results; downwards thus: 5, 8, 12, 6, 1, 2, 7, 10, 3, 4, 9, 11; upwards, 11, 9, 4, 3, 10, 7, 2, 1, 6, 12, 8, 5.

7	2	3	4	5	8	6	12	9	11	10
35	10	33	44	50	72	48	36	36	11	90
56	16	27	16	35	96	18	60	18	132	60
84	24	12	24	45	56	60	108	54	33	70
42	12	15	8	60	40	12	84	90	22	50
7	2	30	4	40	88	36	132	72	121	80
14	4	21	20	25	8	24	144	108	110	40
49	14	6	32	5	32	6	96	99	44	100
70	20	3	48	10	48	66	120	9	88	30
21	6	18	36	15	16	30	72	63	55	110
28	8	36	28	30	80	42	24	81	77	20
63	18	24	40	20	24	72	48	45	66	120
77	22	15	12	55	64	54	12	27	99	10

SECTION V.—WORKING MODELS IN COMMON FRACTIONS.

I. MULTIPLYING AND DIVIDING A FRACTION BY A WHOLE NUMBER.

Note.—There will be no difficulty in lessons like the following, if the teacher will let technical terms alone, take only one thing at a time, and drill upon it until it is fixed in the mind by practice. The first steps must be illustrated by broken crayons or sticks.

Oral Lesson.

1. How many fourths are 2 times $\frac{1}{4}$?
   Ans. Two times $\frac{1}{4}$ are $\frac{2}{4}$, and $\frac{2}{4} = \frac{1}{2}$.
2. What is $\frac{1}{2}$ of $\frac{2}{4}$? *Ans.* $\frac{1}{4}$.
3. What is $\frac{1}{2}$ of $\frac{1}{2}$? *Ans.* $\frac{1}{4}$.
4. Multiply $\frac{1}{8}$ by 3.
5. Divide $\frac{3}{8}$ by 3.

Multiply.	*Divide.*
1. $\frac{1}{8}$ by 5	2. $\frac{5}{8}$ by 5
3. $\frac{2}{9}$ by 3	4. $\frac{6}{9}$ by 3
5. $\frac{3}{10}$ by 3	6. $\frac{9}{10}$ by 3
7. $\frac{2}{11}$ by 5	8. $\frac{10}{11}$ by 5
9. $\frac{7}{20}$ by 2	10. $\frac{14}{20}$ by 3

II. MULTIPLYING BY A FRACTION.

1. *Oral Questions.*

1. What is one half of 4?
2. What is the product of 4 multiplied by $\frac{1}{2}$?
3. What is one half of 12?
4. 12 multiplied by $\frac{1}{2} = $?
5. What is $\frac{1}{2}$ of 5?
6. Multiply 5 by $\frac{1}{2}$.

Exercises.

1. Find one half of each of the even numbers from 2 to 20.
2. Multiply each of the even numbers from 2 to 20 by $\frac{1}{2}$.
3. Find one half of each of the odd numbers from 1 to 19.
4. Multiply by $\frac{1}{2}$ each of the odd numbers from 1 to 19.
5. Find one half of 20, 40, 60, 80, 100.
6. Multiply by $\frac{1}{2}$ each of the following: 20, 40, 60, 80, 100.

2. *Slate and Blackboard Drill.*

1. The question "What is one half of 4" is expressed thus in written arithmetic: Multiply 4 by $\frac{1}{2}$.

Slate Work.—$4 \times \frac{1}{2} = ?$ $4 \div 2 = 2$. *Ans.*

Rule.—Divide the number by 2.

In a similar manner perform each of the following:

1. Multiply each of the even numbers from 2 to 100 by $\frac{1}{2}$.
2. Multiply each of the odd numbers from 3 to 99 by $\frac{1}{2}$.

III. MULTIPLYING BY A FRACTION.

1. *Oral Questions.*

1. What is $\frac{1}{4}$ of 8?
2. Multiply 8 by $\frac{1}{4}$.
3. What is the product of 8 multiplied by $\frac{1}{4}$?
4. How do you multiply 8 by $\frac{1}{4}$?
   Ans. By dividing 8 by 4.
5. Find $\frac{1}{4}$ of 12, 16, 20, 24, 28, 32, 36, 40, 44, 48.
6. Multiply each of the preceding numbers by $\frac{1}{4}$.
7. Find $\frac{1}{4}$ of 40, 80, 120, 160.
8. Find $\frac{1}{4}$ of 9, 13, 17, 21, 25, 29, 33, 37, 41, 45, 49.

2. *Slate and Blackboard Drill.*

Form of Slate Work.

1. Multiply 8 by $\frac{1}{4}$.

   $8 \times \frac{1}{4} = ?$

   $8 \div 4 = 2$.

Rule.—Divide the number by 4.

EXERCISES.

1. Put each of the oral questions in the preceding lesson into slate work.
2. Multiply each of the even numbers from 4 to 100 by $\frac{1}{4}$.
3. Multiply each of the odd numbers from 5 to 99 by $\frac{1}{4}$.
4. Multiply every number that ends with a cipher from 10 to 100 by $\frac{1}{4}$.
5. Multiply every number ending in 5 from 15 to 105 by $\frac{1}{4}$.

IV. DIVIDING BY A FRACTION.

1. *Oral.*

1. How many times is $\frac{1}{2}$ contained in 2?
2. How can you show it?
   Ans. By taking 2 crayons and breaking them into halves. Do it.
3. How many times is $\frac{1}{2}$ contained in 4?
   Show it by drawing on the blackboard a line four inches long, and then dividing into half-inches.
4. Divide 2 by $\frac{1}{2}$.
5. Divide 4 by $\frac{1}{2}$.
6. What is the quotient of 2 divided by $\frac{1}{2}$.
7. Find the quotient of 4 divided by $\frac{1}{2}$.
8. $2 \div \frac{1}{2} = ?$ $4 \div \frac{1}{2} = ?$

Exercises.

Rule.—Multiply the number by 2.

1. Divide each of the even numbers from 2 to 100 by $\frac{1}{2}$.
2. Divide each of the odd numbers from 3 to 100 by $\frac{1}{2}$.
3. Divide by $\frac{1}{2}$ each of the numbers ending in a cipher from 10 to 100.
4. Divide by $\frac{1}{2}$ each number from 15 to 105 ending in 5.

2. *Slate and Blackboard Drill.*

Questions like the preceding are put into the form of written arithmetic according to the following

Model.

1. What is 5 times $\frac{1}{6}$?

$$\tfrac{1}{6} \times 5 = \tfrac{5}{6}. \qquad\qquad \tfrac{5}{6} \div 5 = \tfrac{1}{6}.$$

Require the class to put each of the preceding questions into the form of written arithmetic, and then dictate ten examples, using larger numbers.

SECTION VI.—ANALYTICAL WORK IN FRACTIONS, FOR GRAMMAR-SCHOOL GRADES.

Note.—In undertaking to train pupils to a clear conception of analytical processes in common fractions, it is desirable to proceed slowly, taking a great number of easy operations limited to small numbers upon each new process. In the following lessons the analytical method is pursued exclusively, and only one method is given. Teachers who desire to add other explanations can do so; but, in the beginning, it is best not to confuse the minds of pupils with too many things at once.

I. MULTIPLYING AND DIVIDING BY A FRACTION.

1. *Oral Drill.*

1. What is $\frac{3}{4}$ of 20?

   Analysis.—Since $\frac{1}{4}$ of 20 is 5, $\frac{3}{4}$ will be 3 times 5, or 15.

2. How many times is $\frac{3}{4}$ contained in 15?

   Analysis.—Since $\frac{1}{4}$ is contained 4 times 15, or 60 times, $\frac{3}{4}$ will be contained $\frac{1}{3}$ of 60, or 20 times.

3. What is the product of 20 multiplied by $\frac{4}{5}$?
4. What is the quotient of 16 divided by $\frac{4}{5}$?
5. Multiply 12 by $\frac{3}{4}$.
6. Divide 9 by $\frac{3}{4}$.
7. What is $\frac{5}{8}$ times 24?
8. How many times is $\frac{5}{8}$ contained in 24?
9. Find $\frac{4}{5}$ of 100.
10. How many times is $\frac{4}{5}$ contained in 20?

2. *Slate and Blackboard Drill.*

Multiplication.	*Division.*
Model 1. $20 \times \frac{3}{4} = ?$	Model 2. $15 \div \frac{3}{4} = ?$
$20 \div 4 = 5.$	$15 \times 4 = 60.$
$5 \times 3 = 15.$ *Ans.*	$60 \div 3 = 20.$ *Ans.*
Analysis.—Divide 20 by 4 to find $\frac{1}{4}$, and multiply the quotient 5 by 3 to find $\frac{3}{4}$.	*Analysis.*—Multiply 15 by 4 to find how many times $\frac{1}{4}$ is contained in 15, and divide the product 60 by 3 to find how many times $\frac{3}{4}$ is contained in 15.

Examples.

1. $900 \times \frac{2}{3} = ?$
3. $1200 \times \frac{3}{4} = ?$
5. $\$1600 \times \frac{5}{8} = ?$
7. $\$10.000 \times \frac{3}{5} = ?$
9. $1728 \text{ in.} \times \frac{7}{12} = ?$

2. $600 \div \frac{2}{3} = ?$
4. $900 \div \frac{3}{4} = ?$
6. $\$1000 \div \$\frac{5}{8} = ?$
8. $\$8000 \div \$\frac{3}{5} = ?$
10. $1728 \div \frac{2}{3} = ?$

II. MULTIPLICATION AND DIVISION OF FRACTIONS.

1. *Oral Drill.*

1. What is $\frac{1}{2}$ of $\frac{1}{2}$? *Ans.* $\frac{1}{4}$.
2. How do you find $\frac{1}{2}$ of any number?
    Ans. By dividing it by 2.
3. How do you divide $\frac{1}{2}$ by 2?
    Ans. By multiplying the denominator by 2.
4. In what other way can you show this?
    Ans. $\frac{1}{2} = \frac{2}{4}$, and $\frac{1}{2}$ of $\frac{2}{4} = \frac{1}{4}$.
5. How many times is $\frac{1}{2}$ contained in $\frac{1}{4}$?
    Ans. $\frac{1}{2}$ a time.
6. How do you divide any number by $\frac{1}{2}$?
    Ans. By multiplying it by 2.
7. How do you divide $\frac{1}{4}$ by $\frac{1}{2}$?
    Ans. By multiplying $\frac{1}{4}$ by 2, and this is done by dividing the denominator 4 by 2.
8. In what other way can you show this?

WORKING MODELS IN ARITHMETIC.   221

Ans. $\frac{1}{2} = \frac{2}{4}$, and $\frac{2}{4}$ is contained in $\frac{1}{4}$ as many times as 2 is contained in 1, which is $\frac{1}{2}$ a time.

9. What is $\frac{1}{2}$ of $\frac{1}{4}$?   *Ans.* $\frac{1}{8}$.   Why?
10. How many times is $\frac{1}{2}$ contained in $\frac{1}{8}$?
    Ans. $\frac{1}{4}$ of a time.   Show why.
11. What is $\frac{1}{3}$ of $\frac{1}{5}$?   *Ans.* $\frac{1}{15}$.   Show why.
12. Divide $\frac{1}{15}$ by $\frac{1}{3}$?   *Ans.* $\frac{1}{5}$.   Show why.

2. *Mental Operations.*

Multiplication.

Find the product—
1. Of $\frac{1}{2}$ of $\frac{1}{4}$.
3. Of $\frac{1}{3}$ of $\frac{1}{4}$.
5. Of $\frac{1}{4}$ of $\frac{1}{4}$.

Division.

Find the quotient—
2. Of $\frac{1}{8}$ divided by $\frac{1}{2}$.
4. Of $\frac{1}{3}$ divided by $\frac{1}{4}$.
6. Of $\frac{1}{16}$ divided by $\frac{1}{4}$, etc.

Dictate ten similar examples.

3. *Blackboard Drill.*

Put each of the preceding examples into the form of written arithmetic.

Models.

(1.) $\frac{1}{2} \times \frac{1}{4} = ?$
$\frac{1}{4} \div 3 = \frac{1}{8}$. *Ans.*

(2.) $\frac{1}{8} \div \frac{1}{2} = ?$
$\frac{1}{8} \times 3 = \frac{1}{4}$. *Ans.*

III. MENTAL OPERATIONS.

1. What is $\frac{1}{2}$ of $\frac{3}{4}$?   *Ans.* $\frac{3}{8}$.
2. How is the answer obtained?
   Ans. By dividing $\frac{3}{4}$ by 2, which is done by multiplying the denominator.
3. How many times is $\frac{1}{2}$ contained in $\frac{3}{8}$?   *Ans.* $\frac{3}{4}$ of a time.
4. How is this answer obtained?
   Ans. By multiplying $\frac{3}{8}$ by 2, which is done by dividing the denominator.
5. What is $\frac{1}{3}$ of $\frac{4}{5}$?   *Ans.* $\frac{4}{15}$.   Why?
6. What part of a time is $\frac{1}{3}$ contained in $\frac{4}{15}$?   *Ans.* $\frac{4}{5}$ of a time. Why?

7. What is the product of $\frac{2}{3}$ multiplied by $\frac{1}{3}$? *Ans.* $\frac{2}{9}$. Why?
8. What is the quotient of $\frac{2}{9}$ divided by $\frac{1}{3}$? *Ans.* $\frac{2}{3}$. Why?
9. Multiply $\frac{5}{8}$ by $\frac{1}{3}$? *Ans.* $\frac{5}{24}$. Why?
10. Divide $\frac{5}{24}$ by $\frac{1}{3}$? *Ans.* $\frac{5}{8}$. Why?

IV. MENTAL MULTIPLICATION.

Principle.—Multiplying by a fraction gives a product less than the multiplicand.

Rule.—Divide the multiplicand by the denominator of the multiplier.

Examples.

1. What is the product of $\frac{5}{8}$ multiplied by $\frac{1}{4}$? etc.
2. Dictate ten similar examples.

V. MENTAL DIVISION.

Principle. — Dividing by a fraction gives a quotient greater than the dividend.

Rule.—Multiply the dividend by the denominator of the divisor.

Examples.

1. How many times is $\frac{1}{4}$ contained in $\frac{2}{3}$?
2. What is the quotient of $\frac{2}{3}$ divided by $\frac{1}{2}$?
3. Dictate ten similar examples.

VI. SLATE AND BLACKBOARD DRILL.

Multiplication.   *Division.*

(1.) $\frac{5}{6} \times \frac{1}{4} = ?$ | (2.) $\frac{5}{24} \div \frac{1}{4} = ?$

$\frac{5}{6} \div 4 = \frac{5}{24}$. *Ans.* | $\frac{5}{24} \times 4 = \frac{5}{6}$. *Ans.*

Dictate twenty similar examples.

VII. MENTAL MULTIPLICATION.

1. What is $\frac{2}{3}$ of $\frac{4}{5}$? *Ans.* Since $\frac{1}{3}$ of $\frac{4}{5}$ is $\frac{4}{15}$, $\frac{2}{3}$ will be twice $\frac{4}{15}$ or $\frac{8}{15}$.
2. What is $\frac{3}{4}$ of $\frac{2}{3}$? Why?
3. Multiply $\frac{2}{3}$ by $\frac{2}{3}$.
4. Dictate twenty similar examples.

WORKING MODELS IN ARITHMETIC. 223

VIII. MENTAL DIVISION.

1. How many times is $\frac{3}{4}$ contained in $\frac{2}{3}$?
   Analysis.—Since $\frac{1}{4}$ is contained in $\frac{2}{3}$ 4 times $\frac{2}{3}$, or $\frac{8}{3}$, of a time, $\frac{3}{4}$ will be contained $\frac{1}{3}$ of $\frac{8}{3}$, or $\frac{8}{27}$ of a time.
2. What is the quotient of $\frac{4}{7}$ divided by $\frac{2}{3}$?
3. Divide $\frac{4}{5}$ by $\frac{2}{3}$.
4. What part of a time is $\frac{4}{7}$ contained in $\frac{2}{3}$?
5. Dictate ten similar examples.

IX. SLATE AND BLACKBOARD DRILL.

Multiplication.	*Division.*
Model.	*Model.*
(1.) $\frac{2}{5} \times \frac{2}{3} = ?$	(2.) $\frac{8}{15} \div \frac{2}{3} = ?$
$\frac{2}{5} \div 3 = \frac{2}{15}$.	$\frac{8}{15} \times 3 = \frac{8}{5}$.
$\frac{2}{15} \times 2 = \frac{4}{15}$. Ans.	$\frac{8}{5} \div 2 = \frac{4}{5}$. Ans.
Analysis.—Divide by 3 to find $\frac{1}{5}$, and multiply that quotient by 2, to find $\frac{2}{5}$.	*Analysis.*—Multiply by 3 to find how many times $\frac{1}{3}$ is contained, and divide that product by 2, to find how many times $\frac{2}{3}$ is contained.
(3.) $\frac{3}{8} \times \frac{4}{5} = ?$	(4.) $\frac{8}{15} \div \frac{4}{5} = ?$
(5.) $\frac{5}{9} \times \frac{3}{7} = ?$	(6.) $\frac{4}{7} \div \frac{5}{8} = ?$

Dictate ten similar examples.

X. WRITTEN MULTIPLICATION.

$\frac{2}{5} \times \frac{3}{8} = ?$ *Analysis.*—Since $\frac{1}{5}$ of $\frac{3}{8}$ is $\frac{3}{40}$, $\frac{2}{5}$ is 3 times $\frac{3}{40}$, or $\frac{6}{40}$;
$\frac{2}{5} \times \frac{3}{8} = \frac{6}{40}$ which process is equivalent to multiplying the two numerators together for a numerator, and the two denominators for a denominator.

Rule.—Place the product of the numerators over the product of the denominators.

1. $\frac{2}{5} \times \frac{3}{7} = ?$ 2. $\frac{5}{7} \times \frac{2}{3} = ?$

Dictate twenty similar examples.

XI. WRITTEN DIVISION.

1. Divide $\frac{2}{3}$ by $\frac{3}{4}$.

$\frac{2}{3} \div \frac{3}{4} = ?$ *Explanation.*—Multiply $\frac{2}{3}$ by 4 in order to find how
$\frac{2}{3} \times 4 = \frac{8}{3}$ many times $\frac{1}{4}$ is contained; and divide that result by
$\frac{8}{3} \div 3 = \frac{8}{27}$ 3 in order to find how many times $\frac{3}{4}$ is contained.

XII. METHOD BY INVERTING THE DIVISOR.

Analytical Model.   *Practical Model.*

$\frac{2}{3} \div \frac{3}{4} = ?$ $\frac{2}{3} \div \frac{3}{4} = ?$
$\frac{2}{3} \times 4 = \frac{8}{3}$ $\frac{2}{3} \div \frac{3}{4} = \frac{2}{3} \times \frac{4}{3} = \frac{8}{27}$.
$\frac{8}{3} \div 3 = \frac{8}{27}$. *Ans.*

Rule.—Invert the *divisor*, and place the product of the numerators over that of the denominators.

1. $\frac{7}{8} \div \frac{4}{9} = ?$ | 2. $\frac{5}{6} \div \frac{5}{7} = ?$ | 3. $\frac{9}{10} \div \frac{7}{8} = ?$

SECTION VII.—WORKING MODELS IN MENTAL ARITHMETIC, FOR GRAMMAR-SCHOOL GRADES.

Directions.—Read each question to the class, allow from one quarter to one half a minute for the mental solution, and require each pupil to write his answer on the slate. When the ten questions have been given, let pupils exchange slates, and credit the work as the teacher reads the correct answers.

SET I.

1. What is $\frac{5}{7}$ of 84?
2. How many times is $\frac{3}{4}$ contained in 6?
3. Divide $\frac{6}{12}$ by 4.
4. Multiply $\frac{2}{3}$ by 3.
5. Divide $\frac{1}{2}$ by $\frac{1}{4}$.
6. How many times is $\frac{3}{4}$ contained in $\frac{5}{7}$?
7. Multiply $1\frac{1}{2}$ by $1\frac{1}{2}$.
8. Divide $5\frac{1}{4}$ by $5\frac{1}{4}$.

9. Multiply the decimal .2 by .02.
10. Divide the decimal .2 by .05.

Set II.

1. How many times is $2\frac{1}{2}$ contained in 40?
2. What is $3\frac{1}{2}$ times 75?
3. How many times 6 inches is 50 feet?
4. Sum of $\frac{1}{2}, \frac{1}{4}$, and $\frac{1}{8}$?
5. Difference of $\frac{3}{4}$ and $\frac{1}{2}$?
6. 80 divided by $\frac{3}{4}$?
7. Sum of $\frac{2}{3}$ and $\frac{1}{4}$?
8. How many feet in 10 rods?
9. How many square inches in $\frac{1}{4}$ of a square foot?
10. How many acres in $\frac{1}{4}$ of a square mile?

Set III.

1. Bought a horse for $50 and sold for $75; per cent. of gain?
2. If you answer 5 questions out of 6, what per cent. do you make?
3. What is 300 per cent. of $\frac{2}{3}$?
4. If 10 is 5 per cent. of a number, what is 40 per cent.?
5. What is 500 per cent. of 25?
6. What is $\frac{1}{2}$ per cent. of 200?
7. At $12\frac{1}{2}$ cts. per pound, how much beefsteak can you buy for $80?
8. How many ounces in $4\frac{2}{3}$ lbs. of gold?
9. Find the product of $5 \times 4 \times 6 \times 0 \times \frac{1}{2}$.
10. $3 \times 4 \div 6 - 2 \times 5 + 2 \div \frac{1}{2} = ?$

Set IV.

1. Square the decimal .12.
2. Square root of 625?
3. Square root of .0625?
4. $28 is 175 per cent. of what?
5. Cube root of 1728?
6. Cube of 9?
7. Cube of .6?

8. Cost of 6¼ lbs. of beef at 12½ cents?
9. What part of 4 is ⅔?
10. What per cent. of ¼ is ½?

Set V.—Test Examination.

Time: One quarter of a minute to each question. Only the *answers* to be written.

1. $15 + 12 + 13 + 17 + 11 + 18 + 27 = ?$
2. $21 + 24 + 32 + 45 + 24 + 25 = ?$
3. Divide 18 by ⅔.
4. How many minutes in ⅔ of a day?
5. Cost of 1¾ yards ribbon at 20 cents?
6. 144 is 12/13 of what?
7. Prime factors of 144?
8. G. C. D. of 84 and 144?
9. L. C. M. of 8, 12, and 16?
10. How many tons in 5000 lbs. of iron?
11. Which is the heavier, a pound of silver or a pound of cotton?
12. Which is the lighter, an ounce of iron or an ounce of gold?
13. How many cubic inches in a gallon of water?
14. How many rods in ¾ of a mile?
15. What part of a square inch in a surface ¾ of an inch square?
16. Acres in ⅔ of a square mile?
17. Square of 1.2?
18. Square root of 1600?
19. Cube of 12?
20. Cube root of 125?
21. Cubic inches in a cube of wood whose edges are 8 inches?
22. Sheets of paper in a quarter ream?
23. Inches in the *meter?*
24. How many feet of board measure in a board 18 feet long and 16 inches wide?
25. Multiply 2.5 by 2.5.
26. Divide .25 by .0005.
27. Write in decimal form ¼ per cent.
28. 7 is what per cent. of 8?

29. Find 12½ per cent. of $1600?
30. What is the amount of $48 plus 75 per cent. of itself?
31. From $150 take 20 per cent. of itself.
32. $15 is ¾ of what?
33. $1500 is 75 per cent. of what?
34. What number plus ¼ of itself equals 30?
35. What number increased by 25 per cent. of itself equals 3000?
36. Bought butter at 25 cents, and sold at 30 cents; per cent. of gain?
37. Interest on $240 for 1 year 4 months at 10 per cent.?
38. Interest on $400 at 1½ per cent. a month for 21 days?
39. Cube root of the decimal .125.
40. Inches of surface on a cube whose edge is 10 inches.

Extra Questions.

1. Product of $2.00 by $5.00?
2. Divide $2.00 by $5.00.
3. $25 \times 4 \div 50 - 2 \times 10 \div 2 \times 5 = ?$
4. $10 \times 0 \div 2 + 4 \times 5 \div 2 = ?$
5. Which is the larger, ½ an apple or ⅓ a pear?

SECTION VIII.—WORKING MODELS IN THE TABLES.

I. LONG OR LINEAR MEASURE.

Note.—As introductory lessons, teachers must require pupils to measure with a rule the length of slates, books, desks, blackboards, rooms, etc.; to draw by the eye, and afterwards to measure lines of different lengths on the blackboard, as, 6 inches, 1 foot, 2 feet, 3 feet, etc.; to measure on the floor a rod in length, etc. Such exercises must be repeated and varied until pupils are trained to estimate length with some degree of accuracy. Pupils should also be taught how to make rough estimates by "pacing," by "hands," and by the extended arms.

TABLE.

12 inches (in.) = 1 foot (ft.).
3 feet = 1 yard (yd.).
16½ feet = 1 rod (rd.).
320 rods = 1 mile (mi.).

1. *Oral Questions.*

How many
1. Inches in 4½ ft. ?
2. Inches in 2¾ ft. ?
3. Inches in 1 yd. ?
4. Feet in 2 rods ?
5. Feet in 10 yds. ?

How many
6. Feet in 10 rods ?
7. Rods in half a mile ?
8. Rods in 2 miles ?
9. Feet in 10 fathoms ?
10. Feet in 33⅓ paces ?

2. *Slate and Blackboard.*

1. How many rods in 25¼ miles ?
2. How many feet in 40 rods ?
3. How many inches in 97½ feet ?
4. How many geographical miles in 180 degrees of longitude on the equator ?
5. From the north to the south pole the distance is 180 degrees. How many statute miles ?
6. How many statute miles in length is the equator ?
7. London is in 50° N. L.; how many statute miles from the equator ?
8. What part of a mile in 80 rods ?
9. How many yards in 3530 feet ?
10. How many rods in 2500 miles ?

II. SQUARE MEASURE.

1. Draw on slates a figure one inch square.

2. Draw on slates a figure 2 inches square, and divide it into square inches.

3. Draw a figure 12 inches long and 4 inches wide, subdivide into square inches, and count them.

4. Draw on the blackboard a figure 1 foot square, subdivide it into square inches, and count the squares.

5. Draw on the blackboard a figure 2 feet square, and subdivide it into square feet.

1. *Oral Questions.*

How many square
1. Inches in a figure 6 inches long by 4 inches wide?
2. Feet in a surface 9 by 4 feet?
3. Inches in a surface 12 by 6 inches?
4. Inches in a surface 16 inches by $\frac{1}{2}$ an inch?
5. Feet in a figure 20 by 6 feet?

Rule for Finding the Square Contents, or Area.

Multiply the number representing the length by the number representing the breadth, in the same denomination, and the result will be the square units of measurement.

TABLE.

144 square inches (12 × 12) = 1 square foot (sq. ft.).
9 square feet (3 × 3) = 1 square yard (sq. yd.).
272$\frac{1}{4}$ square feet (16$\frac{1}{2}$ × 16$\frac{1}{2}$) = 1 square rod (sq. rd.).
160 square rods = 1 acre (a.).
640 acres = 1 square mile.

2. *Practical Application.*

Teachers will require pupils to measure, and then find the square contents of—

1. The surface of a school desk.
2. Of the teacher's platform.
3. Of a door.
4. Of a window.
5. Of a blackboard.
6. Of the floor.
7. Of one side of the room.
8. Of one end of the room.
9. Of the ceiling.

3. *Oral Questions.*

1. How many square inches in $\frac{7}{12}$ of a square foot?
2. How many square feet in $4\frac{3}{8}$ square yards?
3. How many square inches in four square feet?
4. How many square inches on one side of a slate 12 by $8\frac{1}{2}$ inches?
5. On both sides of a book 6 by $3\frac{1}{4}$ inches?
6. On the surface of a desk 20 by 18 inches?
7. Square feet on the floor of a room 16 by $10\frac{1}{2}$ feet?
8. Square rods in a field 12 rods by $8\frac{3}{4}$?
9. Acres in 2 square miles?
10. Acres in $\frac{3}{4}$ of a square mile?

Teachers will require each pupil to put to the class a similar question.

4. *Slate and Blackboard.*

1. How many square inches on the surface of a desk $21\frac{3}{4}$ by 16 inches?
2. How many square yards on a floor 33 by $27\frac{1}{2}$ feet?
3. Find the square feet of surface on the ceiling and walls of a room 25 by 20 feet, and 14 feet high.
4. How many square inches of surface on both sides of a sheet of cap paper? Measure it.
5. How many square yards of painting on one side of a house 60 by 30 feet?
6. How many square feet of land in a lot $137\frac{1}{2}$ by $137\frac{1}{2}$ feet?
7. How many acres in 4640 square rods?
8. How many acres in 159,000 square miles?
9. How many acres in a piece of land 1250 rods long by 840 wide?
10. How many square rods in a square mile?

Teachers will dictate five similar questions.

SECTION IX.—THE METRIC SYSTEM.

1. The Metric System, the French system of weights and measures, is based on the decimal scale.

WORKING MODELS IN ARITHMETIC. 231

2. The *Meter*, the unit of the system, is the ten millionth part of a meridian measured from the equator to either pole.

3. The prefixes are:

For *Whole Numbers*. For *Decimal Parts*.

Thousands.	Hundreds.	Tens.	Tenths.	Hundredths.	Thousandths.
Kilo–.	Hecto–.	Deka–.	Deci–.	Centi–.	Milli–.
1000	100	10	.1	.01	.001

LONG OR LINEAR MEASURE.

The meter, the unit of length, is equal to 39.37 inches nearly. The decimeter is about 4 inches. Draw on the board a meter and a decimeter.

Teachers can make a meter correct enough for practical purposes by taking a stick $39\frac{2}{5}$ inches long, and dividing it into ten equal parts, and then subdividing each part into tenths.

Require each pupil to make one.

TABLE.

After each prefix supply the dash by the word meter.

Ten equals one of the next higher.

Prefixes .	Kilo–	Hecto–	Deka–	Meters.	Deci–	Centi–	Milli–
Meters ..	1000	100	10	1	.1	.01	.001
Number .	3^k	4^h	5^d	6^m	7	8	9

1. Practically, the preceding number, written below the table, is read thus: 3456 meters, $78\frac{9}{10}$ centimeters, and is written thus: 3456.789^m; just as we read 345 eagles, 6 dollars, 7 dimes, 8 cents, 9 mills, thus: $3456.78\frac{9}{10}$, three thousand four hundred fifty-six dollars, seventy-eight and nine-tenths cents.

The *dollar*, *dime*, *cent*, and *mill* correspond to the *meter*, *decimeter*, *centimeter*, and *millimeter*.

2. The meter (39.37 in.) is used for measuring short distances.

3. The kilometer (.6213824 mi., or about ⅝ mi.) is used for long distances.

4. Practically, then, this table is reduced to *meters* and *kilometers*, and their decimal divisions, just as our table of currency is practically expressed in dollars, cents, and decimals of the cent.

Practical Questions.

1. Write 18 meters, 2 decimeters, and 5 centimeters. *Ans.* 18.25^m.
   Note.—This may be read 18$\frac{25}{100}$ meters, just as we sometimes read 18\frac{25}{100}$ instead of $18 and 25 cents; or it may be read 18 meters, 25 centimeters.
2. Write 45 meters, 7 decimeters, 5 centimeters, 8 millimeters.
3. Write 85 kilometers, 9 hectometers, 7 dekameters, 6 meters. *Ans.* 85.976^k.
4. Read 3.008^m; 5.0095^m; 275.04^m.
5. Read 42.38^k; 147.3596^k; 4.05^k.

Slate and Blackboard Drill.

6. Mount Everest is 29,600 feet high; find its height in meters.
7. The Column Vendôme in Paris is 40.5^m high: Mount Everest is how many times as high?
8. Cost of 8.5^m of cloth at 5 fr. 40 c. a meter?
9. How many feet and inches in 15.25^m?
10. How many miles in 75 kilometers?
11. How many kilometers in the circumference of the earth — 25,000 miles?
12. The distance from New York to San Francisco, by rail, is about 3000 miles; how many meters?

GENERAL RULE FOR THE METRIC SYSTEM.

Measure all lengths in *meters*, all capacities in *liters*, all weights in *grams*, using decimal fractions only, and saying *deci* for tenth, *centi* for hundredth, *milli* for thousandth, *deka* for ten, *hecto* for hundred, *kilo* for thousand, and *myria* for ten thousand.

Chapter III.

WORKING MODELS IN GEOGRAPHY.

SECTION I.—GLOBE LESSONS FOR BEGINNERS.

Directions.—Place the school globe on the table in front of the class, and require the pupils, one by one, to go up to the globe and point out with the finger what is asked for by the teacher. If one fails to find the place called for, send up another, and so on round the class. Tell the children nothing that any one in the class is able to find out for himself. The German relief globes are the best suited to these exercises.

Lesson I.

1. What is the shape of the school globe?
2. Point out with your finger the parts that represent land.
3. Point out the parts that represent water.
4. Which is the larger, the land surface or the water surface?
5. Turn the globe round once: on what does it turn?
6. In what time does the real earth turn round, or rotate *once?*
7. How often does the sun rise and set?
8. Place your finger on the most northerly point on the globe: what is that point called?
9. Place your finger on the most southerly point of the globe: what is that point called?
10. Put your finger on the black line half-way between the two poles, and follow it all round the globe: what is it called?
11. Find the Pacific Ocean, and turn the globe so that the class can see it.

Lesson II.

1. Point out the Atlantic Ocean.
2. Find the Indian Ocean.
3. Point out North America.
4. Who can point out the land on which we live?
5. Find South America.
6. Find Asia, Africa, Europe.
7. Turn the eastern hemisphere towards the class.
8. Turn the western hemisphere towards the class.
9. Find and tell the names of as many large islands as you can.

Lesson III.

1. In what direction is the north pole from the south pole?
2. The south pole from the north pole?
3. The north pole from the equator?
4. The south pole from the equator?
5. North America from South America?
6. South America from North America?
7. Europe from Africa? Africa from Europe?
8. Asia from Australia? Australia from Asia?
9. In what direction is North America from Europe? Europe from North America?
10. Europe from Asia? Asia from Europe?
11. South America from Africa? Africa from South America?

Lesson IV.

1. Put your finger on Asia; on Europe: which is the larger?
2. Put your finger on North America; on South America: which seems to be the larger?
3. Which is the larger, North America or Europe?
4. South America or Asia?
5. South America or Africa?
6. Africa or Australia?
7. Africa or Europe?

Lesson V.

1. What is the southern point of Africa named? Of South America?
2. Point out and read the names of four large islands between Australia and Asia.
3. Which is the largest of these?
4. Find out the place where North America and Asia come nearly together: what separates them?
5. Which is the largest ocean?
6. Which is the longest and narrowest?
7. What small ocean around the north pole?
8. What ocean around the south pole?

Lesson VI.

1. Find the Amazon River, in South America.
2. Point out the Mississippi, in North America.
3. Find the Nile, in Africa; the Niger.
4. Find some great river in Asia.
5. Find the largest river in Europe.
6. Find any other river that you have ever heard of.
7. Put your finger on the globe where the Amazon seems to begin; follow it down to the ocean: in what direction does it flow?
8. In the same way follow the Mississippi, and tell its direction.
9. Follow down the Nile, and tell its course.

Lesson VII.

1. Find the longest range of mountains in North America; read the name.
2. Follow the range with your finger: in what direction does it extend?
3. Find the longest range in South America; follow it with your finger over its whole length: what is its direction?
4. Look at Asia; see if you can find the Himalaya Mountains.
5. Find the name of any other range in Asia.
6. See what mountains you can find in Europe.
7. In Africa.

Lesson VIII.

1. Find a sea between North America and South America.
2. Put your finger on a sea between Europe and Africa; name it.
3. Point out a sea south of Asia.
4. Put your finger on a sea north of the island of Borneo.
5. Find a sea between Asia and the Japan isles.
6. What long and narrow sea between Africa and Asia?
7. Find a sea north of Australia.
8. Find a great gulf south of the United States.
9. Find a great bay north of the United States.
10. Put your finger on a great bay south of Asia.
11. Find a gulf west of Africa, near the equator.
12. Find and name any other bay, gulf, or sea that you can.

SECTION II.—SECOND SERIES OF GLOBE LESSONS.

Lesson I.

1. Put your finger on the equator, and follow that circle entirely round the globe: in what direction does it extend?
2. Which point is at the greater distance from the equator, the north pole or the south pole?
3. Make up a definition of the equator.
4. Count the small circles between the equator and the north pole; the south pole.
5. There are 360° in a circle: how many degrees is it from the equator to the north pole? The south pole?
6. How many degrees from the equator is the first circle north of it? The second? The third? etc.
7. How many degrees south of the equator is the first circle? The second? The third? etc.
8. What is the use of these circles parallel to the equator?
   Ans. To show the distance of places north or south from the equator.

Lesson II.

1. Put your finger on London, the largest city in the world.

2. Passing near London, north and south, you see a heavily marked black line; follow it with your finger from the north pole to the south pole.
3. What part of the distance round the globe does this line extend?
4. Where does it begin and where does it end?
5. What is this half-circle called?
   Ans. The meridian of Greenwich.
6. See if you can find any other half-circles on the globe.
7. Beginning on the equator, at the meridian of Greenwich, count the half-circles eastward round the globe: how many?
8. Now read the figures on the equator where each of these half-circles crosses it: what is the first numbered east of the meridian of Greenwich?
9. What is the use of these half-circles or meridians?
   Ans. To show how many degrees places are east or west from the meridian of Greenwich.

Lesson III.

Note.—Teachers will now explain the use of the terms latitude and longitude.

1. You will look for the figures showing *latitude* on the meridian of Greenwich; put your finger on the place named, and then follow the parallel passing through or near that place around to the meridian of Greenwich. If you have a meridian globe, bring the place to the edge of the brass meridian. The degree over the place, counted *from the equator*, gives the latitude.
2. In what latitude is London?
3. In what latitude is the northern part of South America?
4. Cape Horn? Cape of Good Hope?
5. The mouth of the Amazon?
6. New York? Philadelphia? Cuba?
7. The Himalaya Mountains? The Isthmus of Suez?
8. For the figures marking longitude, look on the equator, put your finger on the place named, and follow the meridian passing through or near it to the equator, and read the figures.

With a meridian globe, bring the place to the edge of the brazen meridian; the degree on the equator, cut by this meridian, is the longitude of the place.

9. What is the longitude of Cape Horn? Cape of Good Hope?
10. Of Iceland? Of the mouth of the Amazon?
11. Of the Isthmus of Panama?
12. Of the mouth of the Mississippi?
13. Of the Gulf of Mexico?
14. Of the Caribbean Sea?
15. Of the Sandwich Islands?
16. Of the eastern point of Africa?
17. Of the western point of South America?
18. Of the Nile River?
19. What is the greatest latitude any place can have? Why? The greatest longitude? Why?
20. What places have no latitude? no longitude? Why?
21. Where is the place that has neither latitude nor longitude?

Lesson IV.

1. Point out, and follow with your finger around the globe, the dotted circle $23\frac{1}{2}°$ north of the equator; find its name.
2. Point out in the same way the dotted circle $23\frac{1}{2}°$ south of the equator: what is it called?
3. Add $23\frac{1}{2}$ to $23\frac{1}{2}$.
4. How wide is the equatorial, or torrid, zone?
5. Point out and name two large islands in this belt or zone.
6. Find two grand divisions principally within this zone.
7. What great river is entirely within this zone?
8. What important isthmus?
9. What ocean is mainly in it?
10. In what zone is the Niger River?

Lesson V.

1. Find a sea, a bay, and a gulf partly in this zone.
2. Find a sea wholly in this zone.
3. Point out on the globe the dotted circle $23\frac{1}{2}°$ south of the north pole: what is this circle named?

4. What great island does this circle cross?
5. What three grand divisions does it pass through?
6. Near what straits does it pass?
7. Find a dotted circle $23\frac{1}{2}°$ north of the south pole: what is it called?
8. The north temperate zone lies between the arctic circle and the tropic of Cancer; follow it around the globe with your two fingers, one on each circle.
9. Point out a great sea in this zone.

Lesson VI.

1. In what zone is our country?
2. In what zone are the Japan islands?
3. In what zone is London? Paris? New York? Boston? San Francisco?
4. Find the south temperate zone.
5. What great island partly in this zone?
6. Find two cities in this zone.
7. In which zone is Cape Horn? Cape of Good Hope?

Lesson VII.—Map Exercise.

Note. — After finishing the globe lessons, hang up an outline map of the hemispheres, ask as many of the preceding globe questions as are suitable for the map, and require pupils singly to point to the places with a pointer.

Section III.—Lessons in Local Geography.

Note for Teachers.—The following sets of questions are merely suggestive of extended lists to be asked by teachers:

I. First Steps.—The Schoolroom.

1. What is the part of the room over your heads called?
2. What is the part under your feet called?
3. How many sides has this room?
4. How many ends?

5. How many walls?
6. Point out the right wall; the left; the front; the back.
7. How many windows are there?
8. Where are they?
9. How many doors? Where are they?
10. What stand on the floor?
11. What hang on the walls?
12. How long is this room?
13. Measure it by stepping.
14. How many feet do you take in one long step?
15. How wide is this room?
16. Point to where the sun rises; sets.
17. Face north; south; east; west.
18. Where is the sun at noon?

II. LOCAL GEOGRAPHY FOR COUNTRY CLASSES.

Lesson I.

1. What is the name of the town or village in which you live?
2. In what county do you live?
3. In what State do you live?
4. Point to the place where the sun rises.
5. Point to the place where the sun sets.
6. Point towards the north; the south.
7. Point towards the east; the west.
8. In what direction is your home from the school-house? The school-house from your home?
9. How far from the school-house do you live?
10. How long does it take you to walk to school?

Lesson II.

1. Is there any river near your home?
2. Do you know the name of any brook near us?
3. Have you ever seen a spring? If so, where?
4. Have you ever seen a hill? Where? What is its name?
5. Is there any mountain in your town or vicinity? Its name?
6. What is the name of the highest mountain you have ever seen?

Lesson III.

1. What towns besides your own have you ever seen?
2. What towns lie next to yours?
3. Have you ever visited a city?
4. What is its name? And how did you travel there?
5. How does it differ from the place in which you live?
6. Do you know the names of any large cities in your State?

Lesson IV.

1. What farms or ranches do you know of near where you live?
2. What kinds of grain are raised on them?
3. What kinds of animals are raised on a farm?
4. How are they kept during the winter?
5. What are horses used for?
6. Why are sheep raised?
7. Why are cows kept?
8. What kinds of fruit are raised on the farms that you have seen?
9. How are butter and cheese made?
10. What kinds of trees grow in the woods or forests near where you live?

Lesson V.

1. Are there any saw-mills in your town?
2. What kinds of trees are sawed into lumber in them?
3. Are there any grist-mills or flour-mills in your town?
4. Are there any factories, mills, or machine-shops in your town?
5. Did you ever see a blacksmith's shop? Whose?
6. How do the people in your place earn a living?

Lesson VI.

1. Have you ever been a-fishing in any of the brooks, rivers, or ponds in your town?
2. What kinds of fish can you catch?
3. How do you catch fish?
4. Are there any mines in your town?
5. What is got from them?

III. LOCAL GEOGRAPHY FOR CITY CLASSES.

1. In what city do you live?
2. In what State is it situated?
3. In what county is it?
4. Is it a large city or a small one?
5. Is it on a bay, river, or lake?
6. What is the name of the principal street?
7. On what street is your school-house?
8. On what street is your home?
9. On what street is the Post-office? City Hall?
10. In what direction does the principal street extend?
11. Which way does the front of your school-house face?
12. What lies north of your city? South? etc.
13. What railroads, if any, pass through your city or terminate in it?
14. What city have you ever seen besides your own?

Add similar questions until all that the pupils know about their own city is exhausted.

SECTION IV.—CLIMATE AND THE ZONES.

[Introductory oral explanations by the teacher.]

Climate.—The climate of a place depends on the kind of weather that prevails there, whether hot, cold, or temperate.

Hot Climate.—That part of the earth lying near the equator has a hot climate. It is called the Torrid Zone.

Cause.—The cause of this hot climate is the fact that the sun's rays at noonday fall vertically, or nearly so, upon this part of the earth.

Boundaries.—The torrid zone extends $23\frac{1}{2}°$ on each side of the equator. Its boundary circles are the tropics.

Reason.—These circles are $23\frac{1}{2}°$ from the equator, because the earth's axis is inclined $23\frac{1}{2}°$ from a perpendicular to its path around the sun.

Seasons.—The weather in the torrid zone is a continual summer, there being but little change, except from the dry season to the rainy season.

Cold Climate.—Those parts of the globe that lie near the poles have a very cold climate, and are called the Frigid Zones.

Boundaries.—They lie between the poles and the polar circles. These circles are $23\frac{1}{2}°$ from the poles, because the earth's axis is inclined $23\frac{1}{2}°$.

Seasons.—There are only two seasons—a long and freezing winter, and a short, warm summer.

Reason.—The sun's rays fall slantingly, or obliquely, upon these parts of the earth.

Temperate Climate.—Those parts of the earth that lie between the tropics and the polar circles are called the Temperate Zones. These zones have four seasons; what are they?

Reason.—These changes of seasons are owing to the different way in which the sun's rays fall upon the earth at different times during the year.

The teacher will illustrate the effect of the inclination of the earth's axis by means of a globe revolving around a light.

SECTION V.—QUESTIONS ON LOCAL WEATHER CONDITIONS.

[To be given as a basis for conversation lessons.]

Set I.

1. In what country do you live?
2. In what zone is it?
3. In what months does the snow fall?
4. Name the three winter months.
5. The three summer months.
6. When are the days the longer, in summer or in winter?
7. In which month in winter are the days shortest?
8. In which month of the year are the days longest?
9. When are the days coldest?
10. When are the days hottest?

Set II.

1. At about what time does the sun rise and set in the shortest winter days?
2. In the longest summer days?
3. How long are the longest days?
4. How long are the shortest days?
5. How long are the longest nights?
6. How long are the shortest nights?
7. When is the sun more nearly over your head at noon, in summer or in winter?
8. When is the sun lowest down in the sky at noon, in winter or in summer?
9. When does the sun shine the hottest, at morning, evening, or at noon? Why?
10. Does the sun rise at the same point in the horizon in summer as in winter?
11. Does it set at the same point?

Set III.

1. In what seasons is it neither very hot nor very cold where you live?
2. What about the length of the days in spring and autumn?
3. At what time in the year do you have the most rain? The least?
4. How does your climate compare with that of the frigid zones? Of the torrid zone?

SECTION VI.—LOCAL STATE GEOGRAPHY.

[An exercise in general information.]

Set I.

1. Have you ever seen a farm or ranch?
2. Do you know any farmers?
3. What is the work of a farmer?
4. Are there many agriculturists in your part of the State?
5. Are there any manufactories in or near the place where you live?

6. What articles do they make?
7. Have you ever seen a woollen-mill? A cotton-mill? A shoe-shop? A machine-shop? A flour-mill? A saw-mill? A blacksmith's shop? A quartz-mill? A carpenter's shop? A printing-office?
8. Are there any traders or merchants in or near the place where you live?
9. What articles do they keep for sale?
10. What do they buy?

Set II.

1. Have you ever seen a gold-mine? A silver-mine? A coal-mine? An iron-mine?
2. What mines in your State do you know of?
3. Are there any fishermen near where you live?
4. What do they catch?
5. What kinds of fish have you yourself ever caught?
6. Are there any vineyards in or near the place where you live?
7. What is made on those vineyards?
8. How is wine made?
9. Are there any fruit orchards near you?
10. What kinds of fruit are raised?

Set III.

1. Are there any stock-farms, or ranches, near you?
2. What kinds of stock are raised on them?
3. Name any seaport cities in your State.
4. Name any manufacturing cities.
5. In what parts of your State are the best farms?
6. In what parts the richest mines?
7. In what parts the most extensive orchards or vineyards.
8. In what parts are there lumber-mills?
9. In what parts are the largest stock-ranches?
10. In what parts are the largest vegetable gardens?

Set IV.

1. What kinds of forest trees grow in your State?

2. In what parts are the largest forests?
3. What kinds of wood do you burn?
4. Of what kinds of wood is your house built?
5. Name all the kinds of trees that you have ever seen growing?
6. What wild animals are found in your State?
7. Which of these have you ever seen?
8. What birds live in your place?
9. Can you tell the names of any wild flowers growing in your place?
10. What kinds of fishes can you catch in your brooks, rivers, or ponds?

SECTION VII.—COMPOSITIONS ON GEOGRAPHY.

Read this to the class as a model. Let the pupils note on their slates the order of the "heads," and then reproduce from memory, dividing into paragraphs, but omitting the "headings."

I. THE NEW ENGLAND STATES.

1. [*Name.*]—The six Eastern States were named *New England* by the early English explorers and settlers.
2. [*Surface.*]—Along the Atlantic coast there is a narrow belt of lowland, but, in general, the country is either hilly or mountainous. The White Mountains in New Hampshire are noted for picturesque scenery.
3. [*Climate.*]—The winters are long and cold, and in the northern parts of this section snow falls to a great depth. The summers are short, but hot.
4. [*Lakes and Rivers.*]—In Maine and New Hampshire there are numerous small lakes, filling the depressions among the hills and mountains. The principal rivers are the Penobscot, Kennebec, Connecticut, and Merrimac; but there are a great many smaller streams that supply abundant water-power for manufacturing purposes.

WORKING MODELS IN GEOGRAPHY. 247

5. [*Sea-coast.*]—The long line of sea-coast has many deep and safe harbors that afford excellent facilities for commerce.
6. [*Forests.*]—The hills and mountains of the northern parts are covered with extensive forests, which supply great quantities of lumber.
7. [*Occupations.*]—The soil of New England is neither fertile nor easily cultivated. The leading occupations are manufactures, commerce, ship-building, and fishing.
8. [*Cities.*]—The largest city and chief business centre is Boston, which ranks in commerce as the second city in the Union. Among other important places are New Haven, Providence, Worcester, Portland, Lowell, Lawrence, and Manchester.

Exercises on Outlines.

Write short descriptions of the different sections of our country from the following outlines, slightly changed from the preceding.

I. *The Middle States.*—1. Name. 2. Surface. 3. Climate. 4. Lakes and Rivers. 5. Facilities for Commerce. 6. Occupations. 7. Mining. 8. Cities.
II. *The Southern States.*—1. Name. 2. Surface. 3. Climate. 4. Rivers. 5. Agriculture and Products. 6. Cities.
III. *The Western States.*—1. Name and Position. 2. Surface and Soil. 3. Rivers. 4. Agricultural Products. 5. Railroads. 6. Cities.
IV. *The Pacific States.*

II. GENERAL DESCRIPTION OF OUR COUNTRY.

Read to the class and require an abstract from notes.

Name.—Our country is called the United States because it consists of a number of States united into one nation, under one general government.

Rank.—It ranks as one of the most powerful, civilized, and populous nations of the globe.

Position.—It includes the middle part of North America, and extends from the Atlantic to the Pacific.

Mountains.—There are three great mountain systems—the Rocky, the Appalachian or Alleghany, and the Sierra Nevada.

Physical Features.—These mountain ranges make three great natural divisions—the Atlantic Highlands and the Atlantic Plain, the Pacific Highlands and the Pacific Slope, and the Valley of the Mississippi.

Rivers.—The Mississippi is one of the great rivers of the globe. Its chief branches are the Missouri, Ohio, Platte, Arkansas, and Red rivers. The other large rivers are the Columbia, the Colorado, and the Yukon, all of which flow into the Pacific.

Lakes.—Along the northern border there is a chain of great lakes which have an outlet through the St. Lawrence River into the Atlantic.

Occupations.—The Atlantic Slope is the manufacturing and commercial section; the Mississippi Valley the agricultural section; and the Pacific Slope the mining and grazing region.

Climate.—Our country, as a whole, has a temperate climate. The winters in the northern parts are long and cold; in the southern parts, mild and short. The Pacific Highlands have but little rain.

Products.—The farm-products in the northern belt are grain, fruit, and vegetables; in the southern, cotton, sugar, rice, and tobacco.

Mining.—The minerals of the Atlantic Slope are coal and iron, and coal oil, or petroleum; of the Pacific Slope, gold and silver; of the northern part of the Mississippi Valley, iron, lead, and copper.

Exports.—The leading exports are cotton, tobacco, breadstuffs, petroleum, and manufactured articles.

Cities.—The chief seaports are New York, Boston, San Francisco, Philadelphia, New Orleans, and Baltimore. The great inland cities are Chicago, St. Louis, and Cincinnati.

Capital.—Washington, in the District of Columbia, is the seat of government.

Government.—The government is a federal republic. Congress *makes* the laws; the President *executes* them; and the Supreme Court decides questions relating to the laws.

Exercise on Outlines.

Describe the following countries by filling up the outlines given:

 I. France.—1. Rank. 2. Agricultural Products. 3. Manufactures. 4. Exports. 5. Paris. 6. Other cities.
 II. The German Empire.—1. Government. 2. Surface. 3. Rivers. 4. Agriculture. 5. Cities.
 III. Empire of Russia.—1. Size and Rank. 2. Surface. 3. Rivers. 4. Seas. 5. Resources. 6. Commerce. 7. Cities.
 IV. The Chinese Empire.—1. Size and Population. 2. Products and Exports. 3. Cities. 4. People.
 V. Empire of Japan.—1. Position. 2. Products. 3. People. 4. Cities and Commerce.

SECTION VIII.—FACTS ABOUT OUR OWN COUNTRY.

Note. — Require all pupils in the grammar grades to copy these summaries into blank-books, and then to memorize them. Out of the mass of text-book details it is desirable to fix in the mind a few leading facts, so that they will *stay* learned.

I. PHYSICAL DIVISIONS.

1. The Mississippi Valley.
2. The Pacific Highlands and the Pacific Slope.
3. The Atlantic Highlands and the Atlantic Plain.

II. MOUNTAIN RANGES.

1. The Rocky.
2. The Alleghany.
3. The Sierra Nevada.

III. RIVERS.

1. Mississippi.
2. Columbia.
3. Yukon.
4. Colorado.
5. Rio Grande.

Chief Branches of the Mississippi.

1. Missouri.
2. Ohio.
3. Platte.
4. Arkansas.
5. Red.
6. Tennessee.

Rivers Commercially Important.

1. Mississippi.
2. Ohio.
3. Delaware.
4. Hudson.
5. Penobscot.
6. Potomac.

IV. BAYS COMMERCIALLY IMPORTANT.

1. New York.
2. Massachusetts.
3. San Francisco.
4. Delaware.
5. Chesapeake.
6. Mobile.

V. GREAT LAKES.

1. Superior.
2. Michigan.
3. Huron.
4. Erie.
5. Ontario.
6. Great Salt.

VI. CAPES NOTED IN NAVIGATION.

1. Sandy Hook.
2. Cape Cod.
3. Cape Hatteras.
4. Cape Sable.

VII. CHIEF SEAPORT CITIES.

1. New York.
2. Boston.
3. San Francisco.
4. Philadelphia.
5. Baltimore.
6. New Orleans.

VIII. CHIEF INLAND CITIES.

1. Chicago.
2. St. Louis.
3. Cincinnati.
4. Pittsburgh.

Five Largest in Population.

1. New York.
2. Philadelphia.
3. Brooklyn.
4. Chicago.
5. St. Louis.

SECTION IX.—FACTS ABOUT THE CONTINENTS.

[For the Highest Grades.]

THE OLD WORLD.   THE NEW WORLD.

CONTINENTAL DIVISIONS.

Three grand divisions.   *Contrast.*   Two grand divisions.

COMPARATIVE SIZE.

Twice as large as the New World.   } *Contrast.* {   One half as large as the Old World.

SHAPE.

Compact. Length and breadth nearly equal.   } *Contrast.* {   Long and narrow. Length three times the breadth.

GREATEST LENGTH.

East and west, 10,000 miles.   } *Contrast.* {   North and south, 9000 miles.

GREATEST WIDTH.

North and south, 7000 miles.   } *Contrast.* {   East and west, 3000 miles.

MOUNTAIN RANGES.

Extend east and west.   *Contrast.*   Extend north and south.

MOUNTAIN PEAKS.

Highest near the Tropic of Cancer.   } *Contrast.* {   Highest near the Tropic of Capricorn.

PENINSULAS.

Extend southerly.   *Similarity.*   Extend southerly.

THE OLD WORLD.		THE NEW WORLD.
SOUTHERN POINTS.		
Cape of Good Hope.	*Similarity.*	Cape Horn.
PLAINS.		
One third of the surface.	*Contrast.*	Two thirds of the surface.
PLATEAUS.		
Two thirds of the surface.	*Contrast.*	One third of the surface.
CLIMATE.		
Continental.	*Contrast.*	Oceanic.
MOISTURE.		
Scanty rains and great deserts.	*Contrast.*	Copious rains, great rivers and lakes.
LIFE.		
In the ascendant *Animal* life.	*Contrast.*	In the ascendant *Vegetable* life.
TYPICAL WILD ANIMALS.		
The elephant, rhinoceros, giraffe, lion, tiger, hippopotamus, and camel.	*Contrast.*	The buffalo, moose, grizzly bear, sloth, and llama.
NATIVE DOMESTIC ANIMALS.		
The horse, ox, sheep, goat, and hog; hen, duck, goose, and dog.	*Contrast.*	None except the dog and the turkey.
INDIGENOUS PRODUCTS.		
Wheat, barley, rye, oats, buckwheat, rice, pease, and beans; orchard fruits; garden vegetables; spices, silk, cotton, flax, hemp, coffee, sugar-cane.	*Contrast.*	Maize, potatoes, tomatoes, bananas, pineapples, tobacco, cocoa, mahogany.

THE OLD WORLD.		THE NEW WORLD.
	POPULATION.	
1300 millions.	*Contrast.*	100 millions.
	RACE.	
Less than half Caucasian.	*Contrast.*	More than half Caucasian.
	GREAT NATIONS.	
In the temperate zone.	*Similarity.*	In the temperate zone.
	GREAT CITIES.	
In the temperate zone between 40° and 50° N. L. London, Paris, Berlin, Vienna, Constantinople, Peking, Tokio, Liverpool.	*Similarity.*	In the temperate zone between 40° and 50° N. L. New York, Philadelphia, Chicago, St. Louis, Boston, San Francisco, Baltimore, Montreal.

SECTION X.—PHYSICAL FEATURES OF THE GLOBE.

Note.—Pupils in the highest class in a grammar-school ought to have the following leading facts:

1. GRAND DIVISIONS.

EASTERN CONTINENT.	WESTERN CONTINENT.
Asia, Africa, Europe. Twice the area of the Western continent.	North America, South America. Half the area of the Eastern continent.

2. OCEANS.

Pacific and Indian.	Atlantic.

3. CHIEF MOUNTAIN RANGES.

Himalaya, Altai, Alps.	Rocky, Andes, Sierra Nevada, Alleghany.

4. HIGHEST PEAKS.

Mt. Everest, Mont Blanc, Kilimanjaro.	Illampu [or Sorata], Orizaba.

METHODS OF TEACHING.

EASTERN CONTINENT.   **WESTERN CONTINENT.**

5. Highest Plateaus.

Thibet, Abyssinia, Iran.	Pacific Highlands, Mexico, Pasco, Bolivia, Quito.

6. Great Plains.

1. Russia. 2. Siberia. 3. Yang-tse-Kiang.	1. Amazon. 2. Mississippi. 3. La Plata.

7. Chief Rivers.

Yang-tse-Kiang, Lena, Nile, Congo [or Livingstone], Volga.	Amazon, Mississippi, La Plata, St. Lawrence, Columbia.

8. Chief Lakes.

Caspian (salt), Victoria Nyanza, Albert Nyanza, Aral (salt).	Superior, Michigan, Huron, Erie, Great Bear.

9. Ocean Currents.

Pacific Equatorial, Indian Equatorial, Japan Current, Australian, Mozambique.	Atlantic Equatorial, Gulf Stream, Greenland Arctic, Humboldt or Peruvian.

10. Chief Seas.

Mediterranean, China, Arabian.	Caribbean, Behring.

11. Bays and Gulfs.

Bengal, Guinea, Carpentaria.	Mexico, Hudson, Baffin.

12. Peninsulas.

Hindostan, Arabia, Malacca, Spain, Italy, Greece, Scandinavia.	Florida, Yucatan, Alaska, California.

13. Noted Capes.

Good Hope, Verd, Guardafui, North, Comorin, Palmas.	Cape Horn, St. Roque, St. Lucas, Farewell, Mendocino, Barrow, Race, Hatteras.

EASTERN CONTINENT. | WESTERN CONTINENT.

14. Largest Islands.

1. Australia. 2. Papua. 3. Borneo. 4. Madagascar. 5. Sumatra.	1. Greenland. 2. Newfoundland. 3. Cuba. 4. Hayti.

15. Most Important Island Groups.

1. The British Isles.	1. The West Indies.
2. The Japan Isles.	2. The Sandwich.
3. The East Indies.	3. Aleutian.

Section XI.—General Review Questions.

Note. — For high-grade classes. Dictate one set of five questions at the beginning of the week. Let the pupils hunt up the answers from their text-books, and take a written examination at the end of the week, or make the recitation an oral one.

Set I.

1. How is it supposed that the earth assumed the shape of an *oblate spheroid?*
2. Why are the tropics and the polar circles $23\frac{1}{2}°$ from the equator and the poles?
3. What circles on the globe would not exist if the earth's axis were perpendicular to the plane of its orbit?
4. If the rotation of the earth were to cease, what change would be made in the distribution of the water on the surface of the globe? What would be the effect on ocean currents.
5. What three motions has the earth?

Set II.

1. What are the two main causes of a difference in climate?
2. What are the causes of the unequal length of day and night?
3. How is the change of seasons caused?

4. What is the length of the longest day where you live? At the Arctic Circle? At the equator? At the north pole?
5. At what places on the earth is the sun ever vertical at noonday?

Set III.

1. How are trade-winds caused?
2. State the two chief causes of ocean currents.
3. Why is the climate of the western coast of North America milder and more uniform than that of the eastern coast?
4. Causes of the dense fogs that prevail off Newfoundland, the coast of Peru, and Alaska?
5. Cause of the excellent fishing-grounds at the Grand Banks and near the Japan Isles?

Set IV.

1. Name the five chief ocean currents.
2. Describe the Gulf Stream and the Japan Current.
3. What winds chiefly supply rain in the north temperate zone?
4. Why is the greatest rainfall in the tropics?
5. Where are glaciers found, and how are they produced?

Set V.

1. Name the two chief mountain ranges in each of the five grand divisions.
2. Name the highest mountain peak in each of the grand divisions.
3. Name five noted volcanoes.
4. Name the chief river of each of the grand divisions.
5. Name four great rivers flowing into the Arctic Ocean; four into the Atlantic; four into the Pacific; four into the Indian.

Set VI.

1. Name the four chief bays or gulfs in the Eastern hemisphere; four in the Western.
2. Name the four chief island groups in each hemisphere.
3. Name five noted capes in the track of commercial routes in the Old World.
4. Name five noted capes in the New World.
5. Name five rivers noted for great internal trade.

Set VII.

1. Name the five chief cities of the Old World; of the New.
2. Name four large cities in the Southern hemisphere.
3. Name the five chief seaports of the world.
4. Name the five great powers of Europe, and the three chief cities of each.

Set VIII.

1. Area and population, in round numbers, of France, Germany, and Austria.
2. Area and population of China, British India, Russia.
3. Population of each of the grand divisions.
4. Population of the world.
5. Population of the five great commercial cities of the globe.

Set IX.

1. By what three commercial routes can you travel round the world from London?
2. How can a grain-ship sail from Chicago to Liverpool?
3. How could you travel by water from Odessa to St. Petersburg?
4. What five cities would you pass on a steamboat trip from New Orleans to Pittsburgh?
5. How could you go from New York to Melbourne?

Set X.

Geography of our own country.

1. Area, population, and five chief cities.
2. Four physical divisions.
3. Five leading exports.
4. Five leading imports.
5. The five countries with which our commercial relations are most important.

Chapter IV.

LANGUAGE-LESSONS AND COMPOSITION FOR BEGINNERS.

Note for Teachers. — Notwithstanding the extent to which modern elementary text-books on language-lessons have been introduced, there are still many schools where there is nothing in the hands of pupils except the old-style text-book on grammar. The following models and exercises are intended mainly for teachers who have to prepare their own work from lack of a book in the hands of pupils.

SECTION I.—EXERCISES FOR BEGINNERS.

Direction.—Write a lesson on the blackboard, and let your scholars copy it on their slates or on paper. Then let them exchange, compare with the blackboard, and correct.

1. *The Golden Egg.*

There was once a poor man who had a goose that laid a golden egg every day. This man was getting rich very fast, but he wanted to become rich still faster.

So he killed his goose, expecting to find in her a whole nestful of golden eggs. He was rightly punished by finding none at all.

2. *Story of Grip.*

Grip was a good dog that went round the streets of a great city with a poor old blind man. Grip led his master by a string. He would hold the old man's hat in his mouth, and look wistfully at people as if he wanted to say, "Please give my poor old master a little money."

Grip was always true to his master. He often wanted to play with other dogs, but he never once, in all his life, ran away. When the old man could no longer go out of his room, Grip used to take his master's hat in his mouth and go out on the streets to beg for money, which he would joyfully carry to the helpless old blind man.

3. *How to Write Names.*

Rule I.—The particular name given to one person, place, or thing must begin with a *capital* letter.

EXAMPLES.

Persons. { George Washington.
           { Martha Washington.

Places. { London, Paris, Rome.
           { New York, Philadelphia.

Things. { Bunker Hill Monument.
           { The Pyramids.

In a similar manner write your own name; the name of your father and your mother, and the names of five of your schoolmates.

In a similar manner write—

1. The name of the place in which you live.
2. The name of your county and State.
3. The name of any State near yours.
4. The name of any river you know of.
5. The names of three men and three women that you know.

4. *Names of Persons.*

Rule II.—When only the initial letter of a given name is written, put a period after each initial. When a person has two given names, it is customary to write only the initial of the second or middle name.

Models. { Charles Henry Brown = *Charles H. Brown.*
          { James Knox Polk = *James K. Polk.*
          { Ella Maria Smith = *Ella M. Smith.*

In a similar manner write the following:

1. Your own name, your father's name, and your mother's.
2. The names of your brothers and sisters.
3. The names of five of your schoolmates.
4. The name of the President; of the Governor of your State; and of the Superintendent of Schools in your State, city, town, or county.
5. The names of five great men.

5. *Composition Exercise.*

Select one of the following subjects, and write all that you can remember of any story relating to it that you ever read or heard:

1. Story about a Dog.
2. Story about a Lion.
3. Story about a Bear.
4. Story about a Wolf.

6. *Composition Exercise.*

Write any story told to you by your mother or your father. Exchange and correct.

Note.—If it is possible for pupils to provide themselves with a small blank-book, it is a good plan to require the most interesting of the exercises to be copied into it; otherwise pupils should be required to preserve and file their exercises.

7. *Composition Exercise.*

Write a short account of your *last vacation;* stating where you went, what you saw, what you did, and what kind of a time you had.

Directions.

Begin each word of the heading of your composition with a capital—thus: "My Last Vacation." Begin each new sentence with a capital and end it with a period.

Exchange and correct the misspelled words, the mistakes in writing the word *I,* and the errors in the use of capitals.

8. *Criticism.*

Write the following child's composition on the board, and let the pupils criticise it:

MY LAST VACATION. [Sixth Grade, age 8.]

I had a very plesant time in vacation. I went to a picnick and i had a very plesant time, and i went to see the Forth of July to a ladies house, i did not go to the country.—*Louise.*

9. *Apostrophe and s* ['*s*].

Rule III.—When a noun denoting but one person, place, or thing is used to express ownership, the noun must be written with the apostrophe and *s* added—thus: Mary's book; the horse's mane.

EXERCISES.

Copy the following examples, and be careful to write the apostrophe and *s :*

1. I have Henry's slate, George's pencil, and Harriet's reading-book.
2. That is my father's horse.
3. My grandmother's pies are good.
4. I found a robin's nest in my father's orchard.
5. Everybody's business is nobody's business.

Rule IV.—When nouns denoting more than one person, place, or thing, and ending in *s*, are used to express possession, the nouns must be written with only an apostrophe added—thus: Horses' manes; birds' nests.

EXERCISES.

Copy the following examples:

1. My sister attends the Girls' High-school.

2. My brother goes to the Boys' Grammar-school.
3. The girls' compositions were very good.
4. The boys' papers were neatly written.
5. Ladies' shoes and men's boots.

Exercise.

Copy all the nouns denoting ownership from a reading-lesson assigned for this purpose.

10. *Sentence-making*.

Write with each of the following *nouns* a simple declarative sentence by using one *verb* to express the characteristic sound made by each of the kinds of animals named.

Direction.

Each sentence must consist of only two words. Each sentence must begin with a capital and end with a period.

Model Sentence.—Bees buzz.

Bees	Doves	Lambs	Peacocks
Bears	Ducks	Lions	Pigs
Bulls	Eagles	Mice	Robins
Cats	Flies	Monkeys	Sheep
Cows	Frogs	Owls	Snakes
Chickens	Hens	Oxen	Swallows
Dogs	Horses	Parrots	Wolves

Exchange exercises and correct one another's mistakes; then rewrite your corrected sentences.

Exercise.

Change each of the sentences that you wrote in the preceding lesson into an interrogative sentence; that is, one that asks a question.

DIRECTION.

Use only three words in each sentence. Each sentence must begin with a capital and end with an interrogation point.

Model Sentence.—Do bees buzz?

EXERCISE.

Change each of the sentences that you wrote in the preceding lesson into an exclamatory sentence; that is, a sentence expressing wonder or surprise.

DIRECTION.

Use only four words in each sentence. Each sentence must begin with the word *How*, and end with an exclamation mark.

Model Sentence.—How the bees buzz!

11. *The Cries of Animals.*

Make simple sentences by placing the name of the proper animal before each verb.

bray	caw	chirp	grunt
hum	bark	squeak	drum
drone	bay	cluck	croak
growl	howl	neigh	moan
bellow	yelp	whinny	twitter
mew	coo	chatter	growl
purr	quack	baa	gobble
bleat	scream	roar	snarl
pipe	buzz	squeal	sing
crow	croak	hoot	caterwaul
moo	cackle	screech	whistle
low	hiss	talk	

12. *Letter-writing.*

Require the pupils to write a short letter about their school to their father or mother.

CRITICISM.

Put the following first attempt, by a child nine years old, upon the blackboard, and let the pupils point out the mistakes:

My Dear Mamma
   I am a good girl in school And I know my lessons well. This is the first time I ever wrote a letter to you. And I want to write well. I like to come to school. And get my lessons well. We write on the blackboard with chalk and we draw. I am nomber fourteen in my class. I am going to try to get promoted by Christmas. I would like to get some Christmas presence If I can. Please exquse my writing as my ink was black.
                      Your affectionate child
                                  Emma

13. *Punctuation.—The Comma.*

Rule V.—When only two nouns, verbs, adjectives, or adverbs are joined by *and*, they are not separated by a comma; but when more than two are so connected, they must be marked off by commas.

Copy the following examples of the rule:

1. Men and women work in the mill. [No comma.]
2. Men, women, and boys work. [Use commas.]
3. Boys run and play. [No comma.]
4. Boys run, play, jump, skate, and slide.
5. The apples are large and red. [No comma.]
6. The apples are large, red, mellow, and sweet.
7. Hattie writes neatly and correctly.
8. Hattie writes neatly, correctly, and rapidly.

14. *Composition.*

Subject.—An Account of Myself.

Directions.
1. Begin every sentence with a capital.
2. Begin with a capital each word of the subject, except *of*.
3. Do not string sentences together with *ands*.

15. *Composition.*

Subjects.
1. How to set the table. [For girls.]
2. How to behave at the table. [For boys.]

16. *Composition.*

Write from memory a short sketch of any one of the following stories, selecting the one you like best. Teachers will pass the compositions to a higher grade to be corrected.

1. Tom Thumb.
2. Children in the Wood.
3. Robinson Crusoe.
4. Sindbad the Sailor.
5. Any one of Hans Andersen's Tales.

17. *Composition.*

Write a description of the school that you attend. Fill out the following outlines, making a paragraph out of each heading:

My School.—Outlines.

1. *Situation.* In what city or town, on what street, or in what part of the town or village.

2. *Building.* Large or small; of what material; color; number of rooms, etc.

3. *The school.* Number of classes or grades; number of scholars; names of teachers; in what class you are, etc.

4. *Studies.* State what you study; what studies you like best; and anything else of interest.

18. *Observation and Memory.*

I. Write an interesting anecdote or story about any one of the following:

    1. Dogs.   2. Bears.   3. Elephants.   4. Wolves.

II. Write what you know about *how* or *where* any of the following birds build their nests:

    1. Swallows.   2. Crows.   3. Woodpeckers.   4. Orioles.

III. Write what you know about how or where any of the following wild animals live.

    1. Foxes.   2. Rabbits.   3. Squirrels.   4. Deer.

IV. State where each of the following species of fish is found and how caught:

    1. Shiners.   3. Pickerel.   5. Mackerel.
    2. Perch.   4. Trout.   6. Cod.

19. *Wild Animals.*

Write a composition by answering the following questions about such of the following wild animals as live in your part of the country:

    1. In what places are they found?
    2. What do they eat, and how do they obtain their food?

    1. Foxes.   3. Rabbits.   5. Raccoons.
    2. Woodchucks.   4. Bears.   6. Squirrels.

20. *Domestic Animals.*

About the following animals write whatever you have observed that would lead you to think they know anything:

    1. Dogs.   3. Horses.   5. Cattle.
    2. Cats.   4. Hogs.   6. Sheep.

21. *Composition.*

Select one of the most interesting of the following subjects, and write about it the best story that you ever heard or read:

1. Dogs. 3. Wolves. 5. The Lion. 7. Ants.
2. Bears. 4. Horses. 6. The Elephant. 8. Bees.

22. *Composition.*

Write something that you yourself have observed about the actions or habits of any of the following animals:

1. Dogs. 3. Mice. 5. Crows. 7. Bees. 9. Squirrels.
2. Cats. 4. Rats. 6. Robins. 8. Swallows. 10. Foxes.

23. *Composition.*

Write all you know about *how* or *where* the following birds build their nests:

1. Robins. 5. Bluebirds. 9. Sparrows.
2. Swallows. 6. Bobolinks. 10. Humming-birds.
3. Crows. 7. Woodpeckers. 11. Nighthawks.
4. Larks. 8. Golden Robin. 12. Eagles.

24. *General Exercises.*

I. Write a letter to your father or mother, and then compare it with the first one you wrote.
II. Commit to memory, and then write, two stanzas of poetry, assigned by your teacher.
III. Write a letter to anybody you choose.
IV. Write the story of Jack the Giant-killer.
V. Write the story of Cinderella.
VI. Write all you can remember about the "house that Jack built."
VII. Write all you know about the trade or occupation of your father or mother.
VIII. Write about a visit to any of your friends or relatives.
IX. Write a letter to your teacher telling what you intend to do during your next vacation.
X. Write a letter to your doll, telling her how to write a letter to you. [For girls.]

Chapter V.

PRACTICAL COMPOSITION IN GRAMMAR GRADES.

1. *Special Directions.*

I. Avoid "fine writing."
II. Never use two words where one will fully express your meaning.
III. Avoid long and complicated sentences.
IV. Divide into paragraphs and punctuate *as you write*.
V. In correcting your first rough draft, observe the following order:
   (*a.*) Cross out any *adjectives*, or other words, that can be spared.
   (*b.*) Interline any omitted words, or transpose any words, phrases, or clauses to a better position in the sentence.
   (*c.*) Substitute more exact words whenever, by so doing, you can make the sentence clearer.
   (*d.*) Go over your composition very carefully, with reference to—1. Spelling; 2. Capitals; 3. Punctuation; 4. Grammatical correctness; 5. Dot your *i*'s and cross your *t*'s.
VI. Copy in legible hand-writing.

2. *General Principles of Sentence-making.*

1. Every sentence must be complete. It must contain at least one principal subject and one principal predicate, each of which must either be expressed or clearly implied.
2. Explanatory words, phrases, or clauses must be connected as closely as possible to the words which they explain or modify.
3. In simple sentences, be careful about the position of words and phrases; in complex sentences, about the position of clauses and the use of connectives; and in compound sentences, about the use of conjunctions of the *and* type.

4. When there are several adverbial phrases or clauses in a sentence, they should be distributed over the sentence, instead of being crowded together near the close.
5. Avoid writing long complex or compound sentences. It is better for beginners to write short sentences.
6. Use only words whose meaning you fully comprehend.
7. Express simple ideas in plain words.
8. Avoid the use of high-sounding adjectives and high-flown language.
9. Use only words enough clearly to express your meaning.

3. *The Paragraph.*

I. A paragraph is a closely connected series of sentences relating to the same subject, or to some particular part of a subject. Sentences are built up of words, phrases, and clauses; paragraphs are made up of simple, complex, or compound sentences. Composition consists of a succession of connected paragraphs.

II. The art of dividing a piece of composition into paragraphs is best learned by noticing carefully the paragraphing in your readers, histories, or other books; but the following directions may be of use to beginners:

1. In general, make a new paragraph whenever you make a new turn of thought.
2. Denote a new paragraph by beginning the sentence a short space to the right of the left-hand margin.
3. The sentences included in one paragraph should all relate to the same division of the subject.
4. The line of thought should be continued between paragraphs, if necessary, by some such connectives as *and, but, moreover, however, thus, at the same time,* etc.

I. NARRATION AND DESCRIPTION.

Select one of the following subjects, and write an account of where you went, what you did, and what you saw on that occasion. Describe events in the order of their occurrence:

I.

1. The Fourth of July.
2. Thanksgiving-day.
3. Christmas-day.
4. New-year's-day.
5. May-day.
6. My Last Holiday.

II.

1. A Picnic.
2. A Boat Excursion.
3. A Fishing Excursion.
4. My Longest Journey.
5. A Sleigh-ride.
6. My Flower-garden.

III.

1. My Pets.
2. My School and Teachers.
3. My Autobiography.
4. My School Troubles.
5. My Favorite Studies.
6. Housekeeping.

II. LETTER-WRITING.

1. Write a letter to some friend or relative, giving an account of your school-work.
2. Write a letter introducing your friend John Smith to John Brown.
3. Write a letter applying for a position as clerk or teacher.
4. Write an order to some bookseller for some books that you wish to buy.
5. Invite your friend to dine with you.
6. Write a letter of thanks for a present.

III. IMAGINATIVE LETTERS.

1. To Santa Claus.
2. To the Man in the Moon.
3. To Old Father Time.
4. To the Emperor of China.
5. To the author of any one of your school-books, criticising or commending his book.

IV. ABSTRACTS FROM MEMORY.

Read aloud to the class, and let pupils rewrite from memory.

The Ugly Duck.

Towards evening the little Duck came to a miserable hut where there lived an old woman with her Tomcat and her Hen. The Tomcat could arch his back and purr, and the Hen could lay eggs and cluck. They were both very proud of their accomplishments.

In the morning, when they saw the little Ugly Duck, the Tomcat began to purr and the Hen began to cluck. "Can you lay eggs?" said Mistress Hen. "No," said the Ugly Duck. Then the Tomcat, who was master of the house, said, fiercely, "Can you arch your back and purr?" "No," said the frightened Duck. "Then you must hold your tongue when sensible people are speaking," said Master Tomcat.

"I think I would like to swim," timidly said the little Duck. "Ask the Cat about it," said the Hen; "he is the wisest animal I know—ask him if he likes to swim."

"Ask the old woman," said the Tomcat, "there is nobody wiser than she is; ask her if she likes to put her head under water."

"You don't quite understand me," said the poor little Duck. "Don't be conceited," said both the Tomcat and the Hen, with one voice; "only learn to lay eggs and to purr."

EXERCISES.

Write from memory the story of—

1. Bluebeard.
2. Robin Hood.
3. Little Red Riding-hood.
4. Cinderella.
5. The Forty Thieves.
6. Aladdin.
7. A Fairy Tale.
8. Sindbad and the Diamonds.
9. Crusoe and Friday.
10. Crusoe and his Goat.

V. STORIES OF THE IMAGINATION.

Select from the following subjects the one that you like best, and write a story about it:

1. A Ghost Story.
2. A Witch Story.
3. A Fairy Story.
4. My Castle in Spain.
5. What I would do if I were Rich.
6. Autobiography of a Doll.
7. Autobiography of a Dollar.
8. Autobiography of a Spinning-wheel.

VI. SHORT DESCRIPTIONS OF TREES.

Fill out the following outlines:

I. *The Oak.*—Size; height; leaves; varieties or kinds; wood; hardness; toughness. Uses: ships; furniture; farming tools; fuel. Acorns; bark and its uses.

II. *The Pine.*—Where found; size; height; leaves; cones; varieties. Uses: buildings; furniture; ships; masts; fuel, etc.

EXERCISES.

In a similar manner write short sketches of such of the following trees as you have seen growing in your part of the country:

1. The Maple.
2. The Elm.
3. The Beech.
4. The Birch.
5. The Chestnut.
6. The Walnut.
7. The Spruce.
8. The Hemlock.
9. The Sycamore.

VII. METALS AND MINERALS.

Fill out the outlines with all you know about the following metals and minerals:

I. *Iron.*—Where found; how mined. Qualities: tenacity, hardness, etc. Kinds: cast; wrought; steel. Uses: machinery; kitchen utensils; implements; cutlery, etc.

II. *Gold.*—In what countries found; color and qualities. Uses: money; watches; jewelry; gilding; dentistry, etc.

III. *Granite.*—Where found; color; hardness; durability. Composition: quartz; felspar; mica. Uses.

Exercises.

In a similar manner, write all you know about each of the following:

1. Silver.
2. Lead.
3. Copper.
4. Coal.
5. Marble.
6. Sandstone.
7. Limestone.
8. Quicksilver.

VIII. MANUFACTURED ARTICLES.

Reproduce this model from memory:

A Dime.—A dime is a coin made from silver with which is mixed a small quantity of copper. It is coined in the United States Mint. The solid bars of silver, called *bullion*, are melted, refined, and cast into smaller bars, which are then rolled out into long, thin, narrow strips like ribbons. These ribbons are passed under a powerful machine, which cuts out the circular pieces of silver perfectly smooth. These smooth pieces are then stamped in a *die*, which gives them the ornamental impressions seen on a dime.

Exercises.

Write short descriptions of such of the following things as are made in your vicinity:

1. A Nail.
2. A Pin.
3. A Brick.
4. A Boot.
5. A Shoe.
6. A Horseshoe.
7. Cotton Cloth.
8. Woollens.

IX. GEOGRAPHICAL COMPOSITIONS.

My Native Place.

In your description use the following *outlines*, making a paragraph out of each heading. Mark a new paragraph by beginning the first line half an inch to the right of the left-hand margin. At home, ask your parents about what you do not know.

1. *Situation.* { Name of place; in what State and country; on what river, lake, bay, or other water; near what large city or town.

2. *Description.* { Size, population, trade, railroads, steamers, ships, mills, factories, farm-products, lumber, live-stock, etc.

3. *Special.* { Mention any objects of special interest, such as mountains, hills, forests, lakes, ponds, rivers, parks, gardens, buildings, etc. Close with any interesting event in the history of the place.

X. GENERAL EXERCISES.

I. Select your own subject, and write the best composition you can, being particularly careful about spelling, punctuation, and capitals.

II. Write a letter to a friend in the city, describing the appearance of the country at the time you write. [For country scholars.]

III. Write a letter to a friend in the country, telling what is going on in the city. [For city scholars.]

IV. Write a letter to your father, telling him what you have learned during the past year.

V. Composition.—"Our School Games."

VI. Composition.—"Going a-Fishing." [For boys.]

VII. Composition.—"A Fairy Tale." [For girls.]

VIII. Composition.—"How to Make Bread." [For girls.]

IX. My Best Story-book.

X. Write from memory the best piece of poetry you know.

XI. BIOGRAPHICAL SKETCHES.

Reproduce the following from memory, compare with the original, and correct errors:

1. *The Boyhood of Lincoln.*

Abraham Lincoln, the son of a farmer, was born in Kentucky in 1809; but his youth was passed mainly in Indiana. His father had chosen to settle at the farthest verge of civilization. Around him was a dense forest, still wandered over by the Indians. The next neighbor was two miles away. There were no roads, no bridges, no inns.

Abraham had little schooling. Indeed, there was scarcely a school within his reach; and if all the days of his school-time were added together, they would scarcely make up one year. His father was poor, and Abraham was needed on the farm. There was timber to fell, there were fences to build, fields to plough, sowing and reaping to be done. Abraham led a busy life, and knew well, while yet a boy, what hard work meant. Like all boys who come to anything great, he had a devouring thirst for knowledge. He borrowed all the books in his neighborhood, and read them by the blaze of the logs which his own axe split. He entered a small store as clerk, then became a lawyer, next a member of the Legislature of Illinois, and, finally, in 1861, he became President of the United States.

2. *Alfred the Great.*
[Adapted from Dickens's *Child's History of England.*]

This noble king possessed all the Saxon virtues. Misfortune could not subdue him, and prosperity could not spoil him. He was hopeful in defeat, and generous in success. He loved justice, freedom, truth, and knowledge. In his care to instruct his people, he did a great deal to preserve the old Saxon tongue. He made just laws for his people. He founded schools and appointed upright judges. He left England better, wiser, happier in all ways, than he found it.

Under his reign the best points of the English-Saxon character were developed. It has been the greatest character among the nations of the earth. Wherever the descendants of the Anglo-Saxons have gone or sailed, they have been patient and persevering. In Europe, Asia, Africa, America, the whole world over; in the desert, in the forest, on the sea, scorched by a burning sun, or frozen by ice that never melts, the Saxon blood remains unchanged. Wherever the race goes, there law, industry, and safety for life and property are certain to arise.

Write a short account of any one of the following persons whose biography you have read:

1. Benjamin Franklin.
2. Andrew Jackson.
3. James Watt.
4. Horace Greeley.
5. Sir Walter Scott.
6. Napoleon Bonaparte.
7. David Livingstone.
8. Alexander the Great.
9. Mary Somerville.
10. Mary Queen of Scots.
11. Florence Nightingale.
12. Empress Josephine.
13. Joan of Arc.
14. Charles Dickens.

XII. HISTORICAL SKETCHES.

In the two following sketches, adapted from Dickens's *Child's History of England*, take notice of the short, plain, pure English words that he uses. Reproduce from memory and criticise by comparing with the original.

1. *Reign of Queen Elizabeth.*

The reign of Queen Elizabeth was a glorious one. It is made memorable by the distinguished men that flourished in it. Apart from the great voyagers, statesmen, and scholars whom it produced, the names of Bacon, Spenser, and Shakespeare will always be remembered with pride and veneration by the civilized world. It was a great reign for discovery, for commerce, and for English enterprise and spirit in general. The queen was very popular, and, in her progresses or journeys about her dominions, was everywhere received with the liveliest joy. I think the truth is she was not half so good as she has been made out, and not half so bad as she has been made out. She had many fine qualities; but she was coarse, vain, capricious, and treacherous.

2. *The Great Plague of London.*

In 1665 the Great Plague broke out in London. The disease soon spread so fast that it was necessary to shut up the houses in which sick people were, and to cut them off from communication with the living. Every one of these houses was marked on the outside of the door with a red cross, and the words "Lord, have mercy on us!" The streets were all deserted, grass grew in the public ways, and there was a dreadful silence in the air. When night came on, dismal rumblings used to be heard in the streets, and these were the wheels of the death-carts, attended by men with veiled faces, who rang doleful bells, and cried, in a loud and solemn voice, "Bring out your dead!" The corpses put into these carts were buried by torch-light in great pits, without burial service. In the general fear, children ran away from their parents, and parents from their children. In four months more than one hundred thousand people had died in the close and unwholesome city.

Write a short sketch of any one of the following events, selecting the one that you like best:

1. Battle of Bunker Hill.
2. Battle of New Orleans.
3. Paul Jones's Sea Fight.
4. Settlement of Plymouth.
5. Settlement of Pennsylvania.
6. Settlement of your Native State.

XIII. NATURAL HISTORY SKETCHES.

1. *The Mosquito.*—This bloodthirsty insect is common to all parts of the globe. Its noisy buzz and sharp, stinging bite are familiar to all. It lays its eggs, several hundred in number, on the surface of stagnant water. They are glued together so that they float on the surface. In a few days the eggs hatch, and the *larvæ* come out into the water in the shape of *wrigglers*. These, after a life of two or three weeks, change to the *pupa* form, and float on the surface. In a week more the skin of the *pupa* bursts open, and a full-grown mosquito flies away into the air, hungry for blood.

2. *The Frog.*—What boy has not thrown a stone at a frog, and yet how few know anything about the wonderful transformations which this amphibious animal undergoes!

The frog begins life as a *tadpole*, or *polliwig*, hatched from an egg floating in the water. In this state it breathes, like fishes, through its gills. After several weeks it begins to undergo a *metamorphosis;*

that is, a change of form. Two hind-legs begin to grow out, like buds on a tree; then the fore-legs burst through the skin, and the tail dwindles away. The gills are slowly changed into lungs like those of air-breathing animals. The *tadpole* has become a land-animal, living on insects and worms.

Exercises.

Write what you know about the following insects. Exchange and correct; then read aloud in the class:

1. The Butterfly.
2. The Silk-worm.
3. The Bumblebee.
4. The Honey-bee.
5. The Wasp.
6. The Hornet.
7. The House Fly.
8. The Grasshopper.
9. The Ant.
10. The Cricket.

Chapter VI.

WORKING MODELS IN SENTENCE-MAKING.

Note for Teachers.—Many of the exercises given in this chapter do not differ materially from those found in most modern text-books on language-lessons and grammar. But, whatever text-book is used, the teacher needs to supplement it with additional exercises and illustrations. Particular attention is called to the oral exercises under the head of "The Complex Sentence."

SECTION I.—THE SIMPLE SENTENCE.

1. A simple sentence consists of one subject combined with one predicate, making one statement.
2. The *subject* of a sentence consists of a noun, or one or more words filling the place of a noun, about which a statement is made.
3. The *predicate* expresses a statement about the subject, and consists of a verb, or of a verb united with one or more words added to complete the statement.

1. *The Subject.*

The *subject* of a simple sentence may be:

Subject.	Predicate.
1. Children (noun)	play.
2. They (pronoun)	play.
3. To play (infinitive)	is pleasant.
4. Playing in the fields (phrase)	is pleasant.

Exercise.

Write three sentences similar to 1; three similar to 2; to 3; to 4. Exchange and correct errors in spelling, punctuation, capitals, and construction.

2. *The Predicate.*

The *predicate* of a simple sentence may be:

Subject.	Predicate.
1. Scholars	study (verb only).
2. Bees	make honey (verb and object).
3. Roses	are sweet (verb and adjective).
4. Ants	are insects (verb and noun).
5. We	expect to go (verb and infinitive object).

Exercise.

Write two sentences similar to 1; two similar to 2; to 3; to 4; to 5. Exchange, report, and correct.

3. *Sentence-making.*

Write, with each of the following nouns for a subject, a sentence having a predicate consisting of the verb *is* with a noun in the predicate nominative:

Model.—Arabia is a peninsula.

1. The earth.	4. Italy.	7. Russia.	10. Arizona.
2. Greenland.	5. The United States.	8. Germany.	11. Vesuvius.
3. Arabia.	6. New York.	9. Australia.	12. The Sahara.

4. *Sentence-making.*
Exercise I.

With each of the following nouns write the verb *is* or *are* and a noun in the predicate nominative:

Model.—The bee is an insect.

1. The bee.	4. Horses.	7. Iron.	10. Potatoes.
2. The snake.	5. Robins.	8. Water.	11. Apples.
3. The oyster.	6. Hens.	9. Coal.	12. Wheat.

Exercise II.

With each of the preceding nouns put a predicate adjective, instead of a predicate nominative.

Model.—The bee is busy.

Exercise III.

Make a sentence with each of the nouns under 4 by stating that each *does* something.

Model.—The bee makes honey.

5. *The Enlarged Subject.*

The subject may be enlarged in various ways—thus:

Subject Enlarged.	Predicate.
1. The *cunning* fox (adjective)	was caught.
2. The *lion's* roar (possessive case)	is terrible.
3. The roar *of the lion* (phrase)	is terrible.
4. Brown the tailor (apposition)	is honest.
5. Learning to spell (infinitive)	is hard.

Exercise I.

Write a sentence with each of the possessive enlargements of the subject:

Model.—The birds' nests were found.

1. The birds'
2. The parrot's
3. The ladies'
4. The girls'
5. The earth's
6. The sun's
7. The moon's
8. The men's
9. Our teacher's
10. The sheep's
11. James's
12. Charles's

Exercise II.

Change each of the sentences that you wrote under the preceding exercise into a sentence with an adjective phrase, similar to 3.

Model.—The nest of the birds was built in the tree.

Exercise III.

With each of the following nouns write a sentence having a noun in apposition:

Model.—Dickens, the great novelist, is dead.

1. Smith
2. Milton
3. Dickens
4. Burns
5. Whittier
6. Fulton
7. Washington
8. Cicero
9. Daniel Webster

Exercise IV.

With each of the preceding nouns write a sentence having the verb *is* or *was* and a predicate nominative.

Model.—Dickens was a great novelist.

Exercise V.

With each of the following nouns write a sentence having the subject enlarged by an adjective phrase:

Model.—The flowers of the field are beautiful.

1. The flowers
2. The birds
3. The squirrels
4. The corn
5. The mice
6. The wood
7. The snow
8. The ice
9. The study

6. *The Predicate Enlarged.*

The predicate of a simple sentence may be enlarged in various ways—thus:

Subject.	Predicate Enlarged.
1. The sun	shines *brightly* (adverb).
2. The birds	sing *in the morning* (adverbial phrase).
3. The teacher	assigned *difficult* lessons (adjective).
4. We visited	the capital *of the United States* (adjective phrase).
5. The weather	is *exceedingly* cold (adverb).
6. London	is the *largest* city *on the globe* (adjective and adj. phrase).

Exercise I.

Write with each of the following subjects a sentence having the predicate nominative enlarged by an adjective and an adjective phrase:

Model.—The Amazon is the largest river on the globe.

1. The Amazon
2. The Mississippi
3. Mt. Everest
4. Paris
5. New York
6. Boston
7. The Pacific
8. Russia
9. The Nile

Exercise II.

Complete the following sets of sentences by adding adverbial phrases that answer the questions *where? when? how?* Ask your parents about anything you do not know.

Model.—Cotton grows [where?] in the Southern states.

1. Birds fly
2. Coffee grows
3. Tea grows
4. The Missouri rises
5. We export grain
6. Silk is obtained
7. Gold is found
8. Coal is found

Exercise III.

Model.—Plymouth was settled [when?] in 1620.

1. Plymouth was settled
2. Jamestown was settled
3. America was discovered
4. My birthday will come
5. Independence was declared
6. Our school began

Exercise IV.

Model.—We travelled [how?] by rail.

1. We travelled
2. We write
3. The rain fell
4. The soldiers fought
5. They treated us
6. America was discovered

Exercise V.—Adverbial Phrases of Cause.

Complete the following sentences by adding phrases denoting cause, making use of the prepositions *by, through, for, of, from,* etc. :

Model.—Waves are caused by winds.

1. Day and night
2. The seasons are caused
3. They perished
4. He suffered
5. The money was given
6. He became sick

Exercise VI.—Adverbial Phrases of Purpose.

In completing the following sentences, make use of the prepositions or phrases such as *for, in order to, for the purpose of, for the sake of;* or of an *infinitive.*

Models.—1. We eat to live. 2. We eat for pleasure.

1. We live
2. We went
3. They study
4. The boys ran away
5. They went to Europe
6. He went to California

7. *The Enlarged Predicate Again.*

In a simple sentence the predicate may be enlarged by two or more phrases — thus: "We went (1) into the woods (2) with a gun."

Exercises.

Complete the following expressions by adding two or more phrases. Exchange and correct:

1. The sun rises
2. The brook is running
3. I was born
4. I live
5. The Amazon flows
6. The steamer sailed

8. *Order of Phrases.*

When a sentence contains two or more adverbial

phrases, one of them may be used to introduce the sentence — thus: *In the winter of 1812,* Napoleon invaded Russia *with a great army.*

9. *Punctuation of Introductory Phrases.*

Rule. — Introductory adverbial phrases, unless very short, are pointed off by a comma.

EXERCISES.

Complete and punctuate the following:

1. In the winter of 1620, Plymouth
2. In the year 1607, Jamestown
3. In the year 1492,
4. On the Fourth of July, 1776,

10. *Emphatic Order.*

If we wish to make a phrase emphatic, we place it first in order in the sentence.

ILLUSTRATIONS.

1. With a small detachment, Arnold and Allen captured Ticonderoga.
2. Of the laboring classes we know little.
3. With the deepest interest we watched the combat.

11. *Order of Parts.*

1. The common or grammatical order of the main parts of a simple declarative sentence is as follows:

(1.)	(2.)	(3.)	(4.)
Adjective.	*Subject.*	*Predicate.*	*Adverb or Adverbial Phrase.*
Huge	whales	swim	in the ocean.

2. Interrogative sentences are introduced by the helping verbs *be, do, may, can, must, shall, will, have,* etc., and the subject comes

between the helping verb and the principal verb; as, *Do you hear?*

3. The neuter verb *to be*, denoting present or past time, comes first in interrogative sentences; as, *Is* he sick?
4. Exclamatory sentences are introduced by such words as *how* and *what;* as, *How* beautiful is the rain! *What* a hot day it is!
5. In imperative sentences, the verb is placed first, and the subject is, in general, understood; as, Go [you] into the house.

In poetry the grammatical order is often inverted.

Exercise I.

Change into interrogative sentences:

1. We are going to-morrow.
2. We shall start in the morning.
3. He was doing wrong.

Exercise II.

Change into interrogative from imperative:

1. Give me an apple.
2. Obey your parents.
3. Let me go with you.

Exercise III.

Change into declarative sentences:

1. How wonderful is death!
2. How cold you look!
3. What great eyes you have!
4. What a piece of work is man!
5. How like a fawning publican he looks!
6. What a charming prospect!

Exercise IV.

Change into the grammatical order of the prose sentence:

1. Sweet is the voice of spring.

2. Westward the course of empire takes its way.
3. In their ragged regimentals
Stood the old Continentals.
4. Beneath her torn hat glowed the wealth
Of simple beauty and rustic health.

12. *Idiomatic "There."*

In many English sentences the word *there* is used to introduce the sentence, the subject coming after the verb.

EXERCISES.

Change the following sentences into the more elegant form introduced by *there:*

1. A man is in the house.
2. Plenty of money is in the market.
3. No mercy is in his heart.
4. No terror is in your threats.
5. No luck is about the house.

SECTION II.—THE COMPLEX SENTENCE.

1. *Oral Exercise.—Conjunctions.*

Teachers will require each pupil, in turn, around the class, to make up an oral sentence containing the conjunction *if;* such a sentence *must* be *complex*. In the same manner require each pupil to compose a sentence with *though;* with *because, that, than, as*.

Models.
1. If you go, I will go too.
2. I was absent, *because* I was sick.
3. She said *that* she would stay.
4. I am older *than* you are.
5. I will do *as* you direct.

2. Oral Exercise.—Relative Pronouns.

Require each pupil, in turn, to compose an oral sentence containing the relative pronoun *who;* a sentence with *which,* with *what,* with *that.*

Direction.

Make only *declarative* sentences. Interrogative sentences may be simple sentences. Do not use any one of the co-ordinate conjunctions, *and, but, or, nor,* because the sentence would then become *compound.*

Models.
1. The man *who* was sick is dead.
2. I know *who* stole the apples.
3. The horse *which* I bought ran away.
4. I know *what* you want.
5. I go to the same school *that* you do.

3. The Relative "That."

1. The word *that* is a difficult part of speech to deal with, because it has a variety of uses; as,
    1. He said *that* I was wrong [subordinate conjunction].
    2. Please give me *that* book [adjective].
    3. *That* is my father's house [adjective pronoun].
    4. He is the same man that you spoke of [relative pronoun].
2. *That* is correctly used as a relative pronoun instead of *who* or *which*—
    1. After the adjective *same.*
    2. After an adjective in the superlative degree.
    3. To prevent the repetition of *who.*

Illustrations.

1. This is the *same* lesson *that* we had yesterday.
2. He is the *tallest* man *that* I ever saw.
3. It is not always the person who [that] knows most who makes the best teacher.

Exercise.

Require each pupil to compose an oral sentence similar to 1; to 2; to 3.

4. *Oral Exercise.—Relative Adverbs.*

Let each pupil, in turn, compose an oral sentence with each of the following relative adverbs: *when; where; why; how.*

Direction.

Do not make an interrogative sentence, because the adverbs would then become *interrogative* instead of *relative*, and the sentence might be a *simple* sentence.

1. I will go *when* you are ready.
2. We do not know *where* he is.
3. Tell me *why* you are sad.
4. I know *how* you got it.

Leading signs of the complex sentence:

1. If, because, than, that, as [subordinate conjunctions].
2. Who, which, what, that [relative pronouns].
3. When, where, why, while, how [relative adverbs].

Require pupils to write, with each of the signs, a complex sentence. Pupils will exchange papers and correct under the direction of the teacher.

Note.—That, as a conjunction, is used to introduce objective clauses after such transitive verbs as *see, hear, feel, think, wish, hope, fear, ask, say, tell, state, report, deny, direct,* etc.

5. *Order of Parts.*

The grammatical order of elements in the complex sentence is like that of the simple sentence, except that the *clause* takes the place of the *phrase*. Thus:

1. *Subject;* 2. *Adjective Clause;* 3. *Predicate;* 4. *Adverbial Clause.*

Point out the parts in the following sentences:

1. The swallows that live in the old barn migrate when winter comes.
2. The boys whom we met said they were going home.
3. The man who lost his horse rewarded the boy that found it.

6. The subject of a complex sentence may be a *clause.* Thus:
   1. [He] *Who steals my purse* steals trash.
   2. [The time] *When he will go* is uncertain.
   3. [The fact] That you have wronged me doth appear in this.

Note. — Sentences like the preceding are really contracted complex sentences, as will be seen above where the subjects of the principal verbs are supplied in brackets.

7. The predicate may consist of a neuter verb and a noun-clause as the complement, or predicate nominative.
   1. The truth is, he knew nothing about it.
   2. His excuse was that he was poor.
   3. It is uncertain when he will go.

8. *Emphatic It.*

The use of the pronoun *it* to introduce a sentence by standing for a *clause* after the predicate makes a statement emphatic, and changes a simple into a complex sentence.

Simple.	*Complex.*
1. Columbus discovered America.	1. It was Columbus who discovered America.
2. Cæsar conquered Britain.	2. It was Cæsar who conquered Britain.
3. Whitney invented the cotton-gin.	3. It was Whitney who invented the cotton-gin.
4. Washington planned the campaign of Yorktown.	4. It was Washington who planned the campaign of Yorktown.
5. He did it.	5. It was he who did it.

EXERCISE.

Change the following *complex* into simple sentences without *it:*

1. It was in the age of Greece that the seeds of civil strife were sown.
2. It was the Portuguese who took the lead in maritime discovery.
3. It is the brilliant figure of Spain that first attracts our attention at the beginning of modern history.
4. It was in midwinter that the Pilgrims landed at Plymouth.
5. It was Cromwell who said, "Paint me as I am, with all my warts and wrinkles."

9. *Conditional Clauses.*

Clauses of condition or concession are generally placed before the principal statement in order to add force to the expression.

APPLICATION.

Copy the following sentences, and notice that the conditional clauses are marked off by a comma:

1. If he did that, he ought to be punished.
2. Though you have injured me, I will forgive you.
3. Where you go, I will go too.
4. When you are ready, we will start.
5. How you can talk so, I do not understand.

10. *Forms of the Complex Sentence.*

I. ADVERBIAL CLAUSES.

Copy and punctuate the following, and state which are the clauses:

Condition.—If you do wrong, you will suffer.
Concession.—Though he is guilty, he will escape.
Purpose.—He ran away, that he might go to sea.

Cause.—He prospers because he is industrious.
Effect.—You speak so loud that you disturb me.
Manner.—You walk as if you were tired.
Comparison.—The water is colder than ice [is].
" The ice was clear as glass [is].
Place.—I will go where you do.
Time.—Go when you are called.

II. NOUN CLAUSES.

State the use of each clause, whether as *subject, object*, or predicate nominative after a neuter or passive verb:

1. That the earth is globe-shaped has been proved.
2. My reason is, I am tired.
3. Is it true that the moon is made of green cheese?
4. Where the Indians came from is not known.
5. How it was done is a mystery.
6. Who he was nobody knows.
7. "Why do you eat my grass?" said the Wolf.
8. "What long arms you have!" said she to the Wolf.
9. He said that he would try.
10. "I'll try, sir," said the brave boy.

III. ADJECTIVE CLAUSES.

Point out each adjective or relative clause, and tell what it limits:

1. Franklin, *who* invented lightning-rods, was an American.
2. The snow, *which* fell to a great depth, blocked up the railroads.
3. He is the oldest man *that* I ever knew.
4. The time *when* [= at which] we shall start is uncertain.
5. The reasons *why* [= for which] he went are unknown.
6. The place *where* [= in which] he lives is very beautiful.
7. The ship *in which* they sailed was lost at sea.
8. This is the boy *whose* lesson was perfect.
9. It is the most wonderful story that I ever heard of.
10. This is the cow *that* worried the dog *that* killed the cat, etc.

Write a sentence similar to each of the preceding sentences. Exchange and correct.

11. *Contracted Complex Sentences.*

The *clause* in the complex sentence is sometimes contracted by an ellipsis of the verb, the subject, or both verb and subject.

APPLICATION.

Orally, in the class, point out the ellipsis, and explain the punctuation of the conditional clauses:

1. That house, when [it is] finished, will be the finest in the city.
2. If you go, [it is] well; if [you do] not [go], I must go alone.
3. If [it is] required, the money will be furnished.
4. Though [it was] cold, the day was glorious.
5. While [we were] going to New York, we met an old friend.
6. No wind that blew was bitterer than he [was].

SECTION III.—THE COMPOUND SENTENCE.

1. *Oral Introduction.*

Teachers will require each pupil, in turn, to compose an oral sentence which shall contain the co-ordinate conjunction *and*.

Model.—I shall go to-morrow, and you must go with me.

Teachers' Note.—Sentences containing *and* will, in general, be compound, or contracted compound, sentences. The few exceptions must be explained when given by pupils.

EXERCISE.

In a similar manner each pupil, in turn, will compose a compound sentence containing *but;* one containing *or;* one with *nor;* one with *either—or;* one with *neither—nor*.

2. *Exercise in Writing.*

A compound sentence consists of two or more principal statements connected by a co-ordinate conjunction, either expressed or understood.

Leading Signs of a Compound Sentence.

Co-ordinate Conjunctions. { *and; or; either—or; both—and. but; nor; neither—nor; and—then.*

With each of the preceding signs write two compound sentences.

3. *Contracted Compound Sentences.*

Study the changes made in the following sentences, and tell *how* they are made:

Full Compound.	*Contracted Compound.*
1. I can read, and I can write.	1. I can read and write.
2. You must go, or I must go.	2. You or I must go.
3. Mary sings, and Jane sings too.	3. Both Mary and Jane sing.
4. The water is deep, and it is cold.	4. The water is deep and cold.
5. You must not go, and he must not go.	5. Neither you nor he must go.
6. They fought for their country, and they died for their country.	6. They fought and died for their country.
7. I care not when you go, nor do I care how you go.	7. I care not when or how you go.

BLACKBOARD SYNOPSIS FOR REVIEW.

The Sentence......... { Simple. Complex. Compound.

The Simple Subject. { Word: noun or pronoun. Phrase: verbal noun. Clause: dependent statement.

The Simple Predicate. { Intransitive verb.
Transitive verb and object.
Neuter verb and complement.

Subject Modifiers........ { Adjective: word, phrase, clause.
Nouns in apposition, with their adjective modifiers.

Predicate Modifiers.... { Object: words, phrases, clauses.
Adverbial: words, phrases, clauses.

Connectives............... { *Simple Sentence.*—Prepositions.
Complex Sentence.—Subordinate conjunctions, relative pronouns, and relative adverbs.
Compound Sentence. — Co-ordinate conjunctions.

SECTION IV.—EXAMINATION QUESTIONS IN LANGUAGE-LESSONS AND GRAMMAR.

Note.—The following sets of questions are given as suggestive models of practical questions to be used in oral or in written examinations:

I. SECOND SCHOOL YEAR.

1. I. Write your own name. II. The name of your teacher. III. The name of your father. IV. The name of the place in which you live.
2. Write five sentences by telling what the following animals *do:* I. Dogs. II. Cats. III. Horses. IV. Birds. V. Flies.
3. Write five interrogative sentences by asking questions about— I. Fishes. II. Lions. III. Boys. IV. Girls.
4. Make sentences out of—I. My mother. II. My father. III. My teacher. IV. My home.
5. Write the correct form of these incorrect sentences: I. I seen him do it. II. I done the sum wrong. III. 'Tain't right. IV. Ain't you going? Her and me are going.

II. THIRD SCHOOL YEAR.

1. Write the name of (1) a person; (2) a place; (3) the name of a river; (4) the name of an ocean; (5) the name of the State in which you live.
2. Write five sentences, each composed of only two words—a noun and a verb.
3. Change each of the sentences that you wrote above into an interrogative sentence.
4. Write five exclamatory sentences, and remember to punctuate.
5. Correct the following: I. We done wrong. II. Who seen him? III. Does horses neigh? IV. Was you there? V. Does hens cackle?
6. I. What is a name-word? II. What is an action-word? III. Write a sentence having a *quality*-word. IV. Write a sentence with two *nouns* in it. V. Write a sentence with two *verbs* in it.

III. FOURTH SCHOOL YEAR.

1. "The bees were humming among the flowers, and the birds were singing in the trees and bushes." Point out the *name-words* in this sentence.
2. Write two sentences, each containing two *quality-words*, and draw a line under these words.
3. "The boys read well, and the girls sing sweetly." Point out the adverbs in this sentence.
4. "The girls read and write well, but they do not spell well." Point out the *action-words*, or verbs, in this sentence.
5. "The man, woman, and girl were busy at their lesson." Change the *name-words* in this sentence so that they may mean more than one.
6. "—— boys —— fast." Fill the blanks in this sentence. What do you call the last word?
7. "The boys ran from the house through the garden into the field." Point out the prepositions in this sentence.

8. "The good boy speaks well, and the industrious girls read finely." Point out the adjectives.
9. Give a rule for capitals.
10. Give a rule for periods.

IV. FIFTH SCHOOL YEAR.

1. Compare—1. *red;* 2. *good;* 3. *bad;* 4. *pleasant.*
2. Write the sentence "Bees are busy" in each of the six tenses of the indicative mood.
3. Give the present tense and past tense—I. of two irregular verbs; II. of two regular verbs.
4. Write two declarative sentences with the following nouns: 1. Crickets; 2. The gun. Change them into interrogative sentences.
5. Write two exclamatory sentences.
6. Write two rules for politeness, and make them simple sentences.
7. Write four complex sentences, using in each one of the following words: *if, who, when, because.*
8. Write two compound sentences.
9. Write three rules for capitals.
10. Write two rules for the period.

V. SIXTH SCHOOL YEAR.

1. What difference is there in the use of the letter *s* used as a *noun*-suffix and a *verb*-suffix?
2. Compare *fore, worse, far, most, dead.*
3. Punctuate and capitalize—
    1. The lamb said to the wolf who are you.
    2. Be good said a wise man and you will be happy.
    3. I cannot tell a lie said Washington.
4. In the sentence "That life is long which answers life's great end," parse 1. *that;* 2. *is;* 3. *long;* 4. *which;* 5. *end.*
5. Synopsis of the verb *to study* in the indicative mood, third person, singular, passive voice.

VI. SEVENTH SCHOOL YEAR.

1. Give the rules for the verb having two or more singular subjects connected by *and;* by *or* or *nor.* Examples of each.
2. What change is made in the root form of the verb when the subject is in the third person, singular ? When the subject is *thou?*
3. Define (1) a simple sentence; (2) a complex; (3) a compound sentence; (4) a sentence.
4. Write a simple declarative sentence with "Fire" for the subject; change it, first into an interrogative sentence, next into an exclamatory sentence, and then into an imperative sentence. *Punctuate.*
5. What is the grammatical order of parts in a simple declarative sentence?
6. Define the *subject* of a sentence; the predicate.
7. Write a complex sentence with *if;* one with *who;* one with *when;* one with *than.*
8. Rule for the punctuation of introductory or inverted adverbial phrases or clauses.
9. Rule for the semicolon in a compound sentence.
10. Rule for quotation-marks.

VII. EIGHTH SCHOOL YEAR.

After the answers are written, let pupils exchange papers and correct under the direction of the teacher.

Set I.

1. Write four rules for the use of the comma.
2. Write two rules for the sign of the possessive case. Examples.
3. Rule of syntax for collective nouns. Examples.
4. Give a synopsis of the verb *to teach* in the indicative and potential moods, third person, singular.
5. Define each of the four kinds of pronouns.
6. Define a simple sentence; subject; predicate; phrase; clause.

7. Give the leading signs of the complex sentence; the compound sentence.
8. Analyze the sentence "He laughs that wins."
9. Correct the sentence "I thought it was her."
10. Change into the plural form—1. axis; 2. chimney; 3. loss; 4. leaf; 5. rest.

Set II.

1. Analyze the sentence "You or I must go."
2. In the sentence "I supposed it to be him," parse *it* and *him*.
3. Write five rules of syntax.
4. Write a simple, a complex, and a compound sentence.
5. Write four rules of politeness, and state what kind of a sentence each is.
6. Write the correct forms of the following:
    1. My dress fits bad.
    2. I guess its her.
    3. Who did she marry?
    4. Whose there? Its me.
7. Change the sentence "Bees are busy" into each of the tenses of the indicative mood.
8. Write from memory, and punctuate, a stanza of at least four lines of poetry.
9. Write four forms of the complimentary closing of a letter.
10. Write a sentence to show the use of the word *that* as a relative, a conjunction, an adjective, and an adjective pronoun.

Chapter VII.

PUNCTUATION OF SENTENCES.

Note.—These rules are condensed and arranged for use in grammar-school grades.

I. THE SIMPLE SENTENCE.

Rule I.—Declarative and imperative sentences must end with a period; interrogative sentences with an interrogation point; and exclamatory sentences with an exclamation point.

EXAMPLES.

1. A rolling stone gathers no moss.
2. How does a verb differ from a noun?
3. How beautiful the clouds are!
4. Earn your own living.

Rule II.— Adverbial phrases, when introductory, inverted, or very emphatic, are cut off by a comma.

EXAMPLES.

1. In July, 1588, the Great Armada entered the English Channel.
2. Out in the country, close by the road, under two tall elms, there stands a white cottage.
3. Four centuries B.C., Greece was fast outgrowing her ancient faith.

Teachers will require pupils to point out other examples in some assigned reading-lesson.

Rule III.—Participial phrases are, in general, marked off by commas.

EXAMPLES.

1. The birds, singing in the trees, welcomed the rising sun.
2. Disheartened by defeat, the enemy slowly retreated.
3. The British, twice driven back, carried the redoubt on the third charge.
4. The invention of movable metal types, made in 1436, was, next to that of the alphabet, the greatest of inventions.

For other examples study an assigned reading-lesson.

Rule IV.—More than two similar parts of speech, in the same construction, are separated by commas.

EXAMPLES.

1. The four fine arts are architecture, sculpture, painting, and music.
2. Verbs are divided into transitive, intransitive, and neuter.
3. Oranges, lemons, figs, olives, and grapes grow in California.

For other examples study some assigned lesson.

Rule V.—Minor rules for the comma.

1. The words *as, namely,* or *to wit,* introducing examples or illustrations, are followed by a comma.
2. The words "Yes, sir," or "No, sir," take a comma between them.
3. The introductory words *Resolved, Ordered, Voted,* must be followed by a comma.
4. Nouns in apposition, when limited by phrases, or by any adjective except *the,* are marked off by two commas.
5. An explanatory word, following *or,* must be cut off by commas.

EXAMPLES.

1. A noun is the name of anything; as, *London.*
2. Yes, sir, I will do my duty.
3. Resolved, That the schools be closed on Washington's birthday.
4. Washington, the father of his country, died in 1799.
5. The atmosphere, or air, surrounds the globe.

Rule VI.—Minor rules for the period.
The period must be used—
1. After abbreviated words.
2. After initial letters.
3. After a signature.
4. After the title of a book.
5. After the title of a composition.
6. After the numerals 1, 2, 3, etc., when they mark paragraphs or examples.

Teachers will illustrate by examples found in the readers.

Rule VII.—Rules for capitals.
A capital letter should begin—
1. Every sentence, and every line of poetry.
2. Proper nouns and proper adjectives.
3. Names of the Deity.
4. The names of days and months.
5. The first word of direct quotations.
6. Sentences following *Resolved, Ordered,* etc.
7. The pronoun *I* and the interjection *O* must be written in capitals.

Rule VIII.—Other marks.
1. The curves ( ), or marks of parenthesis, are sometimes used to enclose an explanatory word or statement.
2. The brackets [ ] are used to enclose the correction of an error, or an implied or understood word.
3. The dash — marks a broken or parenthetical sentence.
4. The *caret* ∧ is used in manuscript when an omitted letter or word is interlined.

Teachers will call the attention of pupils to the use of *brackets*, to the use of the *dash* in the readers, and to the use of the *caret* in compositions.

II. PUNCTUATION OF THE COMPLEX SENTENCE.

Rule I.—Introductory adverbial clauses are, in general, cut off from the principal statement by a comma.

Teachers will require pupils to copy the examples, point out the clauses, explain the punctuation, and give additional illustrations.

1. Before the storm began, we had built a camp-fire.
2. If this be treason, make the most of it.
3. When a nation wishes to make war, the opportunity is usually found.

Rule II.—Explanatory adjective clauses, introduced by *who* or *which* [="and he," "and it," etc.], are cut off by commas; restrictive clauses [="that"] require no commas.

1. *Explanatory Clauses.*

1. The king, who [= and he] was a merciful ruler, forgave the offence.
2. The Missouri, which rises in the Rocky Mountains, is the chief tributary of the Mississippi.
3. Plutarch, whóse [= and his] *Lives* has been called the "Bible of Heroisms," lived A.D. 100.

2. *Restrictive Clauses.*

1. That is the man *who* aided me.
2. It is the tallest tree *that* I ever saw.
3. This is the book *which* you want.
4. He is the man *whom* we saw yesterday.
5. This is the flower *that* you spoke of.

Rule III. — A noun-clause introduced by a relative pronoun and used as the object of a transitive verb requires no comma.

1. I have told you *who he is.*

2. I know which he will buy.
3. I know who will go.

Rule IV.—A noun-clause used as the subject of a verb must be cut off from the verb by a comma.
  1. That the earth rotates on its axis, was denied by the ancients.
  2. That illiterate electors should be intelligent voters, is not to be expected.
  3. That a piece of amber will attract light bodies, was a fact well known 600 B.C.

Rule V.—When the sentence is introduced by the pronoun *it*, and the noun-clause is put after the verb, no comma is required.

Change each of the sentences under Rule IV. into a sentence introduced by *it*.

Rule VI.—Commas must be used to mark off a parenthetical expression when it comes between the divided parts of a sentence.
  1. He expected, it seems, to surprise the enemy.
  2. The man was murdered, it is believed, by a band of Apaches.
  3. "Beautiful creature," said the cunning fox, "you sing like a nightingale."

III. PUNCTUATION OF THE COMPOUND SENTENCE.

Rule I.—Unless highly contracted, the principal statements, when closely connected, are, in general, cut off by a comma, and are always so cut off when there are more than two principal statements.

EXAMPLES TO BE COPIED.
  1. Napoleon Bonaparte was of Italian blood, and was a native of Corsica.
  2. "Scrooge signed it, and Scrooge's name was good on 'Change for anything he chose to put his hand to."—*Dickens.*

3. Tea comes from China, coffee from Java and Brazil, and sugar from the West Indies.
4. I came, I saw, I conquered.

Study an assigned reading-lesson, and point out five cases in which the preceding rule is applied.

Rule II.—Principal statements, when loosely connected, when very long, or when subdivided by a comma, are separated by a semicolon.

EXAMPLES TO BE COPIED.

1. The history of the Orient is the history of *dynasties;* the history of Greece and Rome is the history of the *people.*
2. The Greeks were indebted to the Phœnicians for the alphabet; the Romans adopted the Greek alphabet, with some changes; the Roman alphabet is the basis of our modern alphabet.

EXERCISE.

From suitable reading-lessons, teachers will point out to their pupils the application of the preceding rule to the punctuation of the piece.

Rule III.—When a compound sentence is highly elliptical, or contracted, the omission of the principal statement before each of a series of clauses is marked by a semicolon.

APPLICATION.

"England has to undergo the revolt of the colonies; [England has] to submit to defeat and separation; [?] to shake under the volcano of the French Revolution; [?] to grapple and fight for the life with her gigantic enemy, Napoleon; [?] to gasp and rally after the tremendous struggle."—*Thackeray.*

Rule IV.—Principal statements and clauses are punctuated according to the rules for the simple and the complex sentence.

IV. QUOTATION-MARKS.

Rule I.—When we use the exact words of another person, we mark off the expressions or sentences with quotation-marks at the beginning and the end.

Rule II.—In general, a quoted sentence begins with a capital letter: Cæsar exclaimed, "And you, too, Brutus!"

Rule III.—In general, a quoted sentence or expression is separated from the rest of the sentence by a comma; as, "I'll try," said General Miller.

Rule IV.—A very formal quotation, placed in regular order in a sentence, is marked off by a *colon;* as, Remember the old adage: "A stitch in time saves nine."

Rule V. — A quoted *clause* introduced by the word *that* is not marked off by a comma and does not begin with a capital; as, It is said that "necessity knows no law."

EXERCISE.

Copy the following examples, and explain how the preceding rules are applied:

1. "Don't give up the ship," exclaimed the dying Lawrence.
2. "What great teeth you have!" said Little Red Riding-hood. "The better to eat you with," said the wolf.
3. "Vanity of vanities," saith the preacher, "all is vanity."
4. "Language," said Talleyrand, "is made to conceal thought."
5. There is a Prussian maxim as follows: "Whatever you would have appear in the life of a nation, you must put into the schools."

Study an assigned reading-lesson, and explain the application of the preceding rules to any quotations you may find there.

Chapter VIII.
RULES FOR WRITING GOOD ENGLISH.

Note.—The following practical directions, including a combination of grammar and elementary rhetoric, are intended for the use of teachers in the highest classes in the grammar-school, as a supplement to text-books on grammar. Let pupils copy the rules into blank-books; the examples may be given orally, requiring pupils to give additional illustrations.

I. WORDS.

1. The leading qualities of good composition are clearness, force, and brevity. These characteristics depend mainly on the right use and right arrangement of words.
2. A knowledge of the exact meaning of words may be acquired in various ways:
    1. By referring to the dictionary.
    2. By studying word-analysis.
    3. By reading good authors.
    4. By conversing with educated persons.
    5. By attention to the kind of words used in writing or in speaking.
    6. By the study of synonyms.

Rule I.—Use the right word to express your exact meaning.

Put in place of each italicized word some word accurately and properly used.

1. Great *quantities* [numbers] of people were there.

2. Give us this day our *diurnal* [?] bread.
3. The earth's daily [diurnal] rotation.
4. Hallowed be thy *appellation*.
5. He was *banished* from school.
6. Napoleon was *sent* to Saint Helena.
7. How dear to my *soul* [?] are the scenes of my *infancy*! [?]
8. I *admire* to hear her sing.

Rule II.—Use words in keeping with your subject. Avoid dressing up little thoughts in big words.

Substitute simpler words in place of those italicized.

1. The half-drowned boy was *resuscitated*.
2. The *conflagration* of the cottage was *extinguished*.
3. The boys *ascended* an apple-tree.
4. The money was devoted to *eleemosynary* purposes.
5. We took a short *pedestrian excursion* in the garden.
6. I *purchased* two apples.

Rule III.—Avoid vulgarisms and slang, whether low or fashionable. Use English expressions in preference to French or Latin.

Substitute in place of each italicized word or phrase some appropriate word or phrase:

1. That resolution, Mr. President, can never be *resurrected*.
2. The laborer is worthy of his *wage*.
3. I was born and *raised* in Kentucky.
4. It is the *ne plus ultra* of stoves.
5. The statue was a *chef-d'œuvre* [masterpiece] of art.
6. In this danger, he behaved with the greatest *sang-froid* [coolness].

Rule IV.—Use no redundant words or phrases; that is, do not repeat the same idea in different words.

Point out the redundant expressions in the following illustrations:

1. He won the *universal* love of *everybody*.
2. She is an invalid *in poor health*.
3. Mr. Speaker, I desire to make a few remarks before speaking.
4. That book is mine, for I own it.
5. The enemy *retreated back again* to their camp.
6. In my opinion, I think you are wrong.

Rule V.—Avoid pairs of synonymous adjectives, strong superlatives, and exaggerated expressions.

Note.—Among the adjectives incorrectly coupled are "lovely and beautiful," "brave and courageous," "cruel and bloody;" among the superlatives, "very," "immense," "stupendous," "enormous," "tremendous;" among exaggerated expressions, "perfectly lovely," "elegant," etc.

Reduce the following to plain English:

1. The morning is *cold* and *chilly*.
2. We were sweltering under a *hot* and *burning* sun.
3. That is a tremendous big apple.
4. We arrived there half starved, and the dinner was *perfectly elegant*.
5. There were *millions* of crows in the cornfield.
6. I have had a *splendid* time.
7. My hair stood on end.

Rule VI.—Use the right preposition and the right conjunction:

1. Your way is different *to* mine [from].
2. My hat differs *with* yours [from].
3. I was *to* a large party last week [at].
4. Are your folks *to* home [at]?
5. We went *in* the garden [into].
6. No other cause was known *but* carelessness [than].

7. You will not trust me, *and* he will [but].
8. I wish I could write *like* you do [as].

II. ORDER OF WORDS.

Rule VII.—Emphatic words should stand near the beginning or the end of a sentence.

Note.—The grammatical order is, the *subject* with its modifiers, verb with its object or attribute, and the modifiers of the predicate. Force or emphasis frequently requires this order to be changed; as,

1. *Proud* though he was, he was at last humbled.
2. *Sweet* is the breath of morn.
3. *Some* he banished, *others* he put to death.

Rule VIII.—Inconsiderable words must be kept from the end of a sentence.

Note.—Among the unimportant words are *prepositions*, the pronoun *it*, a short *predicate*, etc.

EXAMPLES.

1. My brother is the boy whom the medal was given to [to whom the medal].
2. She is a lady whom all are pleased *with* [?].
3. It is a subject which we know nothing *of* [?].
4. He took the city and was afterwards made governor of *it* [?].
5. They will start on a tour round the world *soon* [?].
6. We shall go next week, if it does not rain, probably.

Rule IX.—When the relative *that* introduces a restrictive clause, the preposition is often thrown to the end of the sentence:

1. He is the same boy that I spoke *of*.
2. He is the tallest man that I know *of*.
3. The big boys are the ones [that] you should begin *with*.

4. Where is the girl [that] you were speaking *about?*
5. It is the very best use that you can put it *to*.

Rule X.—When both sexes must be specifically included, it is better, in general, to put the statement in the plural form, instead of the distributive singular, with "his" or "her."

    1. Every teacher must make *his* or *her* report on the first of each month. [All teachers—their reports.]
    2. *Every* boy and girl must study their lesson. [Incorrect, because *every* is singular and *their* plural. We may say *his* lesson, the pronoun standing for both sexes, or put the whole in the plural form.]
    3. Every man and every woman must earn his or her living [?].

Rule XI.—Use the possessive-case form of the pronoun before a verbal noun.

    1. I had heard nothing about his [not him] going away.
    2. What is the use of *our* [not us] trying to learn it?
    3. We read the account of *their* [not them] being lost.

Rule XII.—In order to secure clearness, words, phrases, or clauses should be put as near as possible to the words they limit.

Rearrange the phrases or clauses so as clearly to express the meaning intended:

    1. These drawings were done by a boy that attended school merely for his own amusement.
    2. Wanted, a servant girl to take care of a child skilled in washing and ironing.
    3. A pin was accidentally swallowed by a little child which had no head.

Rule XIII.—In general, put adverbs next to the words they limit; put the adverb *only* immediately before the word intended to be most affected by it.

Put the adverbs in the right place:

1. He was [ ] engaged in the lumber trade *formerly*.
2. Let us drop a tear to his memory *at least*.
3. I *only* whispered [ ] once or twice.
4. We have only to learn two lessons.
5. The two sisters *nearly* look alike.
6. We *not only* intend [ ] to go, but also to remain there.

Rule XIV. — Adverbial phrases or clauses are frequently put at the beginning of a sentence, either to make the statement more forcible, or to secure a pleasing distribution of adverbial elements.

Rearrange the phrases and clauses:

An old clock stopped suddenly early one summer morning before the family was stirring without giving its owner any cause for complaint.

Rule XV.—In conditional complex sentences, put the *if*-clause first:

1. If he is a spy, he should be hanged.
2. Though you have done wrong, I will excuse you.
3. If we fail, it can be no worse for us.
4. Sink or swim, live or die, survive or perish, I give my heart and my hand for this vote.

Rule XVI.—When a participle introduces the sentence, express in the context the noun or the pronoun which the participle is intended to limit.

1. "Climbing to the summit of the mountain, the whole valley of the Sacramento was seen." This may be corrected thus: "*On climbing*—we saw," etc.
2. Ascending in a balloon, the whole country seemed a panorama [?].

Rule XVII.—In adjective clauses, use *who* or *which*

when the evident meaning is "and he," "and it," etc.; in other cases, use, in general, the restrictive *that*.

Note.—When *who* or *which* means *and he, and it*, etc., it introduces an additional or explanatory statement; *that* introduces a clause without which the antecedent is incomplete, and hence is restrictive.

1. I heard the news from my friend, who [= and he] heard it from the passengers *that* [restrictive] arrived last night.
2. He forgot to keep his appointment, which [and this] was a great blunder.
3. We wasted our time on old-style "parsing," which [=and this] is English grammar "run to seed."

Note.—Mark off the *who* or *which* adjective clauses by a comma.

Rule XVIII.—In clauses introduced by *than, as, as well as*, etc., repeat the preposition or the verb when clearness requires it.

1. The city had more attractions for him than [for] his friend.
2. The teacher is stricter with boys than [with] girls.
3. Teachers are stricter with children than parents [are].
4. He likes Maria better than [he likes] William.
5. He likes Maria better than William [likes her].

Rule XIX.—Keep the construction uniform unless a change is unavoidable.

1. Apples are good for *eating* and *to cook*.
2. To-day is warmer and more pleasant [pleasanter] than yesterday.
3. We had good reasons for expecting him, and to suppose [for supposing] that he would come by rail.

III. BREVITY.

Rule XX.—Use the smallest number of words needed fully to express the meaning intended.

Strike out all unnecessary words or phrases, or condense into briefer expressions:

1. His lecture was brief, short, concise, and condensed.
2. The morning was grand and glorious, the air was balmy and sweet with the scent and perfume of flowers and plants, and we rejoiced and exulted in the buoyance and light-heartedness of youth, and the strength and elasticity of youth.

IV. FIGURATIVE LANGUAGE.

[Simplified for Grammar-school Use.]

"Although it is enough for the teacher to have in view the exigencies of grammar, he may also ring a few of the rhetorical changes that are of common occurrence—as inversion of subject and predicate, interrogation, metaphor, and metonymy."—*Bain's Education as a Science.*

1. Both force and brevity of expression are increased by the proper use of figures of speech.
2. The three leading figures of speech are personification, simile, and metaphor.

I. PERSONIFICATION.

Personification is that figure by which animals are represented as speaking like human beings, or by which inanimate things are represented as having life and action. It may be *direct* or *indirect*.

1. *Direct.*

1. "The better to see you with," said the Wolf.
2. The cunning Fox said to the Crow, "Beautiful creature, what a sweet voice you have!"
3. Once upon a time Mr. Fox invited Mr. Crane to dinner.
4. "There is a reaper whose name is Death."—*Longfellow.*
5. "'Death shall reap the braver harvest,' said the solemn-sounding drum."—*Bret Harte.*
6. "I love Freedom better than Slavery; I will speak her words; I

RULES FOR WRITING GOOD ENGLISH. 315

will listen to her music; I will stand beneath her flag; I will fight in her ranks; and when I do so, I shall find myself surrounded by the good, the brave, the noble of every land."—*Baker.*

2. *Indirect.*

1. The trees waved their long *arms* in the air.
2. The *thirsty* flowers were *fainting* in the hot sun.
3. The *giant* mountains lift their *heads* into the skies.
4. The deep-mouthed cannon *spoke* in angry tones.
5. "No wind that blew was *bitterer* than he."—*Dickens.*
6. "There poetry dips its silver oar."—*Baker.*
7. "Near yonder copse where once the garden *smiled.*"

EXERCISE.

Change into plain language the following:

1. The wind is whispering to the trees.
2. The brook came leaping down the mountain.
3. How sweet the moonlight sleeps upon this bank!
4. From peak to peak leaps the wild thunder.

II. SIMILE.

A *simile* is a direct comparison of one thing with another, expressed by the words *like, as, than,* etc.

EXERCISE.

Explain the points of resemblance between the things compared in the following examples:

1. Human life is like a river.
2. "Old Marley was as dead as a door-nail."—*Dickens.*
3. "How like a fawning publican he looks!"—*Shakespeare.*
4. "The liberty of the press is like a great, exulting, and abounding river."—*Baker.*

III. METAPHOR.

A *metaphor* compares two things having some resemblance by stating or implying that one thing *is* the other. Thus the metaphor is only an *implied* simile.

Exercise.

Point out the resemblance between things compared.

1. That man is a bear [*i. e.*, He is as cross as a bear].
2. An idle scholar is a butterfly.
3. "A thing of beauty is a joy forever."—*Keats.*
4. "All the world's a stage, and all the men and women merely players."—*Shakespeare.*
5. "My eyes cloud up for rain."—*Lowell.*
6. "And yet through the gloom and the light,
   The fate of a nation was riding that night."—*Longfellow.*

Exercise.

Change into plain language the following metaphors:

1. The raging sea swallowed up the ship.
2. Death is the brother of sleep.
3. Spring is a beautiful maiden, but winter is an old man with whitened locks.
4. Youth is the morning of life.
5. Old age is the winter of life.

Require each pupil to give and change five additional examples.

Rules for the Metaphor.

1. *In forcible statements, use metaphor instead of literal statement.*
   1. "The ship *ploughs* the sea" is shorter and more striking than "The ship cleaves the waters of the sea as a plough cleaves the land."
   2. The fortress is weakness itself = The fortress is very weak.
2. *Do not confuse metaphors.*
      The following is attributed to Sir Bayle Roche: "Mr. Speaker, I smell a rat, I see him brewing in the air; but, mark me, I shall yet nip him in the bud."

Give five additional examples.

IV. MINOR FIGURES OF SPEECH.

Force, clearness, brevity, variety, or beauty of expression may be attained in various other ways:

1. *By contrasting things:*
    Talent is power, tact is skill; talent knows *what* to do, tact knows *when* to do; talent is wealth, tact is ready money.
2. *By putting the name of one thing for another:*
    1. I am reading Tennyson [*i. e.*, his writings].
    2. The pen [*i. e.*, literature] is mightier than the sword [*i. e.*, military force].
    3. Gray hairs [*i. e.*, old age] should be respected.
    4. The teakettle [*i. e.*, the water] is boiling.
    5. He is fond of the bottle [*i. e.*, liquor].
3. *By the use of particular instead of general terms:*

General.	Particular.
1. I have neither food nor money.	2. I have neither a crust of bread nor a cent to buy one.
3. He is an uneducated man.	4. He can neither read nor write
5. A king in all his glory.	6. Solomon in all his glory.
7. Behold the flowers of the field.	8. Behold the lilies of the field.

4. *By emphatic interrogation.*
    1. Who ever heard of a happy tyrant?
    2. Who's the man would live a slave?
5. *By an exclamation instead of a statement:*
    1. What a glorious sunrise!
    2. "A horse! a horse! my kingdom for a horse!"
6. *By addressing the absent as present, the dead as living, or inanimate as animate:*
    Instance of addressing the absent as present—
    Come, old schoolmates, dear companions,
    Sit around my lonely hearth, etc.
    Of addressing the dead as living—
    Spirit of Washington! again lead our armies; again guide our counsels.

Or in the address to the mummy—
"Speak! for thou long enough hast acted dummy;
Thou hast a tongue; come, let us hear its tune," etc.

Of addressing inanimate as animate—
Speak, marble lips! Proclaim the love of liberty regulated by law.
"Ye crags and peaks! I'm with you once again."
"Roll on, thou deep and dark blue ocean, roll!"

7. *By exaggeration:*
   1. The waves ran mountains high.
   2. Napoleon dashed down into Italy like an avalanche.
   3. He is tall as a pine and straight as an arrow.
   4. I *worship* my father and *adore* my mother.
   5. The very walls will cry out in its support.

8. *By ridiculing under pretence of praising:*
   1. Pretty lords of creation! when they can't take care of an umbrella.
   2. What an honest man! to steal only half.
   3. "They've built us up a noble wall,
      To keep the *vulgar* out.
   4. We've nothing in the world to do
      But just to *walk about.*"—*Holmes.*

Chapter IX.

HISTORY OF THE UNITED STATES.

QUESTIONS FOR WRITTEN REVIEW LESSONS.

Note.—The following specimen sets of questions may be given, one set at a time, to the class, in advance, and the written examination required at the next recitation. They include outlines of main events, which teachers can extend at pleasure.

Set I.

1. Of the five great centres of colonial settlements, state where and by whom each was settled. 1. Jamestown. 2. Plymouth. 3. New York. 4. Pennsylvania. 5. Maryland.
2. Name five important events in the colonial wars.
3. What events in the War of the Revolution were connected with each of these cities: 1. Boston? 2. New York? 3. Philadelphia? 4. Savannah? 5. Trenton?
4. Name five American victories in the Revolutionary War; five British victories.
5. Give a short account of the most important battle of the War of 1812.

Set II.

1. What part did General Scott take in the Mexican War?
2. Name the first and last battle in the War of Secession.
3. Describe the battle of Gettysburg.
4. Name five Union victories in the War of Secession. Five Confederate victories.
5. What was the Emancipation Proclamation?

Set III.

1. What causes led to the French and Indian War?

2. The Revolutionary War?
3. The Mexican War?
4. The War of Secession?

Set IV.

1. When and how was slavery introduced into the United States?
2. When and how was it abolished?
3. What was the Missouri Compromise?
4. What is the Fourteenth Amendment to the Constitution?
5. What is the Fifteenth Amendment?

Set V.

1. Name five American generals in the Revolutionary War.
2. In the War of Secession.
3. Name three leading statesmen of the Revolutionary period.
4. Of the War of Secession.
5. Name five American authors, and five American inventors, stating what they invented.

Set VI.

1. What resulted from these wars: 1. French and Indian? 2. Revolution? 3. Mexican? 4. Secession?
2. Who wrote the Declaration of Independence, who adopted it, and what was it?
3. What do you know about paper money in the Revolutionary War?
4. Who was Robert Morris?
5. What connection did Alexander Hamilton have with the financial measures of Congress?

Set VII.

1. Name five discoverers of the New World, and the parts of America discovered by each.
2. Name five important persons in connection with the first settlements of the United States.
3. Tell what causes led to the settlement of—1. Massachusetts; 2. Rhode Island; 3. Pennsylvania; 4. Maryland; 5. Georgia.

4. Name five of the most important and populous states in 1776.
5. Name one important act performed by—1. Sir Francis Drake; 2. De Soto; 3. Balboa; 4. Champlain; 5. James Oglethorpe.
6. What was the Stamp Act?
7. When and where did the first Continental Congress meet?
8. Tell what important service was performed by—1. Patrick Henry; 2. John Hancock; 3. Benjamin Franklin; 4. Benedict Arnold; 5. Thomas Jefferson.

Set VIII.

1. When and where was the first action of the Revolutionary War? When and where the last?
2. What was the condition of the Americans at the close of the year 1779?
3. In what year did Congress adopt the "Articles of Confederation?" In what year the Constitution?
4. Name five battles in the Revolutionary War in which the British were successful.
5. What was the origin of "Mason and Dixon's Line?"

Set IX.

1. Who invented the cotton-gin? What did it do?
2. When, where, and by whom was the first steamboat run upon American waters? Give an account of the voyage?
3. Prior to what time were there no railroads in the United States? Of what advantage have they been to the country? Why is the Pacific Railroad a remarkable work?
4. When and where was the first telegraph line built? Who invented the electro-magnetic telegraph?
5. Who laid the Atlantic cable? What does it do?
6. Who invented or improved the sewing-machine? To what class is it a blessing?
7. In what respects is the printing-press of to-day better than the press which Franklin used in 1725? How is the world benefited by this superiority?
8. What is the object of American common-schools? Ought they to be well supported? Why?

Chapter X.

PRACTICAL LESSONS IN SCHOOL ETHICS.

I. LESSONS FOR YOUNGER PUPILS.—DUTIES OF CHILDREN.

1. *Respect for Parents.*

Maxims.

1. Honor thy father and thy mother.
2. Obedience is the first duty of a child.

Hints.

1. Always be polite to your parents.
2. Always obey them pleasantly and cheerfully.
3. Perform all your duties faithfully.
4. Your parents provide you with a home, with food and with clothing, and it is your duty to work for them wherever they ask you to do so.
5. Read or tell to your class some suitable story to illustrate the lesson.
6. Put this question to the class: "*Why* is it your duty to obey your parents?" Draw out as many answers as possible, and converse about them.

2. *Gratitude and Love to Parents.*

Maxims.

1. An ungrateful child is despised by everybody.
2. Gratitude must be expressed in *acts* as well as in *words.*

3. *Duties towards Teachers.*

Hints.

Question your pupils and find out what their ideas of school duties are. At the close of your conversation, sum up your statements into directions like the following:

1. Be orderly and quiet.
2. Be punctual and industrious.
3. Try to form good habits.
4. Be respectful and polite.
5. Learn your lessons as well as you can.
6. You are not studying at school merely because your teacher *tells* you to study, but because you go to school for your own good.
7. When you are idle and neglect your lessons, you cheat *yourself*, not your teacher.

4. *Duties to Brothers, Sisters, and Schoolmates.*

I. FORBEARANCE.

Maxims.

1. He is wisest that gives way.
2. In a quarrel, be the first to conciliate.
3. Offer an offender the hand of friendship when he meets you in a friendly spirit.

II. COURTESY.

Precepts.

1. When you do a favor, do it cheerfully and promptly.
2. Share the work as well as the play of your companions.
3. Refuse to take any part in what you think to be wrong.

II. LESSONS FOR OLDER PUPILS.

1. *Choice of Occupation.*

Precepts.

1. First consult your capacity; your inclination will come of itself.
2. Every occupation has its peculiar burdens and disadvantages.
3. Any lawful occupation may lead to success.
4. Whatever you undertake to do, strive to do it to the best of your ability.
5. Aspire to the highest rank in whatever occupation you engage.

Note.—Teachers will find many excellent extracts to be read to a class in Smiles's *Self-help* and Smiles's *Biographies.*

2. Industry.
Maxims.
1. Idleness is the mother of vice.
2. An idle brain is the devil's workshop.
3. A young man idle is an old man needy.
4. Industry makes all things easy.

Note.—Teachers will find interesting extracts in *Franklin's Autobiography*, or Parton's *Life of Franklin.*

3. Economy.
1. Spend less than you earn.
2. Be economical, but not mean, or stingy, or avaricious.
3. Be prudent and saving in youth as a safeguard against need in old age.
4. Personal independence depends largely on the possession of a competence.

4. Order.
Precepts.
1. Put everything into its proper place.
2. Have regular hours for work, study, and play.
3. Make it a point of honor to keep your appointments punctually.

5. Kindness.
Precepts.
1. Kindness is the sunshine of social life.
2. When you have wronged another, do not hesitate to apologize.
3. In conversation, avoid blunt contradictions.
4. A cheerful, pleasant countenance is a good letter of introduction.

6. Ethical Virtues.

[As classified by Dr. Fricke.]

I. VIRTUES OF CHARACTER.

Cardinal Virtues.—Justice, Love [Kindness].

1. Justice:
Out of which grow:

Subjective.	{ Self-knowledge. { Self-restraint.	Temperance. Moderation.	Self-denial. Determination.
Objective.	(Honesty. { Fidelity. (Truthfulness.	Obedience. Punctuality. Conscientiousness.	Impartiality. Unselfishness. Gratitude.

Love [Kindness]:
Whence proceed:

Subjective.	Self-respect.		
Objective.	(Liberality. { Charitableness. (Friendliness.	Kindness. Forbearance. Forgiveness.	Patience. Frankness.

II. VIRTUES OF TEMPERAMENT.

Subjective.	{ Seriousness. { Activity.	Desire to learn. Courage.	Intrepidity. Firmness.
Objective.	{ Cheerfulness. { Calmness.	Gentleness. Discretion.	Modesty. Contentment.

III. ÆSTHETICAL VIRTUES.

Order.	Decency.	Courtesy.
Cleanliness.	Dignity.	Manners.

THE END.

English Grammar

Metcalf's Elementary English . . . . . . 40 cents
Metcalf's English Grammar . . . . 60 cents
    A logical and progressive series based on the inductive method. Adapted for use in graded or ungraded schools.

Maxwell's First Book in English . . . . . . 40 cents
Maxwell's Introductory Lessons in English Grammar . . 40 cents
    A brief graded course for Elementary and Grammar grades.

Lyte's Elementary English . . . . 35 cents
    For use in Primary and Lower Grammar grades.

Lyte's Elements of Grammar and Composition . . . 50 cents
    For use in Upper Grammar grades.

Conklin's English Grammar and Composition . . . 60 cents
    A complete graded course in Grammar and Composition for Intermediate or Grammar School grades.

Harvey's Elementary Grammar and Composition—Revised . 42 cents
Harvey's Practical English Grammar—Revised . . . 65 cents
    A practical and systematic course in language study, including Language Lessons, Composition and English Grammar.

Swinton's New English Grammar . . . . . 56 cents
    A working class book for the study and practice of English.

FOR ADVANCED CLASSES

Baskervill and Sewell's English Grammar . . . . 90 cents
    An advanced English Grammar based on the actual use of the language. For use in High School, Academy and College classes.

Lyte's Advanced Grammar and Composition . . .
    For use in High Schools, Normal Schools and other Preparatory Schools.

Maxwell's Advanced Lessons in English Grammar . . 60 cents
    For use in higher Grammar classes and High Schools.

Copies of any of the above books will be sent prepaid to any address, on receipt of the price, by the Publishers:

American Book Company

New York   •   Cincinnati   •   Chicago

Mental Arithmetic

Bailey's American Mental Arithmetic . . 35 cents
    For Advanced Grammar Classes, High Schools, Academies, and Normal Schools. Though only recently published, this book has met with the highest favor, and is already in satisfactory use in the best schools.

Dubbs's Complete Mental Arithmetic . . 35 cents
    For use in any school where Mental Arithmetic is taught. The rapid introduction of this book on its own merit is the best evidence of its sterling worth.

Milne's Mental Arithmetic . . . . 35 cents
    This book follows the same inductive plan and method of development which has proved so successful in the author's other works.

Ray's New Intellectual Arithmetic . . . 25 cents
    The Mental Arithmetic of Ray's Series of Arithmetics.

Robinson's New Intellectual Arithmetic . . 35 cents
    The Mental Arithmetic of Robinson's Series of Arithmetics.

ARITHMETIC TABLETS AND BLANKS

    NATIONAL NUMBER TABLETS. 12 Nos. . Per doz. 90 cents
    RAY'S TEST EXAMPLE TABLETS. 8 Nos. . Per doz. $1.00
    PIPER'S GRADED SEAT WORK IN ARITH. 4 Nos. Each 8 cents

    These Tablets are very convenient and useful accessories in teaching Arithmetic.

Copies of any of the above Mental Arithmetics will be sent prepaid to any address, on receipt of the price by the Publishers:

American Book Company

NEW YORK • CINCINNATI • CHICAGO

Elementary English

The following books are adapted for beginners in the study of Language and Composition:

LONG'S
    New Language Exercises. Part I. . . . . 20 cents
    New Language Exercises. Part II. . . . . 25 cents
    Lessons in English (Grammar and Composition) . . 35 cents

LYTE'S
    Elementary English . . . . 35 cents

MAXWELL'S
    First Book in English . . . . 40 cents

METCALF AND BRIGHT'S
    Language Lessons. Part I. . . . . . . 35 cents
    Language Lessons. Part II. . . . . . 55 cents

METCALF'S
    Elementary English . . . . 40 cents

PARK'S
    Language Lessons . . . . 35 cents

SWINTON'S
    Language Primer . . . . 28 cents
    Language Lessons . . . . 38 cents

Language Tablets and Blanks

NATIONAL Language Tablets . . . . Per dozen, 90 cents

PATTERSON'S Composition Books
    No. 1. Flexible. 36 pages . . . . Per dozen, 96 cents.
    No. 2. Boards. 60 pages . . . . Per dozen, $1.80
    No. 3. Cloth. 84 pages . . . . Per dozen, 2.70
    No. 4. Extra. 108 pages . . . . Per dozen, 3.60

WARD'S Grammar Blanks. 2 Nos. . . . Per dozen, 90 cents

Specimen copies of any of the above books will be sent prepaid to any address, on receipt of the price, by the Publishers:

American Book Company

New York   •   Cincinnati   •   Chicago

Books for Supplementary Reading

Needham's Outdoor Studies
A Reading Book of Nature Study. By JAMES G. NEEDHAM $0.40

Dana's Plants and their Children
By Mrs. WILLIAM STARR DANA. Illustrated by Alice Josephine Smith 65

Kelly's Short Stories of Our Shy Neighbors
By Mrs. M. A. B. KELLY. Illustrated 50

McGuffey's Natural History Readers. Illustrated
McGuffey's Familiar Animals and their Wild Kindred . . .50
McGuffey's Living Creatures of Water, Land, and Air . .50

Treat's Home Studies in Nature. Illustrated
By Mrs. MARY TREAT. Part I.—Observations on Birds. Part II.—Habits of Insects. Part III.—Plants that Consume Animals. Part IV.—Flowering Plants 90

Monteith's Popular Science Reader
By JAMES MONTEITH. Illustrated 75

Carpenter's Geographical Reader—Asia 60
Carpenter's Geographical Reader—North America 60
By FRANK G. CARPENTER. With Maps and Illustrations.

Payne's Geographical Nature Studies
For Primary Work in Home Geography. By FRANK OWEN PAYNE, M.Sc. Fully Illustrated 25

Guyot's Geographical Reader and Primer
A series of journeys round the world. Illustrated . . .60

Johonnot's Geographical Reader
By JAMES JOHONNOT. Illustrated 1.00

Van Bergen's Story of Japan
By R. VAN BERGEN. With Double Map of Japan and Korea and Numerous Illustrations 1.00

Holbrook's 'Round the Year in Myth and Song
By FLORENCE HOLBROOK. With beautiful Illustrations . .60

Copies of any of these books will be sent prepaid to any address, on receipt of the price, by the Publishers:

American Book Company

New York • Cincinnati • Chicago

School Histories of the United States

McMaster's School History of the United States
By JOHN BACH MCMASTER. Cloth, 12mo, 507 pages.
With maps and illustrations $1.00
Written expressly to meet the demand for a School History which should be fresh, vigorous, and interesting in style, accurate and impartial in statement, and strictly historical in treatment.

Field's Grammar School History of the United States
By L. A. FIELD. With maps and illustrations . . . 1.00

Barnes's Primary History of the United States
For Primary Classes. Cloth, 12mo, 252 pages. With maps, illustrations, and a complete index 60

Barnes's Brief History of the United States
Revised. Cloth, 8vo, 364 pages. Richly embellished with maps and illustrations 1.00

Eclectic Primary History of the United States
By EDWARD S. ELLIS. A book for younger classes. Cloth, 12mo, 230 pages. Illustrated 50

Eclectic History of the United States
By M. E. THALHEIMER. Revised. Cloth, 12mo, 441 pages. With maps and illustrations . . . 1.00

Eggleston's First Book in American History
By EDWARD EGGLESTON. Boards, 12mo, 203 pages. Beautifully illustrated 60

Eggleston's History of the United States and Its People
By EDWARD EGGLESTON. Cloth, 8vo, 416 pages. Fully illustrated with engravings, maps and colored plates . . 1.05

Swinton's First Lessons in Our Country's History
By WILLIAM SWINTON. Revised edition. Cloth, 12mo, 208 pages. Illustrated 48

Swinton's School History of the United States
Revised and enlarged. Cloth, 12mo, 383 pages. With new maps and illustrations 90

White's Pupils' Outline Studies in the History of the United States
By FRANCIS H. WHITE. For pupils' use in the application of laboratory and library methods to the study of United States History 30

Copies of any of the above books will be sent, prepaid, to any address on receipt of the price by the Publishers :

American Book Company

NEW YORK   ♦   CINCINNATI   ♦   CHICAGO

SCHOOL READING BY GRADES

Baldwin's School Readers

By James Baldwin

Editor of "Harper's Readers," Author of "Old Greek Stories," "Old Stories of the East," etc.

In method and in subject matter, as well as in artistic and mechanical execution, these new readers establish an ideal standard, equally well adapted for city and country schools. They possess many original and meritorious features which are in accord with the most approved methods of instruction, and which will commend them to the best teachers and the best schools. The illustrations are an important feature of the books, and are the work of the best artists. They are not merely pictures inserted for the purpose of ornament, but are intended to assist in making the reading exercises both interesting and instructive.

BALDWIN'S SCHOOL READERS—EIGHT BOOK EDITION

First Year,   128 pp. 25 cents   Fifth Year,   208 pp. 40 cents
Second Year, 160 pp. 35 cents   Sixth Year,   240 pp. 45 cents
Third Year,   208 pp. 40 cents   Seventh Year, 240 pp. 45 cents
Fourth Year, 208 pp. 40 cents   Eighth Year, 240 pp. 45 cents

For the convenience of ungraded schools, and for all who may prefer them in such combined form, an edition corresponding to the ordinary five book series of school readers will be furnished as follows:

BALDWIN'S SCHOOL READERS—FIVE BOOK EDITION

First Year,   128 pages . . . . . .   25 cents
Second Year, 160 pages . . . . . .   35 cents
Third Year,   208 pages . . . . . .   40 cents
Combined Fourth and Fifth Years.   416 pages . .   60 cents
Combined Sixth and Seventh Years. 480 pages . .   65 cents

Copies of either edition of Baldwin's School Reading by Grades will be sent, prepaid, on receipt of the price by the Publishers:

American Book Company

NEW YORK • CINCINNATI • CHICAGO

(9)

Penmanship

STANDARD COPY BOOKS

Barnes's National Copy Books.
Eclectic Copy Books.
Harper's Graded Copy Books.

Spencerian Revised Copy Books.
Payson, Dunton and Scribner's National Copy Books.

VERTICAL COPY BOOKS

Barnes's National Vertical Penmanship

Numbers 1 to 6 . . . . . . Per dozen, 75 cents

A new series designed to secure the highest degree of legibility, the greatest facility of execution, and the utmost beauty consistent with legibility and speed.

Spencerian Penmanship—Vertical Edition

Shorter Course. Numbers 1 to 7 . . . Per dozen, 72 cents
Common School Course. Numbers 1 to 6 . Per dozen, 96 cents

In this series of Vertical Copy Books the graceful lines and symmetrical forms which have distinguished Spencerian writing and made it the accepted American Standard of Penmanship, have been applied in an easy and natural way to vertical writing.

Curtiss's Vertical Copy Books

Numbers 1 to 6 . . . . . . Per dozen, 96 cents

A system of writing which combines in the highest degree legibility, ease, speed, and grace in execution.

Curtiss's Semi-Vertical Copy Books

Numbers 1 to 6 . . . . . . Per dozen, 96 cents

The Semi-Vertical Edition is designed to meet the demands of many teachers who are not satisfied with the old system of writing and yet are not prepared to adopt any of the new vertical styles.

Ward's Graded Lessons in Penmanship and Spelling

Small Numbers, 1 to 6 . . . . Per dozen, 72 cents
Large Numbers, 1 to 6 . . . Per dozen, 96 cents

Special Circulars and Specimen Pages of any of the above Copy Books will be sent free on application.

American Book Company

New York • Cincinnati • Chicago

Business Forms and Letters

Eaton's Business Forms, Customs and Accounts
By SEYMOUR EATON, Director of the Department of Business, Drexel Institute. Quarto $1 00

This is a book of blank business forms, being exact facsimiles of those used in common business transactions, such as orders for goods, bills of all kinds, statements of accounts, checks, pay rolls, receipts, bank deposit tickets, telegrams, business correspondence, etc.

Eaton's Exercise Manual of Business Forms
Designed to accompany Eaton's Business Forms, containing appropriate material and directions for filling out each of the blanks in the Form Book. Boards, 12mo, 110 pages . 50 cents

Key to Eaton's Business Forms, etc. . . . 50 cents

Ward's Letter Writing and Business Forms. Four Numbers.
Numbers 1 and 2 . . . . . . Each, 10 cents
Numbers 3 and 4 . . . . . . Each, 15 cents

A graded series of books for elementary schools, designed to teach letter writing, business forms, rules of punctuation, and the proper use of capitals. No. 1 includes letters and bills; No. 2, letters, receipts, and accounts; No. 3, notes, drafts, and letters; No. 4, business correspondence and business forms.

Appletons' Business Series of Copy Books. Three Numbers.
Numbers 1 and 2 . . . . . . Per dozen, $1.20
Number 3 . . . . Per dozen, 96 cents

For the higher grades in public schools, academies, and high schools. The course includes exercises in the different forms of commercial paper, business correspondence, etc.

Spencerian Business Course
Numbers 8, 9, 10, and 11 . . . . Per dozen, 96 cents

A series of copy books for higher grades, uniting business forms and bookkeeping with a practical course in penmanship. No. 8 includes ordinary business writing and business forms; No. 9, single entry bookkeeping; No. 10, connected business forms; No. 11, double entry bookkeeping.

Specimen copies of any of the above books will be sent, prepaid, to any address on receipt of the price by the Publishers:

American Book Company

NEW YORK • CINCINNATI • CHICAGO

Standard School Geographies

SUPPLEMENTED WITH STATE EDITIONS.

APPLETONS'	Elementary	$0.55
	Higher	1.25
BARNES'S	Elementary	.55
	Complete	1.25
CORNELL'S	Primary	.42
	Intermediate	.86
ECLECTIC	Elementary	.55
	Complete	1.20
GUYOT'S	Elementary	.50
	New Intermediate	1.00
HARPER'S	Introductory	.48
	School	1.08
NILES'S	Elementary	.44
	Advanced	1.00
SWINTON'S	Introductory	.55
	Grammar School	1.25

STANDARD PHYSICAL GEOGRAPHIES.

Appletons' Physical	$1.60
Cornell's New Physical	1.12
Eclectic Physical	1.00
Guyot's Physical	1.60
Geikie's Physical	.35
Monteith's New Physical	1.00

GENERAL GEOGRAPHY.

Geographical Reader and Primer	$0.60
Grove's Geography	.35
Johonnot's Geographical Reader	1.00
Long's Home Geography	.25
Patton's Natural Resources of the United States	.35
Ritter's Comparative Geography	1.00
Ritter's Geographical Studies	1.00

HISTORICAL GEOGRAPHY AND ATLASES.

Eclectic Historical Atlas	$1.00
Monteith's Boys' and Girls' Atlas	.40
Putz and Arnold's Ancient Geography and History	1.05
Putz and Paul's Mediæval Geography and History	1.05
Tozer's Classical	.35

Send for Geography Section of the Descriptive Catalogue.

Copies of any of these books will be sent prepaid to any address, on receipt of the price, by the Publishers:

American Book Company

New York ♦ Cincinnati ♦ Chicago

Halleck's Psychology and Psychic Culture

By REUBEN POST HALLECK, M.A. (Yale)

Cloth, 12mo, 368 pages. Illustrated . . . . Price, $1.25

This new text-book in Psychology and Psychic Culture is suitable for use in High School, Academy and College classes, being simple and elementary enough for beginners and at the same time complete and comprehensive enough for advanced classes in the study. It is also well suited for private students and general readers, the subjects being treated in such an attractive manner and relieved by so many apt illustrations and examples as to fix the attention and deeply impress the mind.

The work includes a full statement and clear exposition of the coördinate branches of the study—physiological and introspective psychology. The physical basis of Psychology is fully recognized. Special attention is given to the cultivation of the mental faculties, making the work practically useful for self-improvement. The treatment throughout is singularly clear and plain and in harmony with its aims and purpose.

"Halleck's Psychology pleases me very much. It is short, clear, interesting, and full of common sense and originality of illustration. I can sincerely recommend it."

WILLIAM JAMES,
Professor of Psychology, Harvard University.

Copies of Halleck's Psychology will be sent prepaid to any address on receipt of the price by the Publishers:

American Book Company

New York • Cincinnati • Chicago

Greek Texts and Lexicons.

DEMOSTHENES. Smead's Demosthenes' Philippics, with Notes.
Cloth, 12mo, 220 pages $1.05

HERODOTUS. Johnson's Selections from Herodotus, with Notes. Cloth, 12mo, 185 pages 1.05

HOMER. Johnson's Homer's Iliad. Three Books, with Notes and Selected Passages for Sight Reading, combined with Blake's Lexicon. Cloth, 12mo, 509 pages . . . 1.32

    Blake's Lexicon to the First Three Books of Homer's Iliad.
    Cloth, 12mo, 215 pages 1.00

    Owen's Homer's Iliad, with Notes.
    Cloth, 12mo, 760 pages 1.40

    Owen's Homer's Odyssey, with Notes.
    Cloth, 12mo, 568 pages 1.40

LYSIAS. Wait's Ten Orations of Lysias, with Notes.
Cloth, 12mo, 240 pages 1.25

PLATO. Kitchel's Plato's Apology of Socrates, and Crito, and a Part of the Phaedo, with Notes
Flexible Cloth, 12mo, 188 pages 1.25
The Same. Text Edition 30

    Tyler's Plato's Apology and Crito, with Notes.
    Cloth, 12mo, 180 pages 1.05

SOPHOCLES. Crosby's Sophocles' Oedipus Tyrannus, with Notes. Cloth, 12mo, 138 pages 1.05

    Smead's Sophocles' Antigone, with Notes.
    Cloth, 12mo, 242 pages 1.22

XENOPHON. Harper and Wallace's Xenophon's Anabasis. Seven Books; Books I. to IV. with Notes, Books V. to VII. arranged for Sight Reading. With Full Lexicon.
Cloth, 12mo, 575 pages 1.50

    Boise's Xenophon's Anabasis. Four Books, with Notes and Lexicon. Cloth, 12mo, 309 pages . . . 1.32

    Gleason's Xenophon's Cyropaedia, with Notes and Lexicon.
    Cloth, 12mo, 325 pages 1.25

    Robbins's Xenophon's Memorabilia of Socrates, with Notes.
    Cloth, 12mo, 421 pages 1.40

Sent, prepaid, to any address on receipt of price.

American Book Company

New York   •   Cincinnati   •   Chicago

New Text-Books in German

Keller's First Year in German
    Cloth, 12mo. 290 pages . . . $1.00

Keller's Second Year in German
    Cloth, 12mo. 388 pages 1.20

    By I. KELLER, Professor of the German Language and Literature in the Normal College, New York.

These two books furnish a systematic and thorough course for beginners in German. They combine the best features of both the grammatical and natural methods of teaching. The lessons in each book afford suitable material for practice in reading, for oral and written exercises and translations, for conversational exercises, and for grammatical study. The student is encouraged from the first to speak and write German as the best and shortest means of gaining an intelligent knowledge and use of the language.

Keller's Bilder aus der Deutschen Litteratur

    By I. KELLER, Professor of the German Language and Literature in the Normal College, New York.

    Linen, 12mo. 225 pages . . . . 75 cents

The plan of this work will commend itself to teachers who believe that the teaching of German literature should concern itself with the contents and meaning of the great works themselves more than with a critical study of what has been said about the works. With this aim the author gives a survey of the language and literature at its most important epochs, selecting for detailed study the chief works of each period and writer. A summary of the contents of each work so treated is given, generally illustrated by a quotation from the work.

The simplicity of the treatment and language fits this work for younger students as well as for those of more advanced grades.

Copies of any of the above books will be sent prepaid to any address, on receipt of the price, by the Publishers:

American Book Company

New York   ◆   Cincinnati   ◆   Chicago

www.ingramcontent.com/pod-product-compliance
Lightning Source LLC
Chambersburg PA
CBHW030304240426
43673CB00040B/1055